The World
the Slaveholders Made

TWO ESSAYS IN INTERPRETATION

The World the Slaveholders Made

TWO ESSAYS IN INTERPRETATION

BY EUGENE D. GENOVESE

VINTAGE BOOKS

A Division of Random House / New York

For

SOPHIA LAUTERBACH

VINTAGE BOOKS EDITION, MARCH 1971

Copyright © 1969 by Eugene D. Genovese

All rights reserved under International and Pan-American Copyright Conventions. Published in the United States by Random House, Inc., New York. Distributed in Canada by Random House of Canada Limited, Toronto. Originally published by Pantheon Books in 1969.

Library of Congress Catalog Card Number: 69-15474

MANUFACTURED IN THE UNITED STATES OF AMERICA

Introduction

This book tries to do three complementary things: to extend an analysis of the society of the slave South presented earlier; to contribute to a rapidly unfolding discussion of the comparative study of modern slave societies; and to offer some suggestions for the development of the Marxian interpretation of history.

In 1965, I published a book of essays, *The Political Economy of Slavery*, which advanced a point of view toward the nature of the society of the slave South, and made the mistake of promising a number of supporting studies "soon." The promise was made in good faith, for those studies were indeed well along. One, a study of George Fitzhugh and the logical outcome of the slaveholders' philosophy, was then about finished and is included as the second essay in this book; the other, a study of the black slave, somehow gets bigger and more complicated and has yet to be finished. Part of the delay has been occasioned by the reception of unusually high-level and constructive criticism from many friends and colleagues: the cogency of their arguments, suggestions, objections, and questions has forced me to go slow.

The serious criticism of my earlier work primarily con-

cerned the failure to array sufficient evidence in support of
the theses on the slaveholding class and its regime and the
failure to relate that regime to the other slaveholding regimes
of the New World. I accept the criticisms in principle and
offer the present book as a first installment on an extended
reply. These essays try to do something—not nearly enough
—toward meeting the first criticism and much more toward
meeting the second. No one who remained unconvinced by
the argument of *The Political Economy of Slavery* is likely
to be convinced by this extension, but even the brief discussion of the society of the slave South in the first essay has
provided the occasion for a better balanced statement than
appeared earlier. The thesis that an essentially prebourgeois
ruling class dominated the South has been modified in the
light of criticism. It was never intended to deny the hybrid
nature of the class or the society, and the earlier book does
contain explicit statements to that effect. Nevertheless, zeal
to stress the side that was the less appreciated and yet the
more important apparently led to a one-sided impression,
which a brief general restatement in the first essay and a
fuller discussion in the second may begin to correct. No slave
society in modern times could free itself totally from the
economic, social, and moral influence of modern capitalism;
the problem of evaluation must center on the extent to
which slavery threw up countervailing forces and the extent
to which those forces prevailed over an omnipresent rival
buried deep within its economy and ideology and simultaneously confronting it from without. These essays, hopefully, will also correct the maddening and oft-repeated insistence of even the most careful scholars that I characterized
the slave South as "feudal." How and where such an idea
arose is a mystery to me, but at least this book should end
that misunderstanding.

The first essay attempts to provide a framework within
which the New World experience with slavery may be
studied comparatively and linked to the history of Western
Europe, as well as Africa. It aims to replace the current

viewpoints, which take the race question as their point of departure, with an alternative, which takes the formation and
development of social classes as its point of departure. As
such it has a double purpose: to advance the discussion of
the comparative history of slavery, and to defend the claims
for the superiority of the Marxian interpretation of history.
Despite rapid and impressive strides, the comparative history
of slavery seems to me in danger of bogging down, for the
various interpretations currently informing the discussion are
proving unable to solve any of the vital questions concerning
the place of slavery in the socioeconomic evolution of the
Western world, or even to solve the two major questions to
which they have been specifically addressed—the several
paths to abolition and the patterns of race relations. The
question of abolition has been made a test case by the participants in the debate themselves and ought to be welcomed
as such by Marxists, for the special strength of Marxism
resides in its usefulness as an explanation of transitions from
one social system to another. For reasons that this essay will
try to make clear along the way, the patterns of race relations
must be treated as a series of special cases within a wider
historical process propelled essentially by class forces.

My hopes for offering something useful toward the development of a Marxian interpretation of history rest on an
attempt, made explicit in a general way in Chapter 1 of the
first essay and left implicit throughout the book, to transcend
the narrowly economic notion of class and come to terms
with the "base-superstructure" problem that has plagued
Marxism since its inception. Marxists have tended to let
themselves be suspended between the assertion of the pri-
macy of "material" forces and the necessity to recognize that
ideas, once called into being and rooted in important social
groups, have a life of their own. In recent decades general
theoretical and philosophical contributions, especially those
of Mao Tse-tung and Antonio Gramsci, have pointed to a
way out of the traps implied in the juxtaposition of these
viewpoints. There is, however, a limit beyond which general

theoretical analysis cannot take us. The quality of the contributions of Mao and Gramsci themselves demonstrates as
much, for the advances their work has encouraged would have
been impossible without their careful, empirically based
treatments of such special questions as the class structure of
the Chinese countryside or the place of the Mezzogiorno in
the Italian Risorgimento. The most important work being
done today is to be found in particular historical investigations, rather than in grand theoretical pronouncements; to
the extent that the latter have been forthcoming as serious
efforts at synthesis, in contradistinction to dogmatic asser-
tions, they have come out of hard digging in the sources and
out of attempts to pay respectful attention to the ideas of
major ideological opponents within and without the historical profession. The scholarly work of such exemplary Marxist
historians as Christopher Hill, Eric J. Hobsbawm, and E. P.
Thompson—to name only three prominent Englishmen who
are primarily concerned with their own country in a world
perspective—has contributed, in my opinion, immeasurably
more toward the development of a Marxian interpretation
than have countless volumes on "dialectical and historical
materialism." One need not have illusions about matching
their extraordinary talent to be willing to work in their
spirit.

Specifically, many years of grappling with the problem of
the historical character of the Southern master class have
convinced me that it cannot be understood apart from its
relationship to slaves and nonslaveholding whites, that those
other classes cannot be understood apart from a consideration of the quality and the mechanisms of ruling-class
hegemony, and that none of these classes can be understood
without an appreciation of the uniqueness and particularity
of every social class. Chapter 1 of the first essay tries to work
out some of these ideas in a rough and tentative way. The
remainder of the book tries to work out some of the ramifications.

Acknowledgments

A brief preliminary version of the first essay was delivered to a symposium sponsored by the department of history at Smith College in February 1968, where it was incisively criticized by William Freehling, Herbert Klein, and Arnold A. Sio. I owe a special debt to Professor Sio, who went beyond criticism of content to offer some excellent methodological suggestions. Copies of the paper were sent to a number of friends and colleagues—an increasingly common form of intellectual exploitation that may soon achieve the dignity of surplus-value appropriation—some of whom took more time and care with it than anyone had a right to expect. I am grateful to Roger Anstey, Eric Hobsbawm, Robert Marcus, Magnus Mörner, Arnold Paul, George Rawick, and especially Franklin W. Knight, whose critique of the material on Cuba and Brazil was invaluable to a nonspecialist. Laura Foner offered excellent criticisms of content and, in addition, checked and corrected the citations.

The second essay received a painstaking reading from Carol and Helmut Gruber and from Ann J. Lane. Their undisguised hostility toward Fitzhugh and their disapproval of my affection for him sharpened their normally acute critical sense and added a bite to their extensive remarks that I cannot claim to have enjoyed but do not deny having benefited from. Decidedly more friendly and sympathetic to both Fitzhugh and Genovese were the lengthy criticisms of Warren I. Susman, who offered the brilliant insights his friends now expect from him as a matter of course.

I can only describe the efforts of C. Vann Woodward and Christopher Lasch as having been indispensable. They read the entire manuscript, saved me from blunders, forced many salutary changes, and demanded a degree of clarity and elaboration that I had apparently tried to slip by without. Professor Woodward had, in addition, suffered through almost all of the earlier versions of both essays and had provided an encouragement without which I might well not have been willing to proceed.

Betsey, while still Elizabeth A. Fox, read and reread the manuscript at several stages, offered particularly valuable substantive criticisms of the material on European economic and social history, allowed me to steal from her unpublished work on France and the West Indies, struggled to keep me more or less on schedule, and graciously consented to help me read the proofs on our honeymoon.

Tradition requires that I absolve my critics from responsibility for all errors. Although I deeply respect all tradition as a matter of principle, I see no reason to absolve them. If I have committed blunders, one or another of these learned men and women should have noticed; if they did not, then let them share the disgrace. As for my interpretation and bias, the usual disclaimer is unnecessary since no one in his right mind is likely to hold them responsible for either.

I hope that no violation of protocol has been committed by my selection of the title, which was suggested by one of Gilberto Freyre's lesser known and untranslated books, *O Mundo que o português criou.*

CONTENTS

PART ONE

THE AMERICAN SLAVE SYSTEMS IN WORLD PERSPECTIVE

CHAPTER ONE

Preliminary Observations on Afro-American Slavery and the Rise of Capitalism

I

Let us begin with the masters. The general character of modern slaveholding classes arose from two separate sources: from a common origin in the expansion of Europe, which historically meant the expansion of the world market and, accordingly, established a pronounced tendency toward commercial exploitation and profit maximization; and from the relationship of master to slave, which engendered antithetical qualities. No matter how great the variations and circumstances, the master-slave relationship, which was profoundly different from that of capitalist to wage worker or *rentier* to peasant, left its mark on both participants. Specifically, it engendered a special psychology, mores, economic advantages and disadvantages, and social problems, which appeared in all slave societies, even if only as weakly manifested tendencies. To understand slavery we must trace the fate of these immanent tendencies in specific slave regimes, for their particular combination makes all the difference to a comparative analysis.

All slaveholding classes displayed these two antithetical groups of tendencies, but each combined them uniquely,[1] and the particularity of each combination also derived from two separate sources. First, each slaveholding class, with its European roots, had evolved from a distinct national past, in some cases primarily bourgeois and in some seigneurial; in some Protestant and in some Catholic; in some liberal and in some authoritarian. Within these broadly sketched dichotomies great variations existed; only non-Iberians, for example, could make the mistake of assuming that it made little difference whether the origins were Portuguese or Spanish. Second, the immediate social and economic context—residency or absenteeism of the planters, degree of acculturation of the blacks, nature of the crop, level of technology, type of market mechanism, and locus of political power—provided special qualities in each case. Each slaveholding class carried a particular European inheritance into its American present, but the extent and nature of the transference depended on the immediate context. Race relations, it will be argued, did not determine the patterns of slavery in the New World; the patterns of slavery, as conditioned by past and present, history and ecology, and manifested in particular forms of class rule, determined race relations.

Historians usually treat all slave classes as if they also exhibited monolithic similarity, but few of these historians would adhere to the only principle justifying such a procedure—that blacks are blacks. At one extreme, in the Old South, the blacks were largely creoles (American-born), at least during the mature period of the slave regime. At the other extreme, in Saint-Domingue on the eve of its great revolution, the blacks were overwhelmingly newly imported Africans. Between these two we find various combinations at different times in Cuba, Brazil, Jamaica, and other slave countries. Among the African-born we find quite different peoples, with markedly different political, social, and cultural backgrounds. The mere fact that Bahia, Brazil, witnessed large-scale Moslem-led revolts during the early part of the nineteenth century ought to be enough to put us on our guard.

The differences among the slave classes stemmed from other sources as well. In the Old South, where whites formed a majority, blacks could be excluded from a wide range of occupations, and a free black and colored (mixed) middle class had little room to grow; in the West Indies, the reverse was true. More varied functions of the slave class and the existence of black and colored middle strata seriously affected the life and thought of the slaveholders. Other matters would have to be considered in a full analysis of the class structure of the black and colored communities, but even these elementary observations lead to one major conclusion: no satisfactory assessment of any slaveholding regime or of any slaveholding class will be possible until we retrace its history to take full account of its specific interaction with the other classes in society, whether white or black, free or slave. A ruling class does not grow up simply according to the tendencies inherent in its relationship to the means of production; it grows up in relationship to the specific class or classes it rules. The extent to which its inherent tendencies develop and the forms they take will depend on the nature of this confrontation as well as on the nature of confrontations with other classes outside its immediate sphere of activity.

For reasons common to the slave condition all slave classes displayed a lack of industrial initiative and produced the famous Lazy Nigger, who under Russian serfdom and elsewhere was white. Just as not all blacks, even under the most degrading forms of slavery, consented to become niggers, so by no means all or even most of the niggers in history have been black. That shiftless and unresourceful slave whom we find in all slave societies in turn helped form a common type of slaveholder, as well as vice versa. The great Brazilian abolitionist Joaquim Nabuco, himself a conservative aristocrat, pointedly referred, in his O Abolicionismo, to "two contrary types, and at bottom the same: the slave and the master." W. E. B. Du Bois was probably only half joking when, in Black Reconstruction in America, he solemnly accounted for the lack of a suitable work ethos among the blacks by referring to their tendency to follow the example of their former masters. Every serious student of slavery is forced, in one way or another, to recognize this dialectic. As the Brazilian sociologist and historian of slavery Fernando Henrique Cardoso observes: "Freedom in slave society is defined by slavery. Therefore, everyone aspired to have slaves, and having them, not to work."[2] The aristocratic ideal pervaded slave societies and instilled in the planters the much discussed habit of command, as well as a more complex general psychological pattern that has yet to receive the attention it deserves. This ideal affected every other class in society, including the slaves, although in different ways according to conditions common to the slave position and specific to each such class. American novelists, white and black, have understood this side of Southern life much better than historians. As Ralph Ellison says, "William Faulkner made us so vividly aware . . . that the slaves often took the essence of the aristocratic ideal (as they took Christianity) with far more seriousness than their masters, and that we, thanks to the tight telescoping of American history, were but two generations from that previous condition."[3]

Even on the general level, where we encounter features common to all slave classes, we find a contradictory psychological process. David Brion Davis has demonstrated the existence of a slavish personality wherever slavery has existed throughout history; in the same way one could demonstrate the simultaneous existence of slave rebelliousness. "Slavish personality" must be understood as an expression only of a tendency that often appeared to be dominant, and must not be taken as an absolute—as a living, total "Sambo."[4] All forms of class oppression have induced some kind of servility and feelings of inferiority in the oppressed; failure to induce these means failure to survive as a system of oppression. The slavish personality represents the extreme form of this servility and expresses itself, among other ways, in a longing for the master, understood as absolute other, for this other represents superiority in strength and authority and perhaps even virtue. But this other must also appear as the embodiment of cruelty, arbitrariness, and injustice and must, in reality, prove unattainable to the slave. The act of love is therefore frustrated, collapses into hatred, and generates, at least potentially, great violence. (It is therefore for the best of reasons that the novelist William Styron has Nat Turner attracted to an upper-class white girl whom he must personally kill.[5]) This confrontation is a matter of class; the race question intrudes and gives it a special force and form but does not constitute its essence. White racism in the United States has certainly hardened class lines and given black people a special sensitivity to the feeling of other oppressed peoples and classes. It is not an accident that to hear a ballad like "The Lass from the Low Country" sung in the United States as it ought to be we must go to Odetta or Nina Simone.

If the slave condition in general imparted certain qualities to slaves, and therefore to masters, the particular conditions shaping each slave class also made themselves felt. In a note on Hegel's famous passage on "lordship and bondage," Frantz Fanon writes: "I hope that I have shown that here [in the French islands] the master differs basically from the master described by Hegel. For Hegel there is reciprocity; here the master laughs at the consciousness of the slave. What he wants from the slave is not recognition but work."[6] Fanon says too much, for every master must laugh at the consciousness of his slaves, even as he falls into dependence on it, and every master wants work rather than recognition. Yet Fanon offers us an important insight, so long as we restrict it to the French West Indies and to those slave societies that exhibited certain characteristics. Fanon describes one psychological dimension of one kind of slaveholding class, which in this essay we shall call bourgeois; he does not describe the slaveholders of the Old South or of Brazil. Con-

versely, he describes the experience of only one, or perhaps
several, specific slave classes. On these grounds alone the
whole experience of slave revolt and forms of class struggle
—to take only one set of problems—will have to be reassessed. The extent and depth of the revolts varied greatly
throughout the Americas for a variety of reasons, many of
which have to be subsumed within an analysis of the slaves
as members of specific classes, each of which had its own
history, ideological growth, and type of self-consciousness.

The psychological dimension of the class confrontations
and the confrontations themselves enter into this essay only
sketchily, as hints rather than as extended discussion, and
for this reason alone the essay can at best qualify as a preliminary analysis. It focuses on the slaveholders as self-
determining agents to an extent that can only be justified by
reference to the early stage of the historical debate to which
it is offered as a contribution. If its main argument survives
criticism, it will survive as a deliberately simplified starting
point for a much more complex analysis in which each of
the slaveholding classes is itself reassessed with close attention to what its interaction with particular slave and nonslaveholding classes helped make of it.

I I

During the last decade American historians, sociologists, and
anthropologists have joined their colleagues in Europe, Latin
America, and the Caribbean in an effort to study Afro-
American slavery comparatively rather than in national or
insular isolation. Long before, Manoel de Oliveira Lima,
Gilberto Freyre, and others had pointed the way, but not
until Frank Tannenbaum's challenging essay *Slave and
Citizen: The Negro in the Americas* (1947) did we meet a
forceful demonstration of the value of comparative history.
At that, students of United States history, in contradistinc-
tion to that of Latin America, remained indifferent until one

of their own, Stanley M. Elkins, gave the discussion a new turn in his startling book *Slavery: A Problem in American Institutional and Intellectual Life* (1959). The recognition and acclaim given David Brion Davis' *The Problem of Slavery in Western Culture* (1966) signals the triumph of the comparative method. Clearly, the study of Afro-American history will never be the same.

To realize the possibilities inherent in this advance, we shall have to extend our vision even further and try to discover the place of the slave regimes and of the total slave experience in the general history of the modern world. In view of the rapidity with which scholarly work is proceeding and in view of the magnitude of the task facing those who would attempt a synthesis of the history of four continents during a period of four hundred years, we should not be surprised that few general theses have as yet appeared. Many scholars no doubt consider attempts at synthesis premature, for as Eric Hobsbawm observes in his path-breaking essay on the general crisis of the seventeenth century, "It is always a risky thing to attempt a synthesis towards the beginning rather than the end of a historical debate." Yet, as Hobsbawm's work so impressively demonstrates, the prime function of such an attempt is not so much to settle questions as to provide a framework within which hypotheses for further research may most usefully be formulated and the level of discussion raised. This essay is an attempt to serve that end and is offered without any illusion that it could possibly do more than point a direction.

So far, students have generally worked with two points of view. One, associated with Tannenbaum, Elkins, Freyre, and most recently with Herbert S. Klein, stresses the differences in institutional and cultural history between the Iberian and Anglo-Saxon slave societies; the other, associated with Eric Williams, Marvin Harris, and, with considerably more flexibility, David Brion Davis, stresses the similarities in the nature of slavery as a system of economic exploitation. Both points of view have contributed immensely to our understanding of the slave societies of the Americas, and each is capable of considerable modification. Neither by itself, however, can answer the main questions to which it addresses itself, much less the questions to which we might insist it address itself. Part of the problem arises from their common starting point, race relations. Both have attempted to explain the different patterns of race relations in Brazil, the Southern United States, Jamaica, Cuba, and elsewhere, and both have contributed to the solution of the problem. That solution, however, will have to await the absorption of these contending viewpoints into a more adequate theoretical framework, for each is in itself much too narrow to yield satisfactory results. This narrowness, in addition, has led to their having obscured some of the fundamental features of the slave regimes, as well as the most important questions concerning the place of those regimes in the history of European expansion and the rise of capitalism as a world system.

As Sidney W. Mintz remarks in his critique of Tannenbaum and Elkins, we need to ask about more than the existence or nonexistence of particular traditions; we need to ask about the effectiveness of their transfer to the New World. "The economic and political structures of the metropolises," he adds, "and not only their religious and other ideological systems, were probably important."[7] Even if we look exclusively at the American side, questions arise that quickly break through the familiar categories in which the discussion has been cast. The slave plantations of the New World had much in common, especially in the economic sphere, with subsequent plantations based on formally free labor, but they also offered some striking contrasts. In all cases, the plantation as an institution has inhibited the formation of alternative forms of socioeconomic organization. Eric Wolf contrasts the old, slave-based plantation with the most modern, free-labor ones:

The new-style plantation is an organization which uses money to make more money. Its operation is governed by "rational" cost accounting, and the consumption needs of both owners and workers are irrelevant to its operation. . . . On the old-style plantation, however, labor is not only employed in the fields. A considerable amount of labor-time goes into both feeding the owner and his family, and into the provision of services which may enable him to live in the style demanded by his social position. His workers not only sow and reap; they also serve at table, or curry his horses, or play music on festive occasions. In turn, part of the resources of the plantation and part of the surplus produced is used to cover the subsistence needs of the labor force. . . . The old-style plantation . . . has a split personality. It produces goods for a market, but part of its energy goes into self-maintenance and status consumption.[8]

The plantations of the British Caribbean, even with slave labor, exhibited most of the characteristics of Wolf's "new style" while they did retain certain important features of the old. Even in these, the most bourgeois (or "new-style") of the plantations, the very fact of slave labor introduced pre-capitalist distortions into the economy and into society as a whole.

If we turn to Spanish slavery, with its reputation for mildness, and bracket the question whether or not that reputation has been deserved, we confront similar problems. The common experience of the plantation regimes, especially during the years of an open slave trade and attendant low slave prices, suggests strong tendencies toward cruelty, overwork, and generally inhumane practices. This has led many scholars, most notably Harris, Davis, and C. R. Boxer, to deny or at least to minimize the differences in slave treatment among the several slave countries. Their argument has force, but only to the extent of its being a description of a certain tendency general to all plantation slave regimes, against which specific counter-tendencies operate unevenly from one regime to another. The institutional and moral influences stressed by Tannenbaum and Elkins and the economic and ecological processes stressed by Williams and Harris must both receive full consideration, but neither should be raised to the level of prime mover or presented to the exclusion of the other. To transcend both points of view we shall have to focus on the nature of the constituent social classes. Specifically, without a careful analysis of the legal, moral, religious, and institutional inheritance and its survivals in colonial life, we could not explain the particular history of slavery or of the slaveholding classes in any country. The economic and ecological processes enable us to account for the room given that inheritance to breathe. They provide us with an account of the fundamental tendencies arising from the conditions of material life, but those tendencies operated to set limits to the possible adaptations; they could not and did not determine those adaptations in any absolute sense.

The most striking failure of the present viewpoints appears in relation to the problem of abolition, which they themselves raised as a major aspect of the race question and with which we shall be primarily concerned in this essay. Tannenbaum, in a well-known passage at the beginning of his book, relates the differences in slave systems to abolition as follows:

There is in the history of slavery an important contribution to the theory of social change. Wherever the law accepted the doctrine of the moral personality of the slave and made possible the gradual achievement of freedom implicit in such a doctrine, the slave system was abolished peacefully. Where the slave was denied recognition as a moral person and was therefore considered incapable of freedom, the abolition of slavery was accomplished by force—that is, by revolution. The acceptance of the idea of the spiritual equality of all men made for a friendly, an elastic milieu within which social change could occur in peace. On the other hand, where the slave was denied a moral status, the law and the *mores* hardened and became stratified, and their historical outcome proved to be violence and revolution.[9]

This thesis contains great difficulties and will not bear close examination. If the War for Southern Independence grew out of the failure to recognize the moral personality of the slave, then we need to know the reason why no such war or revolution occurred in the Northern states or in the British or Dutch West Indies, which in terms of the Tannenbaum-Elkins thesis also denied that moral personality. The other country in which abolition occurred amidst fearful violence was Saint-Domingue, which then logically should have stood with the United States at one side of the polarization that Tannenbaum and Elkins posit; in fact, by their explicit account, it stood midway between the Anglo-Saxon and Iberian models. When we turn to the Spanish American mainland, we do not find the smooth transition that has been assumed but a more or less violent and disorderly process. Emancipation received its greatest thrust during the revolutionary wars of independence and was, as Simón Bolívar candidly said, a weapon against the Spanish loyalist slaveholders. In Brazil the vaunted peaceable abolition followed years of major slave revolts, wholesale desertion of plantations, and the growing threat of violence among the whites themselves. In Cuba the Ten Years' War (1868–1878) between the Cuban nationalists and the Spanish and the imperialist rivalry between the United States and Spain, not the culmination of a moral crusade, dealt the deathblow to the slave system. We might grant that, with all these qualifications, a general, qualitative distinction might be made between the Brazilian and the Cuban cases on the one hand and the case of the Old South on the other. We might grant, too, that Davis' proof that no slave system in world history ever failed to take account of the moral personality of the slave could be subjected to discriminating, qualitative distinctions and does not in itself destroy Tannenbaum's argument. We would still be left with a revolution in Saint-Domingue and a nonrevolutionary transition in Jamaica. The Iberian cultures may have been more sympathetic to manumission, but abolition, as a socioeconomic process, began in the Anglo-Saxon world, not the Iberian. The very factors to which Tannenbaum draws attention could be interpreted in an opposite way—as elements of social stability that made Iberian slavery more palatable and less likely to evolve into a higher labor system. Abolition, rooted in the Anglo-Saxon experience, developed into a world-wide process, each advance of which prepared the way for the next.

The economic-determinist alternative explanations, advanced by Williams and Harris, are even less helpful. They see abolition as a political reflex of one or another set of economic changes in Europe or America and deny the importance of cultural, ideological, and moral differences. Such schematic and mechanistic viewpoints create more problems than they try to solve, and they rarely solve any. Having criticized them at some length elsewhere[10] I shall pass over them now. Even if we were to concede more ground to economic determinism than we should, the major problem would remain: Why did some slaveholders prostrate themselves before economic forces, whereas others fought to the death?

This essay offers a different viewpoint. It does not claim to answer all the important questions but does claim to resolve satisfactorily, at least in outline, the problem of the several paths to abolition and to provide the beginnings of a solution to the more general problem that previous viewpoints have obscured or ignored: the problem of the place of slave societies in general and each in particular in the history of the formation of a world market and an integrated international capitalist society. On the race question it argues only that, on principle, no general theory of race relations is possible; it tries to absorb hypotheses already advanced by others into an analysis of class forces.

The most important problems inherent in the study of Afro-American slave societies can only be solved by an analysis of the types of constituent classes, beginning with the ruling classes, and therefore slavery must be understood primarily as a class question and only secondarily as a race or a narrowly economic question. To demonstrate the usefulness of this viewpoint we shall consider the relationship between the American slave societies and their European sponsors; examine the specific slaveholding classes of the hemisphere; and attempt, however crudely, to account for the several patterns of race relations. If the argument proves sound, then almost every important problem, from the general and particular attributes of plantation architecture to the nature and extent of the fundamental tendencies within slave economies, ought to be viewed from this perspective; but we shall restrict ourselves to the problem of abolition as a test case. One observation on the question of slave treatment may be permitted to stand as an illustration of the several directions in which a comparative class approach may take us. As a problem in comparative history, the question of treatment itself becomes enormously complicated and presents great methodological difficulties.[11] But as a problem in the history of social classes it becomes, even if more complex, immeasurably more fruitful. We read a great deal about the brutal way in which Africans were packed into slavers for the Atlantic crossing, but the data have limited significance apart from data on ships carrying European indentured servants and immigrants or on the living conditions of the white sailors working on the slavers and other commercial ships. Similarly, if the proud boast of the Southern slaveholders was correct—as up to a point it was[12]—and their slaves lived as comfortably and were treated as humanely as most European peasants and workers, then it follows that the manifest exploitation and brutality was less a matter of race than of class and that the Africans could not have been so treated unless the groundwork had been laid by the treatment of the white lower classes. These and similar arguments do not imply that Africans did not suffer more than whites, and they hardly absolve white Europeans from their barbarism toward black Africans; they do suggest that that barbarism stemmed much more from an attitude of rich to poor, lord to peasant, bourgeois to human commodity than from an attitude of white to nonwhite. A closer analysis of the historical relationship between class and racial exploitation will, however, have to await a larger and more leisurely study.

III

To proceed, we shall have to consider briefly the two social systems, seigneurialism and capitalism, vying with each other for supremacy at the dawn of the modern era. Karl Marx, Maurice Dobb, and virtually all Marxists use the term "feudalism" or "feudal mode of production," but we shall use "seigneurialism" instead.[13] The substitution represents a grudging, long-resisted capitulation to those medieval historians who bitterly complain about the expropriation of one of their favorite terms. Since "feudalism" continues to define a particular, fairly well delineated political system, even for Marxists, the dual meaning causes unnecessary trouble. As Marx and Dobb themselves show, the mode of production they call feudal does not require the political system of the same name, although some kind of rough historical correlation may be made. The term "seigneurial" expresses the essentials of that mode of production and avoids the difficulty. Seigneurialism is here defined, following Marx and Dobb, as the mode of production characterized by a dependent labor force that holds some claim to the means of production. This definition makes seigneurialism roughly equivalent to serfdom but not exactly so, for it includes regimes in which the lords' claims on the economic surplus are met by payments in money or kind, as well as in labor services. Capitalism is here defined as the mode of production characterized by wage labor and the separation of the labor force from the means of production—that is, as the mode of production in which labor power itself has become a commodity. These definitions constitute an initial approximation designed to establish broad categories and are not intended for purposes of rigid periodization.[14] All such definitions being tools, they should be measured solely by the solutions to historical problems they make possible. Dobb, in *Studies in the Development of Capitalism*, has brilliantly demonstrated the value of these definitions, and we need not pursue the matter here beyond one point of special relevance to the question of slavery. The great value of this viewpoint lies in its focus on human relationships inherent in labor systems. As such, it should be understood to transcend mere economic categories and to define each mode of production as a social rather than as a narrowly economic system. Specifically, it suggests that the relationship of master to slave is fundamentally different from that of capitalist to wage worker and that this difference is decisive for an understanding of ideology and class psychology, as well as of economics.

Colonization and empire building, Richard Pares tells us, constitute economic acts, undertaken for economic motives and seldom for any other.[15] When a Marxist says as much, it is generally taken as new evidence of dogmatism and narrow-mindedness. The good sense of the observation remains, and we may congratulate ourselves for its having Pares' blessing. Good sense or no, the observation, in so stark a form, has its dangers and must not be permitted to obscure the distinction between the discrete processes at work. Economic motives do not equal capitalist motives and do not provide evidence of capitalist expansion. Since every precapitalist society exhibited a search for wealth, individual or collective, the decisive question concerns the social relations in the mother country, for if an alternative criterion is used, then every society, past and present, would have to be considered capitalist and the term would lose all meaning.

If Marxists have been correct in seeking the mainspring of fundamental social change in the relations of production rather than exchange, they have also tended to take too narrow an economic view of the societies in question. This narrowness has naturally accompanied the focus on productive relations, which are at bottom economic, especially since the discussion of the transition from seigneurial to capitalist modes of production remains in an early stage and has been dominated, quite properly, by economists and economic historians. A deeper difficulty arises from the tendency within Marxism itself toward economic determinism, which, when unchecked, does violence to the essentials of Marxian thought. The analysis of the historical transition from one mode of production to the other cannot progress much further until the discussion breaks out of its present economic limits. Some work has been done already, notably by Hobsbawm on the seventeenth-century crisis, by Rodney Hilton on the problem of state power, and by Christopher Hill on English religion and politics; but, as those scholars would undoubtedly be the first to admit, we have hardly begun.

The emergence of capitalism as a dominant mode of production, in contradistinction to a local system of enterprise such as that of the Renaissance Italian cities, required the revolutionary transformation of the social structure as a whole. As Hobsbawm argues, the social division of labor had to be greatly elaborated in order to increase productivity, and the labor force had to be divorced from the soil in order to expand the home market and transfer an adequate portion of the labor force to industry. He adds: "The creation of a large and expanding market for goods and a large and available free labour force go together, two aspects of the same process." One of Hobsbawm's striking advances over previous Marxists —notably Dobb, on whom like the rest of us he builds—is to carry the argument from the sphere of commerce to the sphere of production itself. Whereas Marx and Dobb assign a parasitical and conservative role to the big commercial bourgeoisie and a revolutionary role to the industrial, Hobsbawm insists, from a solid empirical base, that the great industrialists of the period of transition could and generally did stand with their commercial counterparts against the emerging new order. The conditions for capitalist development did not grow up automatically with a capitalist class, except perhaps in the long run. In the short run, he argues, they were often immobilized by the seigneurial structure of society, co-opted, and transformed into supports for the old regime. Research on the industrialists of the Old South suggests that their position corresponded closely to that which Hobsbawm posits for a large section of the big industrialists of seventeenth-century Europe. The impact on the market structure was analogous, although not similar. With a thinly spread market across Europe, Hobsbawm writes, even centers of large-scale production could emerge without effecting a fundamental change in the social structure.[16]

Beyond this line of advance Marxian historians will sooner or later have to turn their attention to the historical formation of the European capitalist classes in their ideological, psychological, and cultural aspects and in order to do so will have to overcome their hostility to the work of Max Weber, who for all his weaknesses asked the big questions. H. K. Takahashi properly chides Dobb, whose point of view he generally supports, for ignoring Weber's insights: "Weber brings out clearly two clashing social systems in that heroic period of English history. The 'capitalist spirit' which appeared in the form of Puritanism was the way of life, the form of consciousness best suited to the class of yeomen and small and middle industrialists of that time, and is not to be found in the mentality of 'hunger for money,' 'greed for gain,' common to monopolist merchants and usurers of all times and countries."[17]

Every social class, and therefore every slaveholding class, is unique. The terms "bourgeoisie," "proletariat," "slaveocracy," or "slave class" are essential in historical investigations, for they provide a starting point and underline common characteristics that lead us direct to the mainsprings of social change. But the bane of Marxian interpretation has been the transformation of that starting point into an end product by the promiscuous application of class labels as a substitute for historical specificity. In the modern world the uniqueness of social classes usually must be understood in a national context; for our immediate problem, no two national slaveholding classes were or could have been exactly alike. They exhibited common traits and embraced some tendencies drawing them together into a single phenomenon, but simultaneously they embraced other tendencies pulling them apart into distinct historical formations. Since all classes combine these tendencies in different ways, each is by definition unique—a definition that need not lead us to deny their universality, which for certain purposes may be of primary importance. The significance of their universality relative to their particularity depends entirely on the problem under investigation, for each has its own legitimate sphere of relevance.

CHAPTER TWO

The Slave Systems and Their European Antecedents

I

The slave regimes rose and fell on the strength of a profoundly contradictory entanglement with their European metropolises. At first glance, the contradiction appears to be merely the ordinary one between an exploiting metropolis and an exploited colony: the metropolis sponsored the colony for its enrichment, but the colony increasingly developed its own interests and sensibilities. We are, however, dealing here with more than a special case or series of cases in the history of the colonial expansion of capitalism; we are dealing with an even deeper contradiction. The slave plantation, as Tannenbaum has eloquently and persistently argued, penetrated every aspect of life—economy and politics, religion and family, sexual mores and social relationships—and generated its own pervasive community ethos. The social, intellectual, and moral tendencies of these regimes developed in reasonable harmony with those of Spain and Portugal but in deepening antagonism to those of England, Holland, and even France. In the latter cases, the antagonism was held in check so long as the mercantilist philosophy of beggar-thy-neighbor held sway, but even then the growth of a many-sided liberal ideology caused severe strains. With the early phase of the industrial revolution and the flowering of liberal bourgeois thought the gap between the two antagonistic world views steadily widened. These ideological currents expose but do not define the essential social process, which was a process of the formation of specific slaveholding classes in relation to metropolitan ruling classes.

The rise of the slave systems in the Americas, in contradistinction to the use of slave labor in a peripheral capacity within an essentially wage-labor system, must be understood as the rise of an essentially archaic mode of production. That the most advanced capitalist countries, notably England and Holland, should have spawned an archaic mode of production at the very moment of the ascendancy of their more advanced mode presents the specific paradox with which we shall have to concern ourselves.

This paradox had a parallel in Eastern Europe, and a comparison of American and Eastern European responses to the changes in the Western European economy shows how the emergence of a world market led to the most diverse social consequences. During the fifteenth and sixteenth centuries, at the very moment of transatlantic expansion, many Western European towns were turning to greater specialization in trade and manufacturing, supported by food imports from the east. This increasing interregional trade developed together with a gradual loosening of seigneurial relations in Western Europe and a reverse tendency in Eastern Europe, where serfdom re-emerged on a large scale. Between the twelfth and sixteenth centuries in Eastern Europe slavery gave way to "free labor," which in reality was dependent labor. As the need for labor on the great estates increased and the supply of slaves fell, the condition of the free peasants deteriorated, so that those rising from slavery met those declining from freedom in a virtual serf status. From the second half of the sixteenth century to the nineteenth, this trend continued and culminated in a "second serfdom." The expansion of the Western European economy encouraged social retrogression and the reinstitution of older modes of production in both Eastern Europe and parts of the New World. The origins of the second serfdom, which may well have been a first serfdom in Russia, are a matter of considerable controversy among specialists, but they need not detain us. There can hardly be much doubt that the developments in Western Europe strengthened the reaction in the east whenever they made themselves felt there. An economic history of the intercontinental and interregional links would be well beyond our present task, but Traian Stoianovich has suggested at least one: "The 'second serfdom' was aggravated ... by a simultaneous long-term rise in prices, caused by the flow of American silver into the eastern Mediterranean and by a growing disparity between prices and wages. . . . The decline in the real wages of unskilled labor made impoverished workers more willing to place their services at the disposal of powerful lords."[1]

Seventeenth century Europe was racked by a general crisis in the international economy, the political system, and moral and intellectual life. At bottom, as Hobsbawm so convincingly argues, it was a crisis of seigneurial social and state power. Hobsbawm draws attention to three secular backlash effects of this crisis in Eastern Europe, and we may note that similar effects appeared in the Americas: the purchasing power of the peasantry remained minimal and offered a poor market for Western goods; the broad-based wealth of the nobility yielded to concentration in the hands of a few great magnates; and the bourgeoisie failed to establish itself or remained feeble. These contradictory features of Western European expansion generated a severe economic crisis during the seventeenth century, which had marked effects in the colonial areas. Although the evidence is by no means firm, it appears that such far-removed areas as the Ukraine and Mexico suffered a decline in population that amounted to a virtual demographic catastrophe.[2] The crisis, however general, did not represent uniform economic retrogression in

Western Europe. Hobsbawm notes and adequately explains the lack of uniformity and specifically analyzes the favorable position of the advanced capitalist countries, particularly England and Holland. The social retrogression in America— the restoration of slavery—whatever its long-run economic deficiencies in providing markets, spelled an enormous economic gain for these countries, particularly in the form of the rapid expansion of sugar production in Barbados, Jamaica, Saint-Domingue, Martinique, St. Kitts, and even Brazil, which felt the Dutch presence during the second quarter of the seventeenth century and the growing, indirect power of the British over the Portuguese metropolis.

The general crisis did not affect Portuguese and Spanish America in the same way. The slave trade, considered as a branch of European commerce, felt its effects, but the impact on the New World far transcended the disruptions in that quarter. As Rolando Mellafe says, "The problem was not a crisis of the slave-trade commerce but a result of the total political and financial situation of the epoch."[3] Agriculture and mining suffered acutely, with a rising desire, if not a rising effective demand, for more slaves to put everything right. Significantly, slave sales to Brazil continued to increase while those to Spanish America fell.[4] The essential difference would appear to be the relatively self-sufficient condition of Brazilian agriculture—a difference that provides a clue, which we shall have to investigate further at a later point, to the difference in class structures.

The seventeenth-century crisis, with its opposite effects on Western Europe and on the rest of the world, was to leave a bitter legacy, as well as to establish the preconditions for extraordinary economic and social advances. Capitalism did not follow the mechanical and logical course of conquering and consolidating each national market before it turned outward. In order to absorb each national peasantry, it often had to bypass it for a given period of time, for the peasants were often strong enough to resist the requisite forms of exploitation. In this sense, capitalism has always manifested an imperialist tendency. The ability of the peasants of Western Europe to resist the worst features of the exploitation inherent in the transition from seigneurialism to capitalism set limits to the pace of bourgeois development. To circumvent these limits the bourgeoisie almost instinctively turned outward. History, Marx and Engels tell us, has been the history of class struggles. They neglected to add that those struggles have been full of ghastly ironies. In this case, the power of the Western European peasants, who for all their misery could and did resist much of the pressure from their lords and from the new exploiters, helped to seal the fate of their weaker counterparts in Africa, the Americas, and Eastern Europe, who in effect were made to take up the slack. The prosperity and growing independence of the Western European peasants in turn rested, or could be made to appear to rest, on the colonial exploitation of others. It has always appeared "logical" that the prosperity of the masses in Western Europe depended on foreign exploitation, as if the very social and economic system responsible for colonialism were not also responsible for that domestic exploitation and misery which colonialism ostensibly has been designed to offset. The campaign to convince the lower classes of the West that their survival and progress depend on mass murder and unspeakable barbarism abroad had, however mindlessly, begun its long course.

I I

England and Holland emerged earliest as capitalist countries; capitalism ripened there during the sixteenth century, and the bourgeoisie began to assume direction of the state and thereby released its potential during the revolutions of the seventeenth century. For these countries mercantilism represented the economic policy most convenient to the period of the primitive or original accumulation of capital, and the

erection of slave plantations represented one device of mercantilist colonial policy. Capitalism then and since has
absorbed and even re-created archaic modes of production in
order the better to exploit less advanced peoples and to ex-
tract from them the largest possible economic surplus. The
force of the world market, supported by the force of bourgeois
state power, has repeatedly imposed this paradox upon the
world, but there was within this paradoxical juxtaposition an
unexpected danger to the bourgeois world: slavery, as an
archaic mode of production, extruded potentially, and under
specific conditions actually, a slaveholding class with interests
and tendencies dangerously antithetical to those of the metropolitan bourgeoisie. For the most part, the bourgeoisie of the
metropolis kept its colonial offshoot in check. Only in the
Southern United States did the slaveholders break free and
follow their own course. In the Caribbean the slaveholders
remained in check for reasons that readily emerge from a
review of the region's economic and social history.

V. T. Harlow's study of the economic and social contours
of the history of Barbados, qualified to take account of such
special circumstances as the size of the island in question and
the moment at which it entered sugar production, telescopes
the history of the British Caribbean as a whole. In 1637,
Barbados had a white population of 37,000—the highest in its
history—and produced tobacco, cotton, indigo, pepper, citrus
fruits, and livestock on small farms. The sugar boom came in
the 1640s and provoked extensive white emigration in the
1650s. Free land had disappeared by the late 1640s, and the
whites moved to Nevis and Antigua. By 1786 only 16,167
whites remained; the stagnation may be readily observed in
the comparable figure for 1922, which was 15,000. The great
plantations ate the island and generated the ills common to
monoculture and slavery. By the end of the century the
island's prosperity lay behind it, and the center of sugar
production had shifted elsewhere.[5]

The Leeward Islands loomed large during the early part of

the seventeenth century, but sugar production leveled off by 1725 and the slave population about twenty-five years later. In 1763 the British added Grenada, St. Vincent, Tobago, and Dominica, which relieved the pressure on the Barbadian planters, but the jewel of their eighteenth-century empire was Jamaica. By the end of the century the Jamaican sugar industry had reached its zenith, and the economy of the smaller islands would probably have been ruined had it not been for the destruction of Saint-Domingue. During the nineteenth century Trinidad and Guiana assumed some importance as slave-plantation colonies, but the closing of the slave trade in 1807 placed severe restrictions on their growth. At their eighteenth-century peak, the West Indian sugar islands accounted for one-fifth of British imports, one-sixteenth of British exports, and one-eighth of total British trade, in comparison with figures of one-ninth, one-eleventh, and one-tenth respectively for the North American mainland.[6] This West Indian contribution to British prosperity came from an economic system based on monoculture, which fostered an enormous waste of human and material resources and left a trail of misery and backwardness in the wake of its moving frontier.

Economic distress did not lead the planters, or at least not many of them, toward a new order, as in Brazil, nor did it provoke them into secession and war against a metropolis that was pursuing policies ostensibly destructive to their interests, as in the United States. With some grumbling they peaceably accepted the abolition of the slave trade, which badly damaged their economic position, and then the abolition of slavery itself, which hurt them even more. This passivity becomes the more striking when we consider certain of the qualities for which the planters had achieved a reputation. Elsa V. Goveia's description of the planters of the Leeward Islands could serve for the planters of the British West Indies as a whole:

> The geography and basic institutions of the islands had long since combined to produce among them a cult of political

individualism and self-assertion and a tendency towards political oligarchy. . . . The group of white colonists who governed the islands did their best to build up their own local
power and to resist the restraints and policies imposed from
outside. . . . The political system of the islands was dominated by a strong tradition of local autonomy, by an habitual
opposition to external direction and interference, and by the
solidarity of a small ruling class. . . . Insularity, colonial
representative government, and slavery were the fundamental
principles. . . .[7]

By the end of the eighteenth century most of the Leewards
had passed into the hands of local legislatures. Even within
this one island group, therefore, a particularism grew strong
and viewed with suspicion not only London but every neigh-
boring island; attempts to organize a joint legislature never
had more than indifferent success. In this way, while the
basic characteristics of plantation slave society fostered common interests among the ruling classes of the various colonies,
they encouraged attitudes and habits antithetical to a broad
class unity. Even the well-known conflicts between the plant-
ing interest and the British government over mercantilist
policies, especially after the American Revolution, never resulted in a sharp break, any more than did the subsequent
liberal policies exemplified by the suppression of the slave
trade and the abolition of slavery. Nor could they have, given
the nature of class power in the islands.

The slaveholders of the British Caribbean, and of the
Dutch and Danish as well, qualify as the most bourgeois of
all modern slaveholding classes.[8] The most important sections
of the planters were absentees, living in the metropolis and
investing abroad in order to acquire big returns from a brutally
exploited colonial labor force. The slave plantation represented to them a distant enterprise in which to produce high
profits; it could not and did not represent a way of life, a
home, a community. Writing of the growth of absenteeism,
D. A. G. Waddell succinctly sums up a situation that con-

tinues to arrest the attention of every historian of the British Caribbean:

> The effect of these practices was cumulative. As more of the property owners came to reside in Europe, absentee ownership became more and more the general aspiration. The very paucity of numbers in the planting class made the islands socially unattractive for its members, and the absence of the most prosperous, the natural leaders of colonial society, made the development of a local community spirit and the provision of social amenities more difficult and less likely.[9]

Three-quarters of the land and slaves in Jamaica belonged to absentee owners, resident in Britain. Absenteeism became acute by 1800 and increased thereafter. For the English investor the islands served to yield quick fortunes, which could be used to establish a social position in the metropolis, not the colony. Orlando Patterson may take too narrow a view when he describes the white Jamaican community as an "absentee society" and traces almost all of Jamaica's ills, past and present, to this condition, but he undoubtedly has a great deal of ammunition on his side of the argument.[10] Added to the main form of absenteeism was what Debien and, following him, Pares call "local absenteeism"—the common practice in the French, British, and we may add the Danish, Caribbean of even a resident planter's having a number of estates on different islands.

The ensuing regime bore the clear stamp of capitalist enterprise. "The business of the islands was business," writes Winthrop D. Jordan, "the production of agricultural staples; the islands were not where one really lived, but where one made one's money."[11] Notwithstanding his bias in favor of his native Georgia, Ulrich Bonnell Phillips put his finger on the essential difference between the plantation social regime of the British islands and that of the Old South:

> On the generality of the [West Indian] plantations the tone of management was like that in most modern factories. The

laborers were considered more as work-units than as men, women, and children. Kindliness and comfort, cruelty and hardship, were rated at balance-sheet value; births and deaths were reckoned in profit and loss, and the expense of rearing children was balanced against the cost of new Africans. These things were true in some degree in the North American slaveholding communities, but in the West Indies they excelled.[12]

The attitudes Phillips describes took such deep root that when the Society for the Propagation of the Gospel in Foreign Parts assumed control of the Codrington estates in Barbados with the intention of turning them into models of humanitarianism, it found itself unable to introduce any significant reform lest it make sworn enemies of the planters.[13]

Absenteeism may not have caused all the ills of the British Caribbean, but all alternative explanations only reinforce our judgment of the quality of the ruling class. Davis argues cogently that resident and absentee owners alike preferred the serene life normally falling to *rentiers* and gave little thought to the expansion of markets, to technological innovation, or to measures to overcome waste. In this respect they resembled planter classes of a decidedly seigneurial type. There was a big difference, for as Davis adds, "When profits declined as a result of falling prices and mounting costs, they speculated in shipping, the sugar commission business, or West Indian mortgages. Finally, when plantations could scarcely pay interest charges on swollen debts, the successful proprietors, such as the Pinneys, transferred their capital to industry and railroads."[14]

When necessary to repel abolitionist attacks, the West Indian sugar planters affected a paternalistic stance and spoke of their role as civilizers of the lower races and guardians of the lower classes. In a large part, these protestations were sheer hypocrisy—lawyers' briefs to be presented to the general public in the forum of bourgeois parliaments reeking with cynicism. To a lesser degree, they sprang from the legitimate soil of the resident planters, who may well have embraced their content honestly, or at least as honestly as any ruling class embraces a self-serving ideology. The preponderance of influence and power did not, however, lie with these resident planters but with the absentees, whose control over the economy grew steadily as time went on.

For the planters as a whole, large-scale absenteeism meant a fundamental division in its own ranks according to place of residence but also, in effect, according to the degree of wealth and the place of Caribbean investments in total worth. Resident planters may or may not have aspired to return to England; some undoubtedly made peace with their lot and settled down to plantation life with a sense of community and home. With representative legislatures, considerable local power passed into their hands. Even when they were rooted to the soil, as were the Brazilian *senhores de engenho* or, in a less stable way, the planters of the Old South—and few appear to have been—circumstances forced them to share power with a wealthy but formally propertyless bourgeoisie of plantation managers and attorneys, who represented the absentees. On decisive questions the local planters could be safely contained. So long as the economic interests of the islands provided the basis for contention with London, no containment was necessary, but when the question arose of accepting abolition with a good grace or resorting to insurrection, the resident planters, who were necessarily acquiring at least some of the attributes of an independent ruling class, learned quickly enough who owned whom.

As a result, the question of abolition in the British West Indies presented itself as an issue internal to the metropolis and its ruling bourgeoisie. We need not follow Eric Williams' extreme economic interpretation here. The existence of colonial slavery proved increasingly galling to the moral sensibilities and liberal pretensions of the metropolitan bourgeoisie. Certainly, the economic interests of its rising industrialists and of those merchants whose position made them hostile to the West Indies group played a decisive role, but without the moral and ideological pressures the industrial bourgeoisie

would have had an immeasurably more difficult time in breaking the back of the West Indian merchant-planter clique.
Those pressures provided the basis for the political coalition
necessary to shift the locus of power to the metropolis. Peaceful abolition in the British Caribbean had less to do with
such mediating institutional and moral influences as those
of church and state, which Tannenbaum and Elkins stress,
than with the class relationships on both sides of the ocean.
Abolition could occur peacefully because it never became a
class question—a question of life or death for a whole class
and therefore for a world view and a notion of civilization. It
was little more than one of those intraclass battles between
interest groups in which some gain and some lose as part of
the give-and-take of national capitalist development. Such
battles may erupt into violence and civil war, but given their
nature, they rarely do. There is simply not enough at stake.

It may properly be argued that other factors were also at
work. Most of the colonies were small islands and could
hardly go it alone, for the means of resistance did not exist in
most of them. The overwhelming preponderance of blacks
over whites—sometimes as high as ten to one—confronted
the planters with the specter of servile war, should metropolitan military power be withdrawn. These factors might be
taken as constituting an adequate explanation of the planters'
capitulation.

Yet certain colonies, such as Jamaica, Guiana, and Surinam,
might well have proved viable. Their first problem lay in
disunity. Planters in some islands actually stood to gain from
compensated abolition by liquidating old debts and reducing
costs under a wage-labor system. In thickly populated islands
where land was scarce, these expectations made great sense
and proved sound, for a sugar revival did follow.[15] Even when
the interests of the planters coincided, the long tradition of
particularism took its toll, and, as in the Southern United
States, this tradition cannot be separated from the plantation
basis of society. But there was a difference. In the Old South,

where the stake of the planters in slavery was total, the tendency toward unity grew strong, whereas in the islands the stake remained primarily economic. Miss Goveia has argued properly that racism exerted its own pull:

> There is a profound irony in the determined resistance of the British West Indian colonies to any form of basic change in their slave system. For the growing density of the slave populations concentrated on their sugar estates and the increasing expense of their traditional methods of agriculture under the slave system were among the most important factors contributing to the lack of competitive efficiency which was already affecting the economic fortunes of most of these territories by the end of the eighteenth century. By that time, however, the West Indian could no longer afford to regard slavery simply as the economic expedient for supplying labour which it had been originally. The slave system had become more than an economic enterprise which could be abandoned when it ceased to be profitable. It had become the very basis of organised society throughout the British West Indies, and therefore it was believed to be an indispensable element in maintaining the existing social structure and in preserving law and order in the community. The idea of a society in which Negroes were released from their subordination and allowed legal equality with whites was so antithetical to the principles on which the slave society rested that it seemed to threaten complete social dissolution and chaos.[16]

Our only quarrel with Miss Goveia's formulation concerns limits. This racism, however intense, did not drive the West Indian planters into a death struggle, whereas in the United States it could be argued, and Phillips and his followers do argue, that it did. Miss Goveia is correct in her assessment but only up to a point, for the "slave society" she describes, unlike that of the Old South, never nurtured a ruling class with a world view setting it apart from the mainstream of capitalist civilization. Her analysis demonstrates the great force of racism but also exposes its secondary character. Disunity had other faces as well. The colored middle strata of the islands, chafing under racist abuses and with enhanced social, economic, and political prospects offered by abolition, stood staunchly loyal to the Crown and confronted the resident whites with a large and dangerous internal enemy.[17]

The danger of slave insurrection remained great. Unlike the United States, the islands had had a long history of massive risings. During the nineteenth century several took place specifically under circumstances in which the blacks thought that local authorities were suppressing news of their emancipation. In 1823, 13,000 rose in Demerara, and in 1831, about 50,000 in Jamaica. Any secessionist *coup d'état* by the resident planters threatened to provoke a recapitulation of Saint-Domingue. After the Jamaica rising some planters did establish communication with the United States with a view toward annexation, but the American response was cool, for war with England would certainly have followed.[18] The opposition of the London interests and of the local colored middle class probably would have sufficed to prevent secession; at least the political position of the diehard slaveholders was clearly precarious.

The question of resistance cannot be separated from the metropolitan orientation, not to say roots, of the planter class. These men could hardly have been expected to move to the colonies to lead a movement of separation from a metropolis that was their home, their nation, and the center of their livelihood. The specter of servile war even more clearly appears as an aspect of the class question, for it quickly reduces itself to a simple proposition: the slaveholders, considered as a class apart from the metropolitan bourgeoisie, could not rule. They constituted, in this sense, not a ruling class at all but a stratum of the metropolitan ruling class.

I I I

The Dutch and Danish West Indies offer variations on the British theme and present only a few special problems, the most important being the social basis of Netherlands expansion. Pouncing on an unnecessary concession from Eric Hobsbawm, who described the Netherlands during the seventeenth century as a "feudal business economy," H. R. Trevor-Roper denies that a capitalist transformation had occurred in the United Provinces and asserts that the economy had returned to the system of the medieval Italian cities. Amsterdam, he concludes, had become a new Venice of the North.[19] Despite the similarities between Amsterdam and the Italian cities of earlier times, Hobsbawm's formulation concedes too much. The landward provinces retained an essentially seigneurial socioeconomic system, and the big bourgeoisie of the West never did secure an adequate hinterland and build up an adequate national market. Even in Holland and Zeeland, where the relations of production in both agriculture and manufacturing had become decidedly capitalist, the power of the guilds, as Pieter Geyl admiringly insists, inhibited the development of a society wholly at the mercy of the market. Only Haarlem and Leiden displayed extensive industrialization and contained a "swarming proletariat."[20] Yet the inhibitions of the guild system were somewhat tempered, for in Amsterdam and presumably elsewhere close municipal regulation of the guilds increasingly turned "from protection of the craftsman in a local market, to control of employment and wages in the interest of employers competing in a world market."[21] We may suspect Trevor-Roper of trying to score polemical points when he writes, "Dutch industry was relatively insignificant."[22] "Relatively" is a big but ambiguous word. Industrial development proceeded rapidly enough in the United Provinces to attract workers from many other countries.[23] Violet Barbour provides an impressive list of industrial enterprises and achievements even for commercial Amsterdam. Closer quantification would doubtless help, but her general evaluation has great force: "The concentration of capital in Amsterdam in this century was great for the time, and would surely have produced catastrophic inflation if this capital had not been drawn off in enterprises both public and private."[24] The formidable industrial strides in Amsterdam resulted from the initiative and investment of the merchants. The investment of Dutch capital in foreign manufactures also reached considerable proportions and deserves careful consideration in any assessment of the revolutionary role of Dutch merchant capital.

Hobsbawm knows all this and undoubtedly takes the stand he does because he also knows of the coexistence of two modes of production in the Netherlands as a whole and especially of the predominance of the commercial over the industrial bourgeoisie within Holland itself. His judgment seems hasty on other grounds. The more advanced city-states of the earlier era could be judged "feudal business economies" not because they did not introduce wage-labor relations into industry or transform agricultural relations from seigneurial to capitalist forms, for, however imperfectly, they sometimes did these things. Rather, they generally proved unable to establish a national state from which to revolutionize the economies they absorbed or penetrated. By the time the Dutch recapitulated their experience, however, the accumulation of capital throughout Europe had proceeded rapidly, no doubt in part because of those earlier, partial contributions. As a result, the outward thrust of Dutch capital could and did play a revolutionary role in helping to bring a world market into being and in stimulating development abroad; even the much discussed Dutch investments in England should be seen in this light. Foreign investments, a commitment to commerce, and the exigencies of a backward hinterland inhibited the full emergence of industrial capitalism in the Netherlands, but this lag, under those specific conditions of the seventeenth century which Hobsbawm so cogently analyzes, should not lead to an underestimation of the revolutionary and bourgeois role of the Dutch in the developing world economy. The sticky issue, which we may happily leave to specialists since it forms no part of our problem, concerns the political and social mechanisms by which state power passed to the bourgeoisie. Undoubtedly, the nobility played a central role in the early phases of the revolutionary crisis of the seventeenth century, but no less marked was the growing power of the essentially bourgeois Regents. The metamorphosis of the nobility of Holland and Zeeland and the rise to power of a new class present formidable problems for a Marxian interpretation of the Dutch experience but need not concern us here, for the regimes built up in the slave colonies clearly followed the dictates of the bourgeoisie.

The limits imposed on Dutch capitalism by its compromised position vis-à-vis the seigneurialism of the landward provinces and the stubborn strength of the guilds even in the advanced towns left their mark on the Dutch performance in the New World. No great Dutch slave plantation colonies emerged despite the central role of the Dutch in the slave trade and despite the ambitions of the capitalists who dominated the West India Company. Slavery in New Amsterdam remained urban and embraced house servants, artisans, and semiskilled workers under a mild regime; and notwithstanding some plantation beginnings, the same proved true in St. Eustatius and Curaçao, which reaped their profits largely from the slave trade.[25] The Dutch conquest of Pernambuco, even under the energetic and imaginative Count Maurice of Nassau, merely superimposed commercial exploitation on a social and economic structure that remained dominated by Portuguese *senhores de engenho*.[26] Only in Surinam do we find a Dutch plantation system of any importance in the New World. Although Dutch presence there dates from the early part of the seventeenth century, not until the arrival of the Dutch and Jewish refugees from Pernambuco in the second half of the seventeenth century did the sugar industry take root. During the next two hundred years Surinam developed into a plantation colony noted principally for its atrocious abuse of slaves. Yet, the importance of the colony should not be exaggerated and might be measured by the 33,621 slaves liberated in the general emancipation of 1863. Of the planters and their "sadistic cruelty, pigheaded selfishness and short-sighted cupidity"[27] little need be said except that in most respects, including their economic and social relationship to the metropolis, both the Dutch and the surprisingly large number of Jews appear to have closely resembled their counterparts in the British islands.[28] The abolition process, therefore, presents no new difficulties.

The economic history of the Danish West Indies, which is to say of the sugar industry there, ran the usual course and reached two peaks. The first was reached in the first quarter of the seventeenth century in St. Thomas, the second at the very end of the eighteenth century in St. Croix. It would be only a slight exaggeration to make this economic history of sugar more or less the social history of the Virgin Islands as well. The islands followed the course of the British islands: "With the increasing size of the plantations absentee landlordism became more general, a larger number of planters was forced to resort to white managers, and in many instances the supervision of the slave was left to Negro drivers."[29] Absenteeism necessarily had to worsen thereafter, for as the plantation system spread from St. Thomas to St. Croix, many planters merely established a second plantation. Politically the Danish government would tolerate no nonsense from the planters about "English liberties," especially since Danes constituted only a minority of the resident whites, but significantly, no slave code ever emanated from Copenhagen. It is true that occasionally the governor might severely punish masters for extreme cruelty,[30] as in St. Croix during the eighteenth century, but in general the government retained tight control over economic relationships while leaving the slaves to the discretion of the master class. If we needed a single circumstance to lay bare the bourgeois nature of the regime, this one would do. The rest followed: increasingly heavy metropolitan investments in the islands, loose lives for resident planters and managers in town, and a general orientation toward Europe and away from local responsibilities.

The plantation regime here too produced patriarchal tendencies. Denmark had the honor of being the first state to forbid its subjects to take part in the slave trade (edict of King Christian VII on March 16, 1792), and the man mainly responsible was a St. Croix planter, Ernest Schimmelmann. Since he was a large planter, we might suspect him of selfish economic motives in wanting to cut off the supply of labor to competitors and to drive slave prices up, but since he also had been a director of a slave-trading company only ten years before and enjoyed a reputation as an especially humane master, this suspicion might well do him a great injustice. These patriarchal tendencies qualified the bourgeois nature of the regime here as elsewhere in the Anglo-Saxon Caribbean, but did not define it.

The abolition process completes the story. The Danish government followed in British footsteps and moved toward gradual abolition with compensation. By the 1840s their sugar islands had long been declining and the metropolitan bourgeoisie had long been in the process of redirecting funds. Before financial matters could be resolved, the blacks, hearing the news and objecting to the plans for a protracted transition, rose in 1848 in a general strike of insurrectionary proportions. The governor, a "friend of the blacks," capitulated with disquieting ease and declared immediate emancipation. Despite howls from the planters, Copenhagen ratified his actions, which ostensibly had saved the planters from the gruesome fate of the French in Saint-Domingue. Perhaps so. But the feeling grew that the Danish bourgeoisie welcomed the chance to cut its losses and bypass the compensation question at the expense of the resident planters.[31]

I V

In discussing the French slave colonies, Tannenbaum describes them as halfway between the Anglo-Saxon and Iberian types, but in the model advanced here they more closely approximate the Anglo-Saxon. The link between the ruling class of the metropolis and that of the islands appears elusive, for the social basis of France during the eighteenth century itself appears so. In general, France provides the best illustration of Engels' characterization of early modern Western Europe as having undergone a revolution in its economy while retaining an essentially seigneurial ruling class that wielded power through an absolute monarchy. By the second half of the sixteenth century the landowners had reversed the trend toward independent peasant proprietorships. Many of the lords had risen from the ranks of the bourgeoisie, but their activity merely strengthened the fundamental structure of the old regime. For example, although the increase in sharecropping might be taken as a sign of progress toward rural capitalism, in fact it generally meant the confirmation of a significant portion of the peasantry in a dependent status, the shift of much of society's economic burden to their backs, and the inhibition of the home market. The attempts of Colbert to break through the economic constraints of the old regime are instructive. If we take the era of Colbert and Louis XIV as a whole, we find a record of some impressive reforms, notably the tariff of 1664, but of general frustration. The state tried to curb the tolls and hindrances to trade between the tree-trade area of the *cinq grosses fermes* and the rest of France, but as Heckscher says, "It is clear enough . . . that it achieved nothing."[32] Toward the end of the reign of Louis XIV, amidst a worsening financial situation, the state doubled river and road tolls under its control. In essential respects little or no political progress toward the organization of a national market occurred until the French Revolution.[33]

E. P. Thompson must nevertheless be taken seriously when he derisively refers to "the quaint notion that peeps from the edges of some Marxist interpretations of the French Revolution that 'feudalism' prevailed in France in 1788."[34] Much may be said for his insistence that the "bourgeois revolution" must be understood as a phased process and not a single stroke. There are, however, two processes requiring our attention, the first being the process of capitalist development of the economy and society, and the second, the revolutionary political process culminating in the effective transfer of state power from one class to another. The second must proceed at a certain pace if the first is not to be aborted. Perhaps Marxists minimize the length of time and the complicated, piecemeal mechanisms normally required for the conquest of state power. They do not err in maintaining that a decisive turn, usually marked by a sharp and open struggle for power, must occur if the antagonism is to be resolved between an increasingly preponderant socioeconomic regime and a state apparatus effectively controlled by a fading ruling class. Without such a turn—the Puritan Revolution in England and the Great Revolution of 1789 in France—the conditions for the uninterrupted development of capitalism could not have been secured. In these terms, Thompson's argument stands, for it draws attention to the limits of such revolutions and warns us against expecting a sudden and total break in the economy or even in the political relationship of class forces.

The planters of Saint-Domingue and the lesser islands were linked to the class structure of France on both its aristocratic and its bourgeois levels. The accumulation of great fortunes in the islands might enable an aristocratic family to reverse its financial decline. In the second half of the eighteenth century a considerable number of impoverished French nobles emigrated to the Antilles, where they served as administrators or military officers and bought slaves and plantations in an effort to recoup fortunes. Carré speaks of two hundred families of noble birth in the area of Le Cap alone and suggests substantial numbers, in proportion, in other parts of Saint-Domingue. Upon returning to France, these nobles were likely to re-establish their social position, as they had their economic, perhaps by marriage into the high aristocracy. Those whose course to economic rehabilitation in the islands included a marriage into a wealthy family there would be no less in a hurry to return to France at the first opportunity.[35] Alternatively, a great plantation fortune might enable a bourgeois family to buy into the *noblesse de robe* or might swell the growing ranks of the *grande bourgeoisie* of Paris or, more likely, Bordeaux. At the other end of the social scale, Debien's researches show that the early *engagés* came from the peasantry of extreme western France in the vicinity of the Atlantic ports. With the conversion from tobacco to sugar, indentured white servitude gave way to black slavery, and the peasant emigration, with a few exceptions, ended.[36] Although most of those who remained in the islands entered the ranks of the *petits blancs,* some did rise into the planter class. In view of their origins and the lure of the ranks to which they aspired, their class attitudes and behavior could not have been much different. We may doubt that it mattered much, so far as the plantation regime in the islands was concerned, whether the planters originated in the aristocracy, bourgeoisie, petty bourgeoisie, or peasantry. As a group they hated the country, left it for Paris when they could, and constituted an absentee class. In general the resident planters, as in Barbados or Jamaica, remained residents only because they could not afford to leave. When they could not resettle in France, they tried to spend several months a year there or as much time as their income and circumstances would allow. The inferiority of living conditions and standards of civilization turned their minds toward Paris; their obsession with Paris diminished their concern with life around them in Saint-Domingue or elsewhere in the islands. They did little to correct a situation in which plantations lay miles apart, connected if at all by bad roads. Their plantation homes, contrary to the usual legends, were poorly furnished temporary stopping places. If the planters could not go abroad, they might at least escape to Le Cap or some other town. As C. L. R. James says: "Seeking to overcome their boredom with food, drink, dice, and black women, they had long before 1789 lost the simplicity of life and rude energy of those nameless men who laid the foundation of the colony. A manager and an overseer, and the more intelligent of their slaves, were more than sufficient to run their plantations. As soon as they could afford it, they left the island, if possible never to return."[37]

No patriarchal plantation regime could grow in this setting, although some tendency in that direction revealed itself even here.[38] If the French islands departed from the Anglo-Saxon model at all, they did so only because the state had a seigneurial and paternalistic bias that theoretically benefitted the slaves and because the Catholic Church was at least nominally present. In fact, neither institution proved effective. The French state had promulgated the relatively humane *Code Noir* in 1685 and improved it later, but by the eighteenth century, when sugar became king, the state had plunged deep into financial crisis. Given these conditions and given the toughness of the colonial residents, who had risen in part from particularly violent buccaneer origins, Paris became increasingly unwilling to interfere in local practices and increasingly content to take its share of the spoils in silence. As for the Church, its position in French life had been circumscribed since the time of Philip the Fair, and its possibilities for interfering were limited. French Catholicism could not play so active a role as could Portuguese or Spanish, for two reasons. As a cultural and ideological force, it had noticeably less effect among the French planters than among the Iberian; for whatever reasons, there can be no doubt of the deeper religious convictions or at least the more active response to Church teachings among the Brazilian planters. As an institution, the Church in France and the French colonies simply lacked the power that it had in Brazil or even Cuba. Whatever possibilities existed for a positive Church role in protecting the slaves in Saint-Domingue ended with the expulsion of the Jesuits, who virtually alone had championed their interests. The case of Saint-Domingue demonstrates as clearly as any how little the institutional framework and traditional ethos counted when not filtered through a ruling class of an appropriate type.

The French colonies, like the English, provided places for investment with an eye toward windfall profits. Investors in Saint-Domingue rarely suffered disappointment. Although the planters established themselves by means of capital advanced by the commercial bourgeoisie of Bordeaux and Nantes, which had an enormous stake in West Indian prosperity by 1789, plantation profits appear to have provided the main source of investment capital from a much earlier point than in the British islands. As a by-product of the fantastic boom, during which sugar production in Saint-Domingue almost doubled in the decade before the Revolution, absenteeism climbed to new heights.[39] For Bordeaux and Nantes the stake far exceeded their direct investments in the islands. An estimated 1,000 ships and 15,000 sailors worked the colonial trade routes, and the direct and indirect profits of the slave trade continued at impressive levels.

The firm link between the bourgeoisie and the planters exposed itself dramatically in the early phases of the French Revolution.[40] In the fall of 1789 the Société des Amis des Noirs frightened Bordeaux by opening a vigorous agitation for abolition. On December 3, Mirabeau drew wild cheers from the Assembly when he presented the abolitionist case. With some difficulty the deputies from Bordeaux had the resolution referred to a special commission, headed by Barnave. The commission fell under extreme pressure not only from the merchant bourgeoisie but from the lower classes of Bordeaux, which linked their own economic prospects to the fate of the Atlantic economy. In March 1790 it recommended that colonies be held at all cost as a matter of economic necessity and that they be left to formulate their own laws and to regulate the status of unfree persons. The planters of Saint-Domingue had won a great, if temporary, victory, thanks to the Girondist bourgeoisie. The victory proved temporary because of the intrusion of the race question into what, for the good bourgeois of Bordeaux, ought to have been understood as a matter of money and morals (to the extent that good bourgeois can recognize a distinction between the two). As soon as the question of the rights of the colonial mulattoes intruded itself, the Girondins remembered some of their principles. The mulattoes were, after all, mostly solid planters and bourgeois themselves, as one dramatic moment will suffice to illustrate. In the 1760s the racist administration at Le Cap prohibited mulatto women, who generally dressed stylishly (that is, impudently), from wearing shoes in the streets. The outraged women won their fight to have the regulation repealed by organizing an orderly march through the city during which, in place of the outlawed shoes, they wore diamonds on their feet. Under pressure from the left, the Girondins drew the line: slavery and the slave trade, yes, for they were good for business; discrimination against the *gens de couleur*, no, for it was not good for business and violated the rights of man. This perfectly natural and sensible combination of attitudes represents the quintessence of what is known as liberal moderation, in contradistinction to extremism, fanaticism, and disorder.

The split between the Girondist bourgeoisie and the planters over the *gens de couleur* illuminates the differences in the character of the two groups. These differences fell into two categories: economic interest and world outlook, which is to say class ideology. Those Girondist principles resulted from a long intellectual and social conditioning and represented a fundamental moral standpoint. The ease with which the Girondist bourgeoisie sacrificed this standpoint when its pocketbook was directly threatened merely tells us that it was a bourgeoisie. The limits to its "realism," which fanatical and insensible leftist critics insist on calling cynicism, were reached when it was asked to sacrifice its moral principles, and therefore its self-respect, simply to flatter the vanity of the colonial *petits blancs*, for whom it had contempt anyway, and to guarantee an unfair competitive advantage to white planters over darker ones. Since for obvious reasons Bordeaux and the emerging party of the Gironde stood for free trade and economic liberalism against the opportunist *étatisme* of the Mountain and its ultra-left *sans-culottes* allies, the pretensions of the colonial whites proved hard to swallow.

If the split between the metropolis and the colony takes on the aspect of a class question, one other point follows. Plantation life in the colonies, even under conditions of extensive bourgeois penetration and fundamental definition, had its own class logic. To the extent that some planters were by choice or, more likely, by circumstance residents and to the extent that some of the others had imbibed the social atmosphere of a plantation society, with its necessarily racist overtones, the planters acquired a class standpoint of their own. This standpoint did not prevail, but its existence reminds us of the tremendous ideological and moral force of the plantation system and reminds us, too, that even in the most "bourgeois" of slave regimes a powerful countertendency, however well kept in check, always remained at work.

The more narrowly economic conflict between the merchant bourgeoisie and the planters shed some light on the nature of colonial resentment and also on the subsequent abolition process. The French West Indian sugar industry, like the British, had originally risen on Dutch capital and entrepreneurship and had quickly become imbedded in an elaborate web of international economic relations. During the seventeenth century Colbert had moved resolutely to secure the insular economies for French capital, and, naturally, his policies and those of his successors had strained relations between metropolis and colony.[41] As Miss Goveia says of the West Indian sugar islands as a whole: "The growth of the sugar industry depended very little on political sovereignty, and, in fact, the economic needs of the industry cut right across the boundaries of political sovereignty. . . . It is therefore possible to speak of a conflict between European political sovereignty and the needs of the West Indian plantation system which were capitalistic and international."[42] The system of taxation, for one thing, vexed the planters, for it included taxes on landowning, with no exemptions, and "the hated poll-tax on slaves."[43] More to the point were the mercantilist arrangements designed to support the interests of the metropolis. According to the terms of the *Pacte Coloniale*, the colonies could only export to and import from France and could not manufacture needed goods. In return, France had to buy its needed tropical commodities only from its own colonies. As a capstone to the arrangement, which caused much colonial discomfiture and bitterness, the French merchant marine would enjoy a monopoly of the trade. Although these restrictions should have proved no worse than those of other powers, in practice the colonists had to carry the burden of the inadequacies of the French merchant marine, which necessarily resulted in heavy additional costs, especially since the French merchants preferred the advantages of higher prices and short supply to a policy of correcting weaknesses. If the antagonisms generated by these conditions did not produce an explosion, it was no doubt because of the prevalence of smuggling and of the Franco-American agreements of 1786-1787, which undermined the *Pacte Coloniale* in essential ways. The system nonetheless took its toll and set the stage for the foolhardy decision of the whites of Saint-Domingue to try to turn the first phase of the revolution in France to their own advantage. They assumed—as is the wont of ruling classes, which invariably believe their own cant—that the slaves were too abject and incompetent to profit from the turmoil. The slaves, notwithstanding their assigned role of perpetual servility and docility, burned down the whole fertile North

Plain, and the day of reckoning arrived. What could be said of the hostility of the planters toward Bordeaux is that it might have produced a sentiment for the transference of the island to Great Britain. Since most of the *petits blancs* probably came from countries other than France anyway, their nationalism was not likely to inhibit the planters from making such a move, but the direct control of investments in the island by Frenchmen and the traditional social orientation of the planters themselves provided formidable obstacles.

Such a transference would not have altered the social structure of the island or immediately compromised its ruling class, as the agreement accompanying the English occupation of 1793 makes clear, for both paralleled those of the British islands. The behavior of the residents of Saint-Domingue in 1793 suggests strongly that had the black insurrection and the war with Britain not intervened, the Jacobin *coup d'état* in Paris would have been enough to drive them to secession. The Jacobins confronted the planters with much more than a wing of the bourgeoisie that threatened to take its moral principles seriously, as they demonstrated when they abruptly abolished slavery; they confronted it with a party that represented the interior, not the ports, and that, as such, could and did thrive politically on the destruction of the Atlantic-oriented bourgeoisie. The Terror sent the Girondists to the guillotine and thereby incurred the everlasting wrath of generations of sensitive scholars. The moral sensibilities of these scholars somehow stop short of passing sentence on people who made their living peddling human flesh not because they believed slavery to be proper and moral—they made it clear that they did not—but because it paid their bills. The fact remains that the death sentence passed on the Girondist bourgeoisie had to fall also on its colonial presence and allies. These speculations alter nothing essential in the principal argument, for had the transfer to Britain occurred, French-speaking planters of a British Saint-Domingue would have found themselves in the same position as the English-speaking planters of Jamaica in the tumultuous 1830s.

Had the black revolution in Saint-Domingue failed and had the island remained French when Napoleon restored slavery, the second abolition (1848) might have been more difficult to effect. But by then the remaining islands, notably Martinique and Guadeloupe, were declining in the face of competition from French beet sugar and Cuban cane sugar, and there is no reason to believe that the outcome would have been substantially different. These two kinds of competition might not have occurred had not Saint-Domingue left sugar production, but given the range of economic forces, the British experience, and the temper of France in 1848, it is difficult to believe that "the most dramatic change in the history of French colonialism," as Gordon Wright calls it, could have been long delayed.[44]

V

When we turn to the Iberian variant we confront more complex issues, beginning with the nature of metropolitan society. Spain qualified as the greatest of powers during the sixteenth century, and the place of American treasure in its performance needs no review. R. B. Merriman, in his classic history of the empire, demonstrated that if the colonies caused Spain's decline, as so often charged, they also provided her with a position from which to decline. As the great colonial power that was pumping gold and silver into Europe and thereby indirectly financing the economic revolution then in progress, Spain was playing a central role in the early history of capitalism. The bases of her social system remained nonetheless seigneurial, although paradoxically, classical Western serfdom had weaker roots there than in the countries to the north. The weakness of those roots did not lead to the early victory of capitalism, as might have been expected, but to the prolongation of the seigneurial regime.

The initial weakness of serfdom grew out of the exigencies of the Reconquest from the Moors. The Christians settled as they advanced, and as a result a free and militarized peasantry dominated much of the landscape. Even many peasants could afford a horse, which enabled them to go to war and affect an almost noble air.[45] The power of the great lords grew slowly. In medieval Castile the prevalence of *mayorazgo* (entail) drove the younger sons of the land-owners abroad but greatly strengthened seigneurial property. Essentially two types of lordship existed in Castile: *señoríos libres* or *behetrías* and *señoríos de solariego*. In the first case, peasants freely placed themselves under the protection of a lord; in the second, which increasingly came to prevail, they received inheritance rights in return for dues and services.[46]

Conditions differed elsewhere in Spain. We may note only Catalonia, which Ferdinand reorganized in order to put an end to a century-long class war between lords and peasants. Among other things, he freed the peasants who had been tied to the land and commutated labor services into cash payments. The Catalonian measures notwithstanding, the era of Ferdinand and Isabella witnessed a great increase in the social and economic power of the nobility. The conquest of Granada ended with the division of Moorish lands into huge entailed estates. "As a result," writes J. H. Elliott, "the late fifteenth century sealed and confirmed the pattern of land distribution that existed in late mediaeval Castile. This meant in practice that 2 per cent or 3 per cent of the population owned 97 per cent of the soil of Castile, and that over half of this 97 per cent belonged to a handful of great families."[47] In the newly occupied lands the nobility had an especially easy time because seven centuries of Moorish rule, with its irrigation, its great state enterprises, and a thoroughly efficient political apparatus, had produced a docile peasantry made to order for incoming feudal lords.[48]

The need for labor on these estates became acute especially after the expulsion of the Moors. As early as the fifteenth century African slaves were pouring into southern Spain, and the Archbishop of Seville himself used large numbers.[49] The Moriscos also remained in a distinctly dependent status and worked the great estates of Catalonia as well as of the south. During the great rebellion of 1568, Christians and Moriscos sold each other into slavery by the thousands. The Spanish freed some 10,000 Christian galley slaves at Lepanto. In short, slavery and virtual serfdom continued to exist for foreign peoples on a large scale while the Spanish peasants, often under seigneurial obligations, aped the cult of *hidalguismo* and sank into misery. As late as the eighteenth century the strength of the higher nobility and the pre-eminence of the grandees rested firmly on their command of land and labor, and four great families reputedly owned one-third of all the land under cultivation in Spain.[50]

A strong Spanish monarchy arose early. Unlike the French and English monarchies, it did not develop in temporary coalition with the bourgeoisie, for which it had to pay a price, but rather because of the inability of the lords to hold power locally without the support of a strong central regime. The social basis of the Spanish monarchy, like that of other absolute monarchies, remained seigneurial. By building an empire, arranging for colonial plunder, and establishing a huge bureaucracy with sinecures for impoverished *hidalgos* and *títulos*, it enabled the lower sections of the aristocracy to survive despite their limited ability to squeeze excessive rents out of the peasants in a period marked by a crisis of seigneurial incomes. For Spain and Portugal colonialism in general and plantation slavery in particular provided the economic surplus necessary for the stability of a ruling class that remained essentially seigneurial.

Just as capitalism has been propelled forward by the law of capital accumulation, so seigneurialism was propelled forward by an analogous law of economic accumulation, requiring the appropriation of an ever larger economic surplus.

In the words of Rodney Hilton: "Fundamentally they [the lords] strove to increase feudal rent in order to maintain and improve their position as rulers, against their innumerable rivals as well as against their exploited underlings. The maintenance of class power in existing hands, and its extension if possible, is the driving force in the feudal economy and feudal politics. For this reason rent had to be maximized."[51] The absolute monarchy emerged as the final bulwark of this old regime. That it had to crush the recalcitrant nobility—those unwilling to surrender ancient liberties —ought not to obscure its role as the ultimate guardian of the social system in which the nobility could remain dominant. Specifically, as Christopher Hill points out, the strengthening of the central state power supported the seigneurial regime from the crisis of the fourteenth century onward by repressing peasant revolts, pumping out the rich peasants' surplus by means of taxation, and subjecting the labor force to national regulation at a time when local power no longer sufficed.[52] The general role of the absolute monarchy has had recent parallels within advanced capitalist society as bourgeois governments have had to curtail sharply the power of individual capitalists and business organizations in the interests of the social system as a whole. The contradictory appearance of the period of absolute monarchy stems in part from the state's having been the vehicle for two different processes. On the one hand, it served the interests of the seigneurial classes in the manner Hilton and Hill suggest; on the other hand, the internationalization of the economy forced it to adopt policies that objectively could and often did strengthen the national bourgeoisie, which had its own sphere of external commercial rivalry, and thereby dug a grave for the system it intended to bolster. Whenever a government, no matter how committed to seigneurial power, had to subsidize maritime, armaments, and other industries in order to secure its country's economic and military power in the international arena, it ran the risk of building up its bourgeoisie both directly and by weakening foreign commercial rivals. The specific contribution of New World colonies and of the slave plantations to European development therefore depended on the nature of the regimes spawning them—on the ultimate use to which the expropriated surpluses were put. In the case of those countries, such as the Iberian, which retained an essentially seigneurial social order, this ultimate use passed beyond the national limits; to the extent that the economic weakness of the old regimes resulted in the siphoning off of accumulated wealth by the bourgeois powers to the north, European capitalism as a whole received a tremendous impetus anyway.

The commercial revolution did not in itself produce capitalism; it prepared the way only where specific developments occurred within the productive sphere. As Pares, to cite a recent non-Marxist authority, observes: "It is beginning to be clear that it was the agricultural rather than the colonial wealth of England that was tapped for industrial development in the later eighteenth century." Pares suggests that colonial plantation profits passed to the metropolitan merchants, who directed them into consumption or plowed them back into commerce.[53] The role of colonial markets nevertheless cannot be ignored. The slave plantations stimulated European industrial production in a limited but important way, as did the slave trade, which established markets for industrial goods on the African coast. Even in the sphere of investment, which is Pares' concern, the crisis of the seventeenth century, with its colonial dimension, did accompany a marked concentration of capital, which, as Hobsbawm notes, set it apart from the seigneurial crisis of the fourteenth century; in the latter case—without here entering into a discussion of cause and effect—we find pressure on seigneurial incomes, a demographic catastrophe accompanying the Black Death, and an acute labor shortage, all of which contributed to a general commutation of labor services and a pronounced tendency toward agricultural decentralization. Colonialism in general and plantation slavery in particular, coinciding as they did with internal structural changes in England and even Holland, undoubtedly contributed significantly—how significantly we do not yet know —to the solution of the problem of capital accumulation for capitalist industry. As Georges Lefebvre argues for the eighteenth century:

> According to a new method of calculating imports, exports, and re-exports, worked out by A. H. Imlah . . . Britain did not grow rich from its balance of trade. Its balance of payments was, nevertheless, favourable, since abundant capital was available for investment in the economy, especially in industry, and was used to underwrite loans asked by the government. Freight service, insurance and commissions undeniably contributed to exports. But during this period England did not furnish capital to continental Europe. On the contrary, the Dutch and Genevans had large investments in England, which weakened the balance of payments. It can therefore be concluded that Imlah's figures prove the essential importance of revenue from overseas territories—from the slave trade, funds tied up in plantations, salaries and pensions of the India Company agents, individual speculations by colonial traders. This was undoubtedly true not only of England but, to a varying degree, of the other colonial powers.[54]

Increased trade under other conditions, such as those in Eastern Europe, strengthened seigneurialism. On the Iberian Peninsula it also strengthened seigneurialism, but with a less disastrous effect on the peasants. The Luso-Hispanic equivalent of the second serfdom emerged, not in Portugal and Spain themselves, but in the colonies when Indian labor was recruited in forms reminiscent of European serfdom and when Negro labor was recruited as direct slave labor. It is especially significant for the history of slavery in the Americas that the use of black slave labor began on the Peninsula itself as the chief means of securing a labor force for the estates of the conquering Christian nobles. In effect, black slave labor in Spain and Portugal did not reconstruct a slave mode of production, but served as an extreme and temporary form of exploitation within a developing seigneurialism. From the beginning, therefore, plantation slavery in the American colonies of Spain and Portugal represented an extension of the essentially seigneurial socioeconomic system of the metropolis; that is, unlike the Anglo-Saxon variant, the mode of production that arose in the colonies proceeded in essential harmony with that of the mother countries, though not without sharp conflicts of interest over the division of the spoils.

Slavery in the Spanish colonies followed two main lines of development. In Cuba it provided the basis for a plantation slave society, albeit one that never wholly dominated the island; elsewhere, on the mainland and in the lesser islands, it provided one form of labor exploitation within a wider system of labor dependency. The second case, being straightforward, creates few problems of interpretation. The large plantations that did exist on the continent and in such lesser islands as Puerto Rico and Santo Domingo formed enclaves within a society that retained a seigneurial mode of production. The large slaveholders constituted part of a seigneurial class with special problems and interests arising from the direct ownership of slave labor, but they did not constitute a class apart except in the narrowest, purely economic sense. The retention of slavery presented itself as a question of convenience, not of class survival. Outside the plantations and mines, the slaveholders could be identified as those who owned artisans and especially domestics for reasons of status and prestige. The wars of independence and subsequent liberalization freed the slaves but created no social chaos because the ruling class was not thereby undermined. All that happened was the conversion of one form of dependent labor into other forms. Except in Cuba, slavery did not create a slave society in Spanish America, and it is within this context, not that provided by the inherited institutional forms per se, that we may find the explanation for the relative mildness of the slave regime there. To understand the social character of the Spanish presence in America, we shall have to begin with Spain itself and with Spanish commercial policy.

Whether one views mercantilism as "the policy of the town writ large in the affairs of the State" (N. S. B. Gras, a well-known economic historian of the last generation), or as a "weapon in the struggle against the foreigner, a tool of war and foreign policy" (Trevor-Roper), or as "primarily an agent of unification" (Heckscher), or as a policy appropriate to the primary or original accumulation of capital—views that are by no means incompatible—the essential question of the social basis of state power remains. The rise of powerful national states, the gradual formation of a world market, and the internationalization of military technology forced on all states policies that were superficially similar. Just as the great rivalry of our own day has forced both capitalist and socialist countries to borrow heavily from each other's methods and techniques, so the great commercial and religious rivalries of the early modern period forced every country to try to offset the measures taken by others. Notwithstanding appearances, the emergence of similar policies has not produced a "convergence" of capitalism and socialism in our own day; it has introduced serious distortions (or, for those who prefer, improvements) into each system, the class basis of which—private versus social property and surplus appropriation—has remained distinct, despite all Swedish pretenses. Since every important power during the seventeenth century had to accept a strong dose of economic *étatisme* to survive, the century exhibits an apparent uniformity that should not be taken at face value. As the economic policy of a national state desirous of pressing its claims against recalcitrant nobles at home and enemies abroad, mercantilism looks the same throughout Western

Europe. Yet some did it better than others, and as Heckscher shows, the Spanish and Portuguese interpreted the task quite differently from the English. Where the economic policy of the state could be brought into harmony with the needs of the bourgeoisie, as in England or Holland, the road to capitalism lay open; where those policies diverged in essential respects, as in Spain and Portugal, the road remained barred.

The state, Heckscher writes, had to assert itself against both medieval universalism and particularism, but especially the latter. "The greater power of mercantilism was directed inwards and not outwards, against the still more narrowly confined social institutions, cities, provinces and corporations which had dominated medieval social activity. . . . Its first object was to make the state's purposes decisive in a uniform economic sphere. . . ."[55] In this sense Spanish policy proved to be almost antimercantilist and represented an up-to-date medievalism.[56] Some of the city-states of medieval and Renaissance Europe may be classed as protocapitalist or as capitalist enclaves, but without political and economic domination of a national market, they could not transcend the seigneurial limits which encased them and could not revolutionize society as a whole. The rise of absolutism and the national state provided essential preconditions for the development of a European capitalist mode of production. Internally, it advanced the process of creation of a national market; externally, it made possible overseas expansion and the creation of an international market.[57] For the rest, everything depended on the progress of the bourgeois currents within the nation and, finally, on the conquest of state power by those willing to remove the fetters on capitalist development.

Spanish policy, externally and internally, demonstrates how thoroughly the monarchy protected the social and economic interests of the nobility while curbing its political pretensions. Colonial plunder, to no small extent, went into shoring up a decaying *hidalguía*. One of the most conspicuous forms of aristocratic waste was the enormous collection of servants and retainers, who probably could be supported from the income of the estates of the great lords, although under conditions of entail financial problems had to accrue even for the sons of the higher nobility. For the lower nobility and *hidalgos*, they were always serious. The state's task was to provide a suitable payroll and positions of local economic power: municipal offices continued as "the characteristic activity of the provincial nobility well into the nineteenth century."[58] From the mid-seventeenth century on, poorly educated students whose social position rendered them hostile to work plagued the country with their search for sinecures. The state obliged by providing the civil service and opening the way to "a frenzied rush for office, to which the suggestive name *empleomanía* has been given."[59] By the middle of the eighteenth century this swollen and parasitic bureaucracy came to be viewed by some as a major cause of Spain's decline. In the time of Philip IV the number of tax farmers and collectors was estimated at between 60,000 and 160,000.[60] Under such a regime it is not to be wondered at that when sharp struggles broke out between landowners and tenants, the Crown almost invariably favored the landowners. Describing the agrarian changes of the eighteenth century, Richard Herr writes:

> This oligarchy of *regidores* and other owners of large *mayorazgos*—that part of the old *hidalguía* that had known how to profit from changing circumstances—was running the countryside in alliance with the monasteries and cathedral chapters and the new *caciques*, while the titled nobility and the great *señores* lived in Madrid and the large cities on the income their overseers, large *cacique* tenants, or dues-paying tenants provided them.[61]

Spain's bourgeoisie, especially its industrial bourgeoisie, hardly had a chance to develop. The inflow of American treasure did stimulate industry—textiles, silk, Toledo blades, ceramics, leather, even iron—but virtually every industry looked to the export market and could rely on little support at home. One might have expected a major breakthrough, for the peasants' ties to the land were weak, and a labor force ought to have been available. The looseness of the *behetría* left many free to leave the land, and many did so, but they did not normally go into an industrial reserve army. They begged and loafed. Although local authorities sometimes rounded them up for factory work, the normal practice was to leave them alone, for Church and Crown defended the honorable rights of beggars. The pretensions of *hidalguismo*, to which all classes subscribed, bore fruit. Those who would dismiss the historical debate on the "spirit of capitalism" as mere metaphysics might ponder the combined effects of this pre-bourgeois Luso-Hispanic ideology and psychology.[62] A single illustration taken from Brazil may suffice. Brazil too was full of beggars, one of whom, in Rio de Janeiro, owned two slaves who carried him through the streets in a hammock while he asked for money. A French traveler suggested that he might sell the slaves with a view toward establishing a means of support. The beggar replied, "Senhor, I am asking you for money, not advice!" Throughout the Iberian world the Church assumed, as best it could, its responsibility to provide charity. The contrast with the English experience favors Latin-Catholic humanity but Anglo-Saxon Protestant business sense.

Other factors help to account for the strangulation of Spanish industry. Bullion in the long run destroyed the export trade, for with prices in Spain higher than elsewhere, others sought to sell but not buy there. The *hidalgos*, living on fixed incomes from rents and government salaries, fought with an adequate degree of success to reduce prices. The tax burden on the bourgeoisie and the peasants, their potential market, was crushing. The transportation system remained appalling. The guild system, encouraged by Ferdinand and Isabella and their successors, kept industry locked into a pre-capitalist mold. In a word, the seigneurial nature of society—

its ideology, its economic arrangements, and above all its state power—contained the bourgeoisie within the narrowest of limits. Notwithstanding the reactionary features of such sixteenth-century revolts as those known in Spanish history as the *comuneros* and the *germanía*, their victory might have made a great difference; their defeat sealed the fate of the middle classes for centuries to come.[63] The outcome may be gleaned from the demands advanced by the Spanish revolutionaries of 1812, which included abolition of tithes and feudal dues, permission for enclosure, repeal of a mass of absurd restrictions on internal commerce and agriculture, suppression of seigneurial jurisdictions, and the like. Long before, the price revolution, as Elliott shows in his critique of Earl J. Hamilton's massive study, had ruined Spain only because internal conditions had already prepared the way and had set industry on a course of decline. Let the last word be spoken by J. H. Plumb: "The dynamic explosion of Spain's energies in the sixteenth century had taken place within the firm structure of mediaeval thought and belief and had not altered them one iota. . . . What worked like yeast in the societies of Britain and the Netherlands crystallised in the joints of Spain and rendered it arthritic."[64] Not until the reforms of the Bourbon monarchy in the late eighteenth century did capitalism begin to struggle forward in a significant way; for the most part, the changes engendered came too late to affect appreciably the slave regimes of the New World except for the interaction between the revolutionary crisis of the early nineteenth century and the situation in Cuba, which requires a separate analysis.[65]

Eric Williams suggests that American slavery ought to be understood as part of the growth of European mercantilism, which he identifies as a phase of capitalism. More recently, Andre Gunder Frank, in his provocative book *Capitalism and Underdevelopment in Latin America*, has argued that the entire history of the Americas must be understood as the development of colonial capitalism and that neither seigneurialism nor an equivalent precapitalist system ever emerged from the European conquest. Frank is not directly concerned with slavery, which he treats as one form of colonial exploitation, but by implication he has provided, at least in outline, the kind of rounded theoretical schema in which Williams' formulation could take on genuine significance. A full critique of Frank's thesis would take us too far afield, but we might note certain intrinsic theoretical and historical difficulties. Frank is forced into a dubious reading of Iberian social and economic history and into oscillation between two untenable theses. The first thesis would have Spain and Portugal capitalist rather than seigneurial during the fifteenth and sixteenth centuries and therefore societies that merely exported their socioeconomic system in a particularly exploitative and retrogressive form. The second thesis would concede the possibility that Spain and Portugal had remained seigneurial but would maintain that colonization grew out of their mercantile-capitalist sectors and assumed the character of those sectors. The principal difficulty with such arguments lies in their identification of capitalism with merchants' capital and extensive, long-distance trade; this identification constitutes a serious error for reasons that Marx and Dobb have presented with theoretical cogency and vigorous empirical defense. Beyond this general difficulty lies a specific one in connection with Frank's theses on the social system of the Iberian Peninsula, especially with the second one. They obscure the nature of class rule and present us with two insoluble problems, the first being the impossibility of locating the process by which the bourgeoisie assumed state power in Spain and Portugal, and the second, the impossibility of accounting for the acquiescence of a seigneurial state in an economic process sponsored by and primarily benefitting the bourgeoisie. Even in France, where economic development proceeded much more rapidly, the growth of the Atlantic ports during the old regime was tolerated rather than fostered, and at that, only so long as their interests could be subsumed within those of an essentially agrarian and seigneurial empire. Spanish and Portuguese history cannot be made intelligible in Frank's terms, but an alternative viewpoint can satisfactorily account for the developments. Frank's trenchant analysis centers on the development of the world capitalist market and of the metropolis-satellite pattern of exploitation. For him the entire history of New World colonization should be understood as a function of the expansion of capitalism, and accordingly, he vigorously attacks all theses that include a feudal or seigneurial dimension. Frank's work has undoubtedly made possible a deeper understanding of the nature of metropolis-colony relations than we have hitherto had, but it accounts for only one side (the international) of a dual process. That one side, is, however, especially significant since it necessarily leads us into a direct appreciation of the unity of modern history—of the extent to which developments within Atlantic civilization formed part of a single process of capitalist development.

Another matter of special gravity in Frank's work invites comment for its bearing on general problems of Marxian historical interpretation and current politics. As a revolutionary socialist as well as a professional economist, Frank argues convincingly against the notion that the national bourgeoisie —that favorite strumpet of the right-wing communists—can any longer play an anti-imperialist role in Latin America. He thereby assumes a position compatible with that of Mao or Fidel Castro and at variance with that emanating from Moscow and adhered to by most Latin American Communist parties. Unhappily, Frank finds it necessary to interpret all Latin American history from this point of view, as if the whole revolutionary Marxist position had to stand or fall with it. But one could easily accept his diagnosis of the present crisis and even much of his revolutionary strategy flowing from it and yet arrive at them by an alternative historical route. The distinguished authority on nutrition and former chairman of UN-FAO, Josué de Castro, in his stimulating book *Death in the Northeast*,[66] adds a touch of unintended humor. Without mentioning Frank's work, De Castro manages to stand it on its head. For him, those who interpret Brazilian history as a capitalist rather than a feudal process play into the hands of the counterrevolution by obscuring the need for revolution as opposed to reform of the capitalist system. His logic is at least as good as Frank's. The juxtaposition of their views might seem to prove—although it does not—that history ought to be left to historians.

Entertainment aside, Frank's insight betrays him, for even if we grant that capitalism, not seigneurialism, shaped the economy, we could not accept his thesis without inviting a political debacle. The strength of capitalism on the countryside of regions like the Brazilian Northeast lies precisely in its ability to harness archaic forms of economy. Under these conditions capitalism has cut the peasant off from access to a market mentality and a bourgeois ethos while drawing his labor into a market economy. Unless the ideological ramifications of this process are understood, socialists will wait a long time for a peasant revolution to develop.

Continental Spanish slavery did not create a slave society—that is, a society dominated by slaveholders and marked principally by the pervasive influence of the master-slave relationship—but it did make possible enough concentrations of plantations and mines using black labor to create substantial pockets of masters and slaves within the wider society. During the mining boom blacks were brought in to supplement Indian labor and to serve as guards and gang leaders over the Indians. Although occasionally slave labor proved enormously profitable, for the most part a large Indian population, working under a different kind of unfree labor system that proved favorable to the mineowners, rendered it generally inconvenient.[67] Black slaves worked the export-oriented coastal plantations of Venezuela and Central America as well as the units designed to supply nearby cities. The areas near the cities were depopulated of Indians fairly early, and even smallholders, taking advantage of good prices in nearby markets, often bought two or three slaves to help them work their farms. As time went on, the agricultural slaves were concentrated in the plantation-export sector, but their owners nowhere on the mainland played a major independent role as slaveholders in society. Rolando Mellafe conveniently summarizes the other groups most desirous of holding slaves: officials and local leaders who needed servants, artisans, and construction workers for various projects; religious orders, notably the Society of Jesus, which used both farm workers and domestic servants; merchants who needed carriers; institutions such as hospitals and townships, which had various odd jobs to be filled; and even individual Indians and collective Indian villages. The gateway to freedom by self-purchase, good works, or sentiment often swung open to slaves in these categories, especially after the Cuban practice of *coartación*, which permitted slaves to buy their own freedom, spread to the mainland during the eighteenth century.[68]

Slavery did not fully disappear from the mainland until after the mid-nineteenth century, despite the progress made toward abolition during the wars of liberation. With a large section of the big slaveholders being *peninsulares* or first-generation creoles loyal to the Crown, Bolívar, San Martín, and other leaders lost nothing by offering freedom to slaves who joined them; they were sufficiently in touch with the liberal influences emanating from revolutionary Europe and North America to have been comfortable doing so. The ensuing years nevertheless brought great trials and reversals to the abolitionist cause. In general, if we except the plantation pockets, slavery in mainland Spanish America existed on the periphery of society, and its abolition ought to have been easy. Slavery in Chile or Mexico strongly resembled slavery in New York or New England. There was a difference, which made matters harder and easier. Slavery was harder to abolish because it formed a long-sanctioned part of an accepted stratification in society; if it served no indispensable end, neither did it represent a great evil in the eyes of men who might fight for political change but wanted no part of unnecessary tampering with the social order. Slavery was easier to abolish because once ideological pressure did build up, there was no deep class interest to check it, and because society had long been prepared to accept the Negro as a man. The peaceful abolition of slavery in South America leads to two apparently contradictory but quite compatible conclusions, the first being that the ideological and material attachment to slavery grew strong even where it was a peripheral institution, for although slavery disappeared from Spanish South America with relative ease, it nevertheless displayed a psychological tenacity far stronger than mechanists and economic determinists can appreciate. Second, with or without this tenacity the bitterness was unlikely to lead to war because no class interest was at stake.[69]

By extension, and with proper qualification for the fundamental difference in social structure, these generalizations apply to the Northern United States. The two leading explanations for the nonviolence of abolition there—unprofitability and ideological pressure—do not carry us far. The traditional economic argument of unprofitability is easily refuted since slavery remained profitable for some, and especially since so many slaves were nonproductive servants and status symbols anyway. The moral-ideological explanation has greater force, but only because society was of a kind to provide ample room for an antislavery morality and because no specifically slaveholding class had ever arisen to project a world view and appropriate morality of its own.

The Cuban case raises the difficult problems and continues to evoke fierce arguments among learned scholars. The central problem, briefly, is this: granted that Cuba deserved its reputation as a mild, patriarchal slaveholding country during the eighteenth century, to what extent did commercialization and the sugar boom offset and reverse the patriarchalism generated by the institutional and earlier economic framework and the moral inheritance? We may recall that the reputation of the Cuban slaveholders during the nineteenth century could hardly have been worse and that they were held up in horrible contrast to the ostensibly beneficient slaveholders of Mississippi. Allan Nevins goes so far as to describe Cuba at mid-century as "an outrage upon the name of Christian civilization."[70] Elkins and, more recently and thoroughly, Herbert S. Klein have cast doubt on this nineteenth-century reputation and have turned the argument around. In effect, they claim that the moral inheritance and institutional framework greatly inhibited the evil tendencies produced by the sugar boom and are to be congratulated for having minimized the brutality and inhumanity, the existence of which they do not deny. Nothing in their work contradicts the evidence that the sugar planters were extremely brutal and indifferent to their slaves. The burden of their argument falls elsewhere, for Klein takes pains to show that Cuban slavery retained its previous character outside the sphere of sugar production. He argues that about half the slaves on the island remained outside the sugar-plantation sphere even at the peak of the preabolition sugar boom; that a large proportion of these slaves lived in cities and survived as artisans and skilled workers in the face of growing competition from immigrants; that the greatest period of sugar expansion came after abolition; that the blacks on the sugar plantations, who were harshly treated, were mostly newly imported Africans, whereas the creole blacks remained in more secure positions elsewhere; and that in short the sugar plantation, however important, was not even roughly equivalent to the slave regime as a whole.

Klein's viewpoint has been seriously challenged, most notably by Franklin W. Knight, who insists that in fact Cuban slavery did dominate society, especially in the sense that the slaveholders commanded insular politics. He notes that 80 percent of the Cuban slaves worked in agriculture, that sugar amounted to 75 percent of the island's exports, and that almost 60 percent of all slaves worked in sugar estates.

He is also critical of Klein's work on other important questions and observes, for example, that the geographical distribution of priests casts grave doubts on the notion of a large clergy protecting the slaves against unscrupulous masters.[71] Knight does, I believe, have much the better case, but even if Klein were to be proved right, his own account demonstrates the rapid development of a highly exploitative sugar sector in the heart of the slave regime.

From its origins as a Spanish colony until the latter part of the eighteenth century, Cuba avoided monoculture, excessive land monopoly, absentee landlordism, and many of the worst effects of colonial status. If it had the appearance of backwardness, it also showed great vitality within its assigned limits. A variety of circumstances combined to create "a class of large-scale and small-scale proprietors who were descended from the first settlers and who were deeply attached to their native soil."[72] For about two hundred years, from the middle of the sixteenth century to the middle of the eighteenth, Cuba remained largely isolated from the world market and became covered with huge cattle estates, which, like the early sugar industry itself, actually fostered settlement and land division instead of the reverse. Spanish trade restrictions inhibited the growth of the sugar latifundia, whereas coffee and especially tobacco production rose and fell on much smaller units.[73] Slavery, whether in agriculture, domestic service, or artisan production, grew up in a manner analogous to that of Spanish South America—in an economy and society only partially driven by the pressures of the world market.

The second half of the eighteenth century changed everything. The British capture of Havana in 1762 had a considerable effect, but probably not nearly so considerable as was once thought. The British introduced 10,000 slaves almost overnight and gave the island a taste of a freer trade policy. Well before the occupation, however, the Bourbons had begun to discuss measures designed to foster large-scale landholdings in order to promote sugar production. The industrial revolution in England radically shifted the world demand curve and, together with the French Revolution, encouraged liberal economic ideas; the American Revolution and the subsequent Anglo-American trade rivalry in the Caribbean led to an expansion of Cuba's illicit trade; and the great rising in Saint-Domingue destroyed the world's greatest sugar industry and opened the way for Cuban ascendancy. These and other less momentous events propelled Cuba into the heady prosperity of the sugar boom and into a fateful commitment to a new colonialism, far more insidious and destructive than the old, which lasted until the communist revolution of the 1950s. Cuba did not move easily into that sugar-based prosperity: world market conditions and internal and external politics resulted in a zigzag economic course until well into the nineteenth century. Not until the demise of slavery and the penetration of American capital at the end of the century did the sugar industry come to dominate Cuba, but it is enough for our purposes that it made impressive strides during the century and introduced a new and vicious slave-driving system.

During the nineteenth century new men brought sugar to supremacy in Cuba in the face of great obstacles. A weak transportation system, even after the introduction of railroads in the late 1830s, and other difficulties slowed the pace of development until mid-century, when sugar exports doubled during the period 1840–1860. A slump in prices and vigorous competition from European beet sugar forced early technological innovation and large-scale production. Deerr writes:

> Cuba was the first sugar-producing area to recognise the economic effect of large capacity, and dating from 1831, when *Alava*, the first of the great sugar centrals, was built by Zulieta, Cuba was far in advance of any other country in this respect. Not only so, but Cuba was a leader in the application of new inventions. The steam engine was naturalised in Cuba, the vacuum pan was generally adopted at an early date. . . .[74]

This technological advance proceeded hand in hand with

foreign investment and investment by wealthy creole businessmen, who probably played the leading role. The great sugar plantations required hundreds of slaves and tremendous outlays of capital; the older class of slaveholders could hardly have accumulated such sums or had access to adequate credit. As Fernando Ortiz says, "Foreign predominance in the sugar industry was always great, and now [first half of the twentieth century] it is almost exclusive."[75] Some regions of Cuba were considered more American than Spanish as early as the second quarter of the century, and investments by Northern United States businessmen probably matched in amount those of Southern slaveholders.[76] The ensuing regime, with its unprecedented but far from complete absenteeism, its reliance on newly imported African labor, and its profit-maximization outlook, took on much of the character of the slave system of the British islands. Whereas until the mid-1830s coffee, grown on small and medium-sized slaveholdings under resident planters, predominated, afterwards sugar, grown on large plantations under planters of a decidedly bourgeois type, came into its own. The rise of the sugar plantations meant the rise of a new regime. Cuban slavery became simultaneously the mildest and harshest of slave systems; it yielded to and yet effectively opposed the old institutional restraints; it did and did not transform itself under the pressure of commercialization. Two systems, in short, had arisen side by side. The new regime for the most part grew alongside of, not out of, the old and was the creation of a new class.

The Cuban course to abolition proved long and tortuous, being intertwined with the politics of national independence and relations between Spain and the United States. Corwin and Foner have admirably traced this complicated story, and we may restrict ourselves to a few observations.[77] The anti-Spanish reform movement went through three phases. The first, led by Arrango y Parreño, defended slavery and the slave trade; the second, led by Saco, defended slavery but opposed the slave trade; and the third, emerging in the 1860s under the leadership of some of the island's wealthiest planters, opposed both. These men understood the importance of general economic renovation and the extent to which slavery inhibited it. The effective end of the slave trade in the 1860s raised the cost of labor and added to the pressures for increased capital intensity. The collapse of the Confederate States of America ended the last hopes of the diehard slaveholders. Increasingly, independence from Spain, economic rehabilitation, the promotion of needed European immigration to staff a technologically advanced industry, and every measure required by the great entrepreneurs pointed to abolition. Already, white workers were working alongside slaves during the grinding season. The Ten Years' War (1868–1878) created havoc. The great Negro revolutionary leader, Antonio Maceo, freed slaves where he could, even while others temporized; Spain, under pressure from Washington, promulgated the weak Moret Law of 1870 to begin a gradual emancipation; and the creole planters moved as quickly as possible toward free labor. The process was complicated, and we do not yet know enough about the class alignments. It is clear, however, that the sugar planters had a purely economic stake in slavery and that when that stake waned, they could move into a wage-labor system. The process was protracted primarily because of the wider political implications. One occurrence may illustrate the ideology of the great sugar planters: they supported the Union side during the North American war in the belief that its victory would result in the destruction of the Louisiana sugar industry. For the most part they felt no strong class identification with the Southern slaveholders, as they certainly would have if the survival of slavery as a social system had been uppermost in their minds.

In sum: the rise of the sugar *ingenio* in nineteenth-century Cuba represented the rise of a new class of capitalist slaveholders for whom slavery was an economic expedient. Cuban slavery experienced a process of bourgeois penetration akin to that of the Anglo-French Caribbean. Foreign capital made its appearance, and the already well-developed creole bourgeoisie intruded itself. As a result, we may postulate the coexistence of two radically different slave regimes. In this setting, the movement of many of the creole sugar planters toward free labor, internal reform, and independence from Spain may be explained as a single process of the maturation of a Cuban bourgeoisie, albeit one well on its way to a comprador status of junior partnership with American capitalism.

V I

Brazil, as a projection of sixteenth-century Portugal, presents special problems. Portugal underwent a peculiar development in the late Middle Ages. On the one hand, the commercial bourgeoisie manifested great strength, and the nobility displayed far less aversion to trade than in most other countries; on the other hand, commercial capital did not revolutionize the mode of production, which remained backward and largely seigneurial, never quite able to make the leap into a capitalist social order. As Gilberto Freyre points out, Portuguese expansion coincided with internal agricultural decay and the commercialization of the nation "to the point where it became one big business house with the King and the leading nobles transformed into business men."[78]

As early as the thirteenth century, well before the rise of the House of Aviz, the Portuguese Crown interested itself in commerce, tried to check the economic power of the Church, and showed sympathy for the mercantile sector. The reigns of Afonso III and his talented son, Diniz, were marked by sharp conflicts with the Church, the growth of towns and trade, and the waning of serfdom. During the fourteenth century the merchants of Lisbon, with royal consent, signed their own trade agreements with Edward III of England. When João of Aviz claimed the throne and sought to block the claims of Castile, he received the support of the bourgeoisie and the lower classes, whereas the nobility rallied to the Castilians. The battle of Aljubarrota, in which the Portuguese smashed the pride of the Castilian chivalry, represented as great a victory for João over his own nobility as over Castile. To all appearances, the bourgeoisie was on the road to power. At best, however, the long evolution of the Portuguese nation and the dramatic ascendancy of João of Aviz had only created favorable conditions for the revolutionary transformation of Portuguese society.

A new nobility replaced the old, and if it had strong ties to merchant capital and lacked the usual prejudices against commerce, it also had or quickly struck deep seigneurial roots. The decline of serfdom did not signal the end of seigneurial obligations, and the conquest of the Moslem south led to the extension of the old regime. The nobles received large tracts of land, for which they recruited African slave labor. The first African slaves arrived as a curiosity in 1441; three years later several hundred were brought in for domestic service, and before long they were coming in large numbers to work the estates. R. Trevor Davies accepts the figure of 10,000 imported slaves per year at the time of the accession of Philip II of Spain and notes that competition from slave-worked estates seriously reduced the standard of living—and therefore the purchasing power—of the peasants.[79] The strength of seigneurialism appeared in the arrangements for the settlement of Madeira and the Azores, which prefigured the subsequent westward expansion. Prominent families received concessions on the condition that they agree to settle their retainers there.[80]

The distinguished historian H. V. Livermore, evaluating late medieval and early modern Portuguese history, denies the widely made contention that by the end of the fourteenth century the landed nobility had fallen from power and been replaced by a mercantile bourgeoisie. Mercantile expansion, he points out, grew primarily out of the efforts of the Crown, not the middle class.[81] The king not only subsidized shipbuilding, he built ships as a royal venture. From the time of

Afonso III, if not earlier, the king was a businessman in a way that no English or Dutch ruler ever was.[82] Heckscher describes Portugal as the country tied most closely to "pure state trading" and, significantly, in his theoretical section argues convincingly that mercantilism did not sympathize with state enterprise but rather with state-supported private monopolies. The contrast which Heckscher himself makes between Portuguese and Anglo-Dutch practices is striking, whether or not one follows him in declaring the former essentially unmercantilist or chooses instead to view mercantilism as an economic policy capable of adaptation to both bourgeois and seigneurial regimes.[83]

Portugal, notwithstanding its high level of commercial development and its breathtaking rise as a colonial power, had avoided rather than solved its secular economic problems. Instead of cutting its peasantry loose from the soil and releasing it for industrial wage labor, it reintroduced slavery, drastically undermined the dignity of labor, and found new ways to exploit its formally free peasants within a web of seigneurial relations. Instead of creating a home market and developing industry to absorb the wealth, especially gold, taken from Brazil and other colonies, it maintained an old order that acted as a center for the re-export of expropriated funds to Northern Europe. Even during the boom period of Brazilian sugar others siphoned off a large part of the profits. "The production phase," writes Celso Furtado, "was in the hands of the Portuguese, whereas the Flemish would load the crude product in Lisbon, to be refined at home for distribution throughout Europe."[84] Without an adequate industrial bourgeoisie or a substantial home market, even when the small size of the country is considered, Portugal had to rely on Dutch and Flemish capital, entrepreneurship, and access to Northern European markets. By the second half of the eighteenth century, the last phase of Portuguese history that bears on our own concerns, not even a tough and enlightened quasi-dictator like the Marquês de Pombal could effect a breakthrough. Acute political weakness after the separation from Spain in 1640 had led Portugal into a series of compromising treaties with England (1642, 1654, 1661, and especially the Methuen Treaty of 1703), and by Pombal's time the semicolonization of Portugal had been accomplished. The Methuen Treaty permitted the Portuguese to sell their wines much more easily in the British market, but the *quid pro quo*—the opening of Portugal to British textiles—dealt a hard blow to hopes for industrialization. The effects of the treaty came to be felt at the very moment that Brazilian gold began to flow in. "Thus," writes Furtado, "almost impromptu the required conditions for enforcing the treaty were created, so as to make it operate as a mechanism for reducing the effect of gold as a multiplier over and above the level of economic activity in Portugal."[85] Pombal's reforms failed to lead the old regime into the new, and Portuguese seigneurialism subsequently had to evolve into capitalism painfully and with serious distortions. Down to the *Grito de Ipiranga* and Brazil's declaration of independence in 1822, where we may leave it, Portugal had much the aspect of what Hobsbawn has called, in a more doubtful connection, a "feudal business economy."

The Brazilian case has a certain similarity to the Cuban in that here, too, either the slaveholding class underwent an astonishing metamorphosis between, say, 1750 and 1850 or, as seems more likely, two kinds of slaveholding classes emerged. During the last forty years Gilberto Freyre has been advancing the notion of a patriarchal, paternalistic slaveholding community, which bound master to slave and black to white, but during the last decade revisionist scholarship has painted a grim picture of the slave regime.[86] The difficulty in evaluating the two viewpoints at the moment stems largely from the curious way in which the discussion has proceeded, for in fact it has been less a discussion than the presentation of separate arguments on separate subjects. Neither line of thought has as yet directly confronted the other. Freyre's work has been on the Northeast during the colonial period, especially the seventeenth century. It is true that he carries the story into the nineteenth century in *The Mansions and the Shanties* and glances at the coffee-growing South, but the relationship he posits between the old regime of the sugar-growing Northeast and that of the newly developed regions is ambiguous. At some points he implies that the South was a new formation with only tenuous connections with the patriarchalism of the Northeast and that the two regions present a sharp contrast; at other points he implies that the South was recapitulating the Northeastern pattern but that since it had not attained maturity by the second half of the nineteenth century, its patriarchalism was undeveloped and much buffeted by the pressures of commercial and frontier life. The revisionists have centered their attention entirely on the South during the nineteenth century and have only implicitly suggested skepticism about Freyre's view of the Northeast. C. R. Boxer, in *The Golden Age of Brazil*, does examine the Northeast, but even he focuses on the period of its decline and the attendant rise of mining in Minas Gerais and bypasses Freyre's main argument for the Northeast. Basically, what Boxer does, and what Caio Prado Júnior also does in *The Colonial Background of Modern Brazil*, which analyzes society at the beginning of the nineteenth century, is to document the contemporary assertion that Brazil was a "hell for blacks." Since Freyre's thesis, as both Boxer and Prado acknowledge, focuses on the pattern of life generated in the Big House, it is or can be rendered sufficiently flexible to include the essence of their criticisms.

The Northeastern regime that matured in the seventeenth century met almost all the preconditions necessary to substantiate Freyre's thesis of patriarchalism. It grew out of a seigneurial if highly commercial Portugal; it developed under the tutelage of an international church that was at the core of the seigneurial structure of Europe; and it arose on the basis of a labor system that, if not itself seigneurial, was wholly compatible with seigneurial power, values, and tradition. For

Gilberto Freyre the Portuguese who settled Brazil brought with them "a love for display and grandeur and a distaste for manual work, which are to be explained, in large part, by their having had, for nearly a century, most of their domestic work done by Negro slaves and, for many centuries, some of their most difficult agriculture provided by the Moors."[87] Caio Prado Júnior is less sure that Brazilian patriarchalism came from Portugal and deliberately bypasses the question, for, he insists, "what really determined its splendid flowering in Brazil was the local background from which it emerged. . . . It sprang from the economic regime, from the plantation system. . . ."[88] This agreement by these two outstanding, ideologically opposed scholars on the outcome should cause no surprise, for the patriarchalism—or as others might call it, paternalism, medievalism, corporatism, seigneurialism—of the sugar-growing Northeast constituted the most obvious feature of the social regime. The Church played its part. In a stratified society it offered a haven for the intelligence and culture of the ruling class and a road upward for the ambitious and fortunate of the lower classes; simultaneously, it provided organizational as well as ideological bonds to keep all social classes together. Despite corruption, the priesthood commanded the genuine respect of the *senhores de engenho* (sugar planters, or literally, lords of the sugar mill), as well as of the masses, and mediated as best it could between them.[89] This patriarchalism had to proceed in the face of powerful tendencies toward commercial exploitation, reinforced by the roughness of frontier life, and it remains an open question as to just when the regime mellowed. There is, in any case, no doubt any longer that field slaves lived under a stern regime, rendered all the sterner by an open slave trade and an attendant low cost of labor, until the sugar economy entered a period of decline in the eighteenth century. As everywhere else, slavery in Brazil exhibited tremendous internal social and ideological strains, for the pressures to maximize income and the ideological pressures toward paternalism remained locked in an incessant conflict.

Freyre, the great interpreter of Brazilian patriarchalism and himself a product of the Northeast, speaks of the persistence of the old regime even within the new and recalls having read somewhere: "*Une cuisine et une politesse! Oui, les deux signes de vieille civilisation.*" The *senhores de engenho*, whom Furtado roughly but plausibly estimates to have earned 90 percent of the sugar income, have been described often, both in the contemporary literature and by later writers. Alexander Marchant's summary serves well:

> In the course of running his property for his own interests, safety, and convenience he performed many of the functions of the state. He was the judge: he settled disputes among his followers. He was the police: he kept order among a large number of people, many of whom were his slaves. He was the Church: he named the chaplain, usually some near relative with or without religious training, to care for his people. He was a welfare agency: he took care of the sick, the aged, the orphans. He was the army: in case of uprisings of slaves or raids by Indians or feuds waged by other great families, he armed his kin and retainers as a private militia. Moreover, through what became an intricate system of marriages, kinship, and sponsorship (*compadrio*), he could appeal for support if need be to a large number of relatives in the country or in the towns who possessed property and power similar to his own.[90]

Absenteeism diluted this paternalism somewhat, but not in any way remotely resembling that of the Caribbean. The sugar boom of the early period produced some *senhores de engenho* like João de Paus, who reputedly owned eighteen *engenhos* and 10,000 slaves; clearly, he could not have been everywhere at once. By the second half of the eighteenth century an increasing number of *senhores de engenho* preferred to spend more time in their town houses than in the country.[91] The quality of life in these towns represented an extension of the rural regime; the influence of the bourgeoisie was minimal, especially since it was largely foreign (i.e., Portuguese, not Brazilian) and was held in contempt. Relatives of the *senhor* generally looked after his *engenho* when he was away, and he rarely remained away for very long.

More than any other slaveholding regime in the New World, that of the Brazilian Northeast approached autarky. Even in the nineteenth century the plantations produced clothes for the slaves, handicrafts, farm equipment, and food, either directly by slave labor or indirectly through formally free squatters and dependent peasants who were tied to the *senhor* by a complex of economic and social relationships.[92]

The economic history of Brazilian sugar during the seventeenth century reveals a good deal about the social nature of the regime. The first half of the century witnessed a buoyant economy, but during the second half the volume of exports fell by 50 percent, relative to the levels reached about 1650, and the real income to the *senhores de engenho* fell by 75 percent or more. Celso Furtado, arguing quite properly that the slave economy depended on external demand, notes that such slumps in no way "present the catastrophic character of modern economic depressions." He makes a number of important points: monetary income from exports consisted entirely of the planters' profits; fixed outlays comprised virtually the whole cost of the enterprise; and therefore, the planters always found it to their advantage to remain in production during periods of falling prices.[93] Furtado, whose excellent economic history of Brazil is generally marred by its excessive attention to the purely economic factors in economic development,[94] offers a dubious interpretation:

> The profitability of the sugar business was inducive to specialization, and it is not surprising from the economic standpoint that the entrepreneurs avoided diverting production factors into secondary activities, at least at times when the prospects of the sugar market seemed favorable. . . . The extreme degree of specialization of the sugar business is in itself proof that it was remarkably profitable.[95]

Notwithstanding the attempt at qualification, Furtado has

somehow lost his own insight. Further along in the same book he returns to that insight: "The great-landlord class, which was largely self-supplied by its own estates and whose monetary expenditures were cushioned by the slave-labor system, was relatively little affected by the consequences of the issuing of paper money."[96] In short, the cost of production consisted of fixed outlays only because of the high level of self-sufficiency, which did not form a necessary ingredient of this seigneurial class rule but which certainly strengthened it enormously.[97]

The competitive pressure of the world market, the greed of the metropolis, and the parvenu character of the rising planters combined to establish powerful tendencies toward capitalistic exploitation and against patriarchalism, but once the foundations of the regime had been laid, the struggle necessarily had to prove unequal. The *senhores de engenho* were residents, not absentees; their lives were intimately bound to those of their slaves; the patriarchalism engendered by this relationship extended itself to embrace white and colored *moradores* and *lavradores*, who made up formally free but actually dependent strata within the domain and under the protection of the landowner. The *moradores* settled as subsistence farmers on the *senhor*'s land in return for occasional labor services and dues, usually in kind. Although they technically paid feudal dues, more often than not these were waived, so that the payments in kind, generally much needed foodstuffs, represented a gift from the *morador* to the *senhor*. Unlike the *morador*, the *lavrador* used the *senhor*'s land to raise sugar cane, which he agreed to send to the *senhor*'s mill on a sharecropping basis.[98] By the turn of the nineteenth century, if not earlier, many "contract fazendas" had arisen. Tenants kept half the sugar proceeds, less a rent, and were supplemented by free copyholders who owned land but sent their sugar to the *engenho* of their choice on a half-share basis without further dues. Prado estimates, from scattered data, that these smallholders raised up to one-third of the Brazilian sugar crop.[99] The copyholders sometimes became rich and achieved slaveholder status; in any case, they doubtless stood socially much closer to the *senhores de engenho* than to the tenant farmers. These arrangements strengthened the *senhor's* control of the sugar crop, provided food for local towns and possibly the *engenhos* themselves, took care of the old or favored manumitted slaves and retainers, gave the *senhor* a source of supplementary labor for emergencies, and enormously enhanced his prestige and power, especially since most of the *roças* (small holdings) were occupied by custom rather than deed. In return the smallholder or tenant got the *senhor's* protection, which was by no means a minor matter. Among other things, he could always count on the *patrão's* help should illness, crop failure, or some other catastrophe strike his household. The whole system made possible and was in turn strengthened by the *corpos de ordança*, local militia charged with certain administrative tasks and the maintenance of public order. As military units they were a joke, but as instruments of seigneurial power they kept the peace, advanced the prestige of the *senhor*, and created another institutional tie between lord and retainer. Josué de Castro surveys these relationships with a critical eye and, as it were, presents the harsher side of the same case: "Whether he was a slave or serf, farmhand or leaseholder, the Brazilian peasant, at least in the Northeast, has always been accustomed to forced labor, hunger and misery."[100]

The ideological and psychological tendencies inherent in these relationships proved infinitely stronger than those generated by commercial connections, no matter how harshly the economic logic of seigneurialism drove the *senhores de engenho* to raise the rate of exploitation. The bond between the *senhores de engenho* and their laborers grew increasingly personal, especially as creole Negroes slowly replaced Africans in the Northeast, and the link received extraordinary reinforcement from the prevailing social ethos and from the Church. It provided an impressive barrier to the ascendancy

of the capitalist market mentality; it might bend considerably
under severe strains in the market, but it was not likely to
break.

The eighteenth and especially the nineteenth century ushered in a new era, marked by the rise of a new slaveholding
regime in the South. The slaveholders of Southern Brazil
drove their slaves hard and acquired a reputation for being
profit-hungry consumers of human flesh. Two interpretations
are possible. The first possibility is that the coffee planters
were still too new, still too much under the pressure of the
coffee boom, still too close to the frontier stage, to have re-
constructed the Northeastern regime, but that they were in
effect recapitulating its early phase. If so, then they resembled
the Mississippi slaveholders of 1830, relative to those of
Virginia and South Carolina, and, given another generation
or two, could have been expected to end in the same place.
The second possibility is that the coffee planters were new
men in a different sense—not merely parvenus but agrarian
capitalists who constituted a class of a new type in Brazil.
Both possibilities in fact obtained: the first might reasonably
be applied to the planters of the Paraíba Valley, whose flush
times in the 1850s passed into a pronounced secular crisis.
They had begun early, before the effective closing of the slave
trade and the defeatism engendered by the progress of abolition in the countries to the north. In attitudes and embryonic
style of life, "The coffee *fazendeiros* of the Paraíba Valley
had much in common with the *senhores de engenho* of the
Northeast."[101] The second possibility clearly applies to those
self-proclaimed heirs of the *bandeirantes*, the Paulistas. If we
place ourselves in the tumultuous 1880s and glance backward, the story, at least in outline, becomes clear.[102]

By the 1870s the planters of the Paraíba Valley, the center
of the coffee economy, were in trouble, and the next decade
would see the shift of the coffee boom to São Paulo. This
development represented far more than an economic shift,
such as the movement of the center of the cotton economy of

the United States from South Carolina to Mississippi; it represented a momentous change in the nature of the planter class itself. This metamorphosis was inseparable from the shift in economic importance from sugar to coffee—from the Northeast to the South—which began earlier and proceeded simultaneously. We shall have to dispose, at the outset, of that vulgar economic-determinist interpretation which frequently occurs in one form or another and which ought not to have appeared in the work of so sophisticated a Marxist as Perry Anderson: "Modern Brazilian capitalism is the accidental product of an import-substitution process dictated by the interests of the patrimonial coffee oligarchy of São Paulo."[103] That God is good we need not doubt; that he is quite so good we may consider less certain. The shift from the Paraíba Valley to São Paulo occurred after the effective, as distinct from the legal, closing of the slave trade, after the fall of the Confederate States of America—the last hope of the remaining slaveholding classes—after the emancipation of the Russian serfs, and after the virtual triumph of the anti-slavery ideology in the world.[104] The ghastly Paraguayan War left its own scars, to which we shall return; it also represented Brazil's end of isolation. The forces it unleashed, combined with the steady political, economic, and ideological pressure of the British, whose commanding position in Brazilian affairs is well known, presented the Paulistas with an unprecedented situation: the Paulistas entered coffee production at the very moment when everyone knew that the death knell of slavery was sounding. The planters of the Paraíba Valley in many ways stood closer to the old regime than the new, but they also represented a continuation of the social process begun in Minas Gerais a century earlier.

The mining boom in central Brazil indirectly eased the transition from a slave-labor to a wage-labor economy. Taken as a whole, the experience helped dissolve the old ways of living and thinking and prepared the way for new men, or at least a new mentality. This process had no abstract in-

This is interesting) almost ect clocher but seems more aut ect clocher tha historical

evitability about it; it had these effects not because mining and a gold rush necessarily had to act as a dissolvent—the reverse might easily have proved true—but because it took place within a definite national and international framework and formed part of a great historical conjuncture. The mineowners in fact often considered themselves planters of a kind and affected the old way of life, when they could afford it. They commanded slave labor and belonged in material interests and in spirit to the old regime, although some, who had come from the cities and the more fluid South, were no doubt of a different type. The mining boom did, however, generate a bourgeoisie. Mining created a big demand for food and supplies, which stimulated commercial activity, artisan workshops, and small-scale farming for market. These elements received encouragement from the Crown, which saw a chance to clip the wings of the haughty *senhores*. Although slave labor prevailed, its foundations underwent dangerous erosion. Mining attracted adventurous free men, and, in contrast to the Northeast, at no time did slaves constitute a majority of the population. Slaves worked under special conditions designed to encourage their initiative. They moved, with new freedom of action, in a more complex environment, and many won or bought their freedom by participating in gold discoveries.

Uncertainty, mobility of capital, labor, and entrepreneurship, high profits, and increasing specialization marked the emergence of a new economy. Average income in the mining economy probably fell below that of the sugar economy, but it was broadly based rather than sharply skewed. The foundations of a diversified and quasi-free economic system were being laid. The entire region developed a speculative psychology, for mines were exhausted quickly and progress came in waves. Speculation, wasteful measures, and other factors led to a sudden collapse during the eighteenth century. When it came, little remained as a monument to the boom.

The story might easily have had a socially retrogressive

rather than a progressive ending. Instead of releasing capital, labor, and entrepreneurship and a new spirit to build up agriculture and fledgling urban industries in the South, the events described might have reinforced the decadent patterns of the Northeast. In fact, the story ended both ways. Prado has shown how the collapse of the mining boom resuscitated agriculture in the Northeast.[105] The gold boom had a loosening effect and helped pave the way for a new order by creating favorable conditions for the advance of capitalism, but by itself it could never have produced the transition. In the Northeast, where the *engenhos* survived in the old way, the influx of resources strengthened the old regime; in the South, where new forces were at work, it played a different role.

The planters of the Paraíba Valley followed the same course. Left to themselves in a static world, they probably would have recapitulated the regime of the Northeast. The patriarchalism was there: the rootedness in the land, the nightly benedictions for the slaves, the aristocratic power over the countryside—in short, the plantation as a way of life. The roughness, cruelty, and barbarism that marked the regime might well have passed with time. Unfortunately for the *senhores*, they had no time. No sooner had the area begun to mature and perfect its social system than it plunged into depression and faced the world-wide onslaught against slavery. The depression was not like that of the sugar-growing Northeast; it did not result from a decline in the demand for coffee. On the contrary, the international market had never looked better; the world-wide demand for coffee was rising. The trouble lay in soil exhaustion and the ruin of a particular region. With the demand high, the planters responded by driving their slaves unmercifully. Notwithstanding the patriarchal features of the system, the planters pushed the rate of exploitation to the breaking point and drove an ever deeper wedge between themselves and their slaves.

The Valley remained the stronghold of the diehards. They

found themselves chained to their labor force—compelled to rely on labor-intensive methods—by economics, sentiment, and tradition. They above all other sections of the planter class had to fear the effects of abolition, for their relationship with their slaves could only produce the expectation of a mass exodus of the labor force once it was free. To complete their economic misery, the impending end of slavery naturally destroyed their chances for borrowing the capital needed to tide them over or even, if they were so inclined, to enable them to change methods. Few bankers were so reckless as to make loans to men whose only collateral was a slave force that might be emancipated at any moment. Had the planters of the Valley had their way, there might well have been a repetition of the United States experience of 1861–1865, despite the lack of a contiguous slaveholding territory and despite the utter hopelessness of the cause. They never had the chance, for the planters of São Paulo, for different reasons, deserted them, and their own position as an undeveloped patriarchy produced serious desertions from their own ranks. Those semicapitalist origins took their toll; for many, the transition was psychologically easy, even if, for most, it produced anguish.[106]

São Paulo rose on new men, whose conversion made abolition possible. The Brazilian legislature was notoriously a planters' club; without the support of the São Paulo coffee planters abolition might have come anyway, probably with far greater violence and social convulsion, but certainly not in the form of the *Lei Aurea* of May 13, 1888, which ended slavery in one stroke and without compensation. The Paulistas provide the key to the puzzle, for a puzzle it is unless we are prepared to believe that ruling classes turn their backs on their interests, tradition, and ideology because philanthropists convince them that they have been living immorally.

São Paulo emerged as the center of coffee production in the 1880s, when slave labor did not come easily. The closing of the slave trade did not lead to substantial measures to stimulate the natural increase of the slaves. The planters of the Valley took opposite measures and drove their slaves harder than ever. The Northeast, which had sent large numbers of surplus slaves to Minas Gerais and farther south in earlier times, continued to export, but within limits, for as we shall see, economic pressures and the social structure militated against a wholesale transfer. From the beginning São Paulo faced a labor shortage, which drove the planters into mechanization. This development coincided with, in part resulting from and in part stimulating, an expansion of banking, insurance, and manufacturing, especially of hats, textiles, and processed foods.[107] The abolition of the slave trade in 1850 had released between $8.7 million and $11.6 million for other investments. The bulk went into commerce, but a significant portion went into the infrastructure and some into manufacturing.[108]

All of these changes, by themselves, might have produced different results and even strengthened the old order; that they did not leads us to consider the new men. The coffee-boom profits in São Paulo accrued to men of diverse origins and, more important, of diverse economic interests. Many of these men came from the city—merchants, professionals, former slave traders, and livestock dealers, who retained urban business connections and saw coffee growing as one more way to make money.[109] Others were small farmers who made good quickly on virgin soil. Had they done so earlier, they might have become old-style *senhores*; as it was, they entered the ranks of the planter class at the historical juncture marked by a growing bourgeois ideology and the impending end of slavery, and they immediately came under the influence of the first group, which had already established its pre-eminence and had the prestige and power accruing to substantial, prior-accumulated wealth. No doubt planters from the Valley and even the Northeast joined them, but these were likely to have been the younger, bolder men—the ones, as Robert Brent Toplin points out in his study of the abolition process, who could change.

The Paulistas encouraged European immigration and prepared to abandon slave labor. With greater capital intensity they had good reason to prefer Europeans to blacks, especially since the long period of African importations meant that few of those blacks available to them came from well-acculturated creole families. The antislavery men in Rio Grande do Sul, according to Cardoso, advocated immigration and free labor in order to instill a new attitude toward work and to regenerate and "civilize" social life. There was plenty of free labor in Rio Grande do Sul and probably a good deal in São Paulo, but centuries of seigneurial traditionalism and a slave environment had rendered it close to useless. Immigrants, when they did come, came as part of a changing order. Even the great changes in transportation must be seen in this light. Normally railroads and better roads would have strengthened the old regime, much as they strengthened the cotton regime of the Southern United States, but in Brazil they appeared at a moment of tumult and change. Among other effects, they made it possible for immigrants to settle and build up an alternative economic order.[110]

The link between immigration and emancipation appears clearly in the measures of 1870 and 1871. In 1870 the imperial government agreed to defray the transportation costs of immigrants going to the coffee estates; in 1871 the Rio Branco Law, theoretically at least, committed Brazil to gradual emancipation.[111] Still, the Paulistas strongly opposed abolition as late as the beginning of 1887 because of the labor shortage. Their switch in 1888 resulted from a powerful offensive by the abolitionists, which threatened a blood-bath and large-scale disruption of the economy and society. The Paulista planters were not abolitionists, although they were prepared to ease into the new order, but they could accept abolition under pressure because slavery did not provide the basis for their community and way of life. Their qualms were those of businessmen who do not want to rush into adventures or take unnecessary risks. By 1888 the risks had become not only necessary but urgent. At that moment they voted for emancipation and even opposed compensation. After all, they were well along toward conversion to free labor. Why should they pay to subsidize their reactionary competitors in the older regions?

The Brazilian planters as a whole knew that slavery was living on borrowed time. The Paulistas displayed greater flexibility than others, but it would be difficult to say whether their capitalist spirit directed their economic course or whether their economic course, as a product of circumstances, shaped their spirit. In either case, a new class was born, the spirit of which gave form to its content. Warren Dean's view of the process, although perhaps one-sided, deserves attention as the considered judgment of one who has studied the Paulista planters closely:

> It might be more easily argued that the shift to capitalist forms of land and labor utilization came at the beginning of the Paraíban coffee expansion rather than at its end. In the Paraíba Valley many of the early estates were assembled by merchants from the city of Rio or by men who had possessed mining interests to the north. By the second quarter of the nineteenth century their land acquisitions were greatly augmented as a result of laws in 1835 and 1850 that abolished primogeniture and substituted cash payments for grants in the distribution of crown lands.
>
> The willingness to shift to free labor, however, did not necessarily imply a more rational or humane approach to its utilization on the part of the Paulistas. Apparently they originally intended to deal with the new European workers as ruthlessly as they had with the slaves whom the immigrants replaced, but in time the constant shortage of labor forced the planters to relax their hold. A standard labor contract evolved, and the terms of payment expanded sufficiently to discourage debt servitude. To a degree, therefore, the free labor system stimulated a capitalistic outlook, rather than vice-versa.[112]

Dean claims too much. The men of São Paulo, unlike those of the Valley, had been forced early into mechanization and into viewing their ventures as strictly business, and we may assume that circumstances were not much different from those of Rio Grande do Sul, where the old slaveholders wallowed in misery during a long and painful readjustment, while new men rebuilt the economy on a wage-labor basis. There too they tried to treat wage earners like slaves, and Dean's point cannot be ignored. But when disabused, some men fretted, sulked, and went under and others learned fast and did well. Prior ideological and psychological conditioning had their role, if only in providing greater or lesser receptivity to economic realities.[113]

The Paulista gamble, if a gamble it was, paid handsomely. Brazil's coffee supremacy dates from the 1870s; its share of world production reached 57 percent in the 1880s and 75 percent during the twentieth century.[114] Brazil's ascendancy in coffee production, like Cuba's in sugar production, largely followed the abolition of slavery. As a consequence of abolition, the old coffee areas declined more sharply and the ex-slaves were expected to shift to the new. They failed to do so, for European immigrants seized the opportunity, and the blacks sank into subsistence economy. In general the economy did advance. "The rapid expansion of the internal market in the coffee region," writes Furtado, "was bound to have favorable effects on the productivity of the subsistence economy, chiefly concentrated in the state of Minas Gerais."[115] The ex-slaves provided a loose manpower pool for construction and other rough work and thereby depressed wages in the coffee sector. Notwithstanding serious deformations, Southern Brazil had entered the capitalist era.

What of the Northeast, which had long been absorbed into the world market via its dependence on the export sector but which had built up a precapitalist mode of production? Despite invigoration following the collapse of the mining sector, the economy of the Northeast continued to wallow in secular decline and was abandoning slavery voluntarily much more rapidly than the South. A simple economic explanation, however attractive superficially, does not answer the big questions. For an alternative we must return to a consideration of the traditional ruling class and the social order it had built. It rested on a straightforward slave-labor system but had once constituted part of a seigneurial ruling class of the Portuguese Empire. Slavery had never evolved fully into a separate mode of production because in the modern world no system could. It had come close enough. The seigneurial features of the regime supplemented but did not define the basic social regime. Social relations in the postabolition Northeast displayed strongly seigneurial features and revealed much about the world out of which they grew. Euclides da Cunha has given us an unforgettable picture of a patron-client psychology among the people of the stock-raising Sertão in his *Rebellion in the Backlands*. Roy Nash, writing in 1926, could say of the ostensibly free Brazilian peasant:

> No retainer of medieval Europe ever belonged to plumed and mail-clad knight more completely. The colonel is the political chief of the river, a *poderoso*; his word is law. His "protection" is the most valuable asset a serf can possess. Without it, life here would be as cheap as it is twenty miles up the Gongogy, beyond the colonel's reach.[116]

The slaveholders confirmed their power during a series of political crises, most notably during the transfer of the Portuguese monarchy to Rio de Janeiro (1808), the *Grito de Ipiranga* (1822), and the overthrow of Dom Pedro I (1831).[117] The world they made represented a compromise between seigneurialism and slavery. For most purposes, the mode of production in the Northeast may be considered slaveholding, but its seigneurial features, which were fundamentally compatible with its slave base, eased its way into the future.

Confronted with poor prospects in the world market, the *senhores de engenho* had sold their surplus slaves south for some decades, much in the manner of Virginia or Maryland.

By the second half of the nineteenth century there was not much of a surplus left to sell. Favored and old slaves had increasingly been emancipated and settled on small plots of land under the *senhor*'s protection, and the ranks of *moradores* and *lavradores* had swelled. Under conditions of labor surplus and with the alternative social relations not genuine wage labor but a familiar seigneurial dependency, the *senhores* had little to fear. In the long run abolition would undermine the patriarchal regime, but that seemed a very long run, and few *senhores* had reason to tremble. For the blacks the change meant little more than that they could now choose their own *patrão*. Another development in the Northeast helped to ease the transition. The appearance of *engenhos centrais* (central sugar mills) and *usinas* (big mills), largely financed by foreign capital, was appreciably weakening the old regime in a manner suggestive of the Cuban experience but on a much smaller scale. Thus, slavery gave way to a seigneurialism already well on its way toward a capitalist transformation.

The abolition of slavery or the simple and steady personal emancipation of the slaves assumed the character of an economic question. Although not without some moral aspects, it never developed into a profound moral question for the slaveholders, as it did for some of their enemies, because it never constituted a genuine class question. The *senhores* were heir to a Catholic tradition that called slavery into question as an unnatural if tolerable human relation, and their own class position and attendant self-image depended on the general features of lordship in a highly stratified society rather than on slavery per se. For them, patriarchal lordship might appear as a moral issue—as the only proper basis for civilized living—but slavery was merely one possible form of it. The transition to ostensibly free labor was in fact a transition to various forms of dependency that long before had struck roots alongside slavery itself. It did not threaten the hegemony of the regional ruling class; it strengthened it in the short run while establishing preconditions for its long-run absorption into a national capitalist ruling class to which it contributed a number of seigneurial distortions.

Social and economic developments in São Paulo and the Northeast tell us that the planters could swallow abolition and even turn it to advantage; they do not reveal the reason that the planters abruptly switched sides in 1887–1888. The pressures were many, but generally they coalesced into one political form: the rise of a powerful abolitionist movement, with widespread support, prepared to carry the fight from parliament to the streets and to the plantations themselves. The celebrated "peaceful" abolition of slavery in Brazil came amidst a wave of violence and the threat of much greater violence. As the planters dragged their feet, especially after the manifest failure of the Rio Branco Law of 1871 to effect a gradual emancipation, the urban-based abolitionist movement began crying out in frustration against the arrogance and greed of the "feudal barons." The planters began to face an all-out class war with their rebellious slaves and with other classes in society at the same moment. Whatever the diehards might say, the great majority of planters understood that the game was not worth the price. Neither the Paulistas of the South nor the *senhores de engenho* of the Northeast, for different reasons, saw the end of the world in front of them; the alternatives looked palatable and even promising, although certainly disquieting. The events of 1887–1888 drove these men to cut bait.

The slaves and free blacks provided the most dramatic feature of the period. With the open and enthusiastic support of the latter, the former left the plantations in droves; they killed overseers in substantial numbers; and they rose repeatedly in violent, if local, insurrections.[118] The free blacks could not have been so bold and the slaves could not have expected success had they not been certain of enormous assistance from the nation. They had it: abolitionists scarcely deigned to dissemble their incitement to insurrection, organized not-so-underground railroads, provided for escaped slaves, deliberately fomented violence against particularly obnoxious slaveowners, and finally, after years of pleading, negotiating, and temporizing, made it clear that it would be war to the death.

The urban bourgeoisie and its intelligentsia provided the backbone of this intransigent abolitionism. Although, as might be expected, important sections of the bourgeoisie, especially the commercial, took a different view, the new men of the cities saw their chance. The relationship between the end of slavery and the opening of a new era for Brazilian capitalism was clear even to the most dense. The moral indictment of slavery, which had been growing, provided the passion, even in an aristocratic conservative like Nabuco, and the direct participation of the free blacks and mulattoes in large numbers helps account for the increasingly militant and impatient tone. The working class rallied to the slaves. In 1884 seamen and port workers began a trend by shutting down the port of Fortaleza in Ceará until their refusal to transport slaves received sanction. Before long, the coastal slave trade had been smashed, and Ceará became a haven for runaways. Similar action by railroad workers, who as a group had an abolitionist reputation, received support from company managers. By 1886 refugee slaves were being carried by railroad to cities like Santos, where they found protection. The nation had risen.[119]

In the face of so powerful a coalition, with the planters themselves divided, with the royal family quasi-abolitionist, and with civil war threatening, the police and the military stood by and either refused to intervene or intervened halfheartedly. The police never had a chance; things had gone too far. The army presents a more complicated and revealing case. The officer corps originated in the cities and recruited its members from the wealthier strata of the bourgeoisie and intelligentsia; the rank and file came from the lower classes, largely black and colored. For years the army had avoided slave hunting and antiabolitionist activity; finally in 1887 the Club Militar politely petitioned the princess regent to be excused from such degrading activity. The Paraguayan War

(1865–1870) had had its effects. About 6,000 slaves had fought in the Brazilian army and won their freedom thereby; a total of 50,000 troops of all colors had fought alongside Uruguayan and Argentine troops, who chided them for retaining so barbarous an institution. To make matters worse, little Paraguay had fought with incredible courage for its war lord, Francisco Solano López. The Paraguayans put one-fifth of their population, including women and children, under arms and persisted almost literally to the death. At that, disease rather than Brazilian and Argentinian military prowess probably did them in.[120] R. A. Humphreys writes of the Paraguayan War's effects in Brazil:

> The war bred friction between civil and military authorities. It left a sinister legacy of military discontent, a contempt among military men for the ways of civilians, a surplus of officers with too little to do; and the army, in the years of peace, came to entertain an exaggerated idea both of its own importance and its own neglect. It was the army, in 1889, that made the revolution [which overthrew the Empire].[121]

The Paraguayan War revolutionized the Brazilian military much as the Palestinian War of 1948 revolutionized the Egyptian: the army's humiliations and setbacks, although in this case within the context of ultimate victory rather than defeat, were laid, with good reason, at the doorstep of a decadent economic and social order. We need not wonder that in the years between the war and 1888 the military schools became centers of abolitionist sentiment. Nor need we wonder that those planters who could make the adjustment did so with as much grace as possible. The principle was simple: If you cannot beat them, join them. Their own metamorphosis, in its particular national and international context, had given them the chance to apply the rule.

The totality of national and international conditions formed that historical context and produced the sense of borrowed time and with it the sense of slave labor as a mere economic expedient. The Brazilian South, like the Northeast, used slave labor, but unlike the Northeast it did not produce a slave or seigneurial mode of production. The peaceful drift of a substantial section of the Southern slaveholders into conversion to free labor presents no special problem, and we may readily understand that the argument against abolition had to be couched almost exclusively in economic terms—that is, in terms of providing adequate time and compensation to avoid collapse of the coffee sector. As Furtado says:

> Considered from a broad point of view, abolition was a measure of political rather than of economic nature. Slavery was more important as the basis of a regional system of power than as a form of organization of production. Once slave labor was absolutely abolished, almost no changes of true significance took place in forms of production organization or even in distribution of income. Nevertheless, one of the basic mainstays of the regional system of power established during the colonial era had been eliminated. It had survived for nearly the entire nineteenth century, acting as a stifling influence on the economic development of the country.[122]

Furtado treats the planters as a single class, but we need not do so to appreciate the force of his remarks. The main objection is that the continuity he sees had a different social content in different parts of the country. From this point of view, we may accept the proposition advanced by Octávio Ianni that the use of slave labor and the wider development of Brazilian capitalism generated the fundamental contradiction propelling the historical events of the period, for in these terms that contradiction may be located, as Ianni does locate it, within the process of world-wide capitalist development itself.[123]

VII

The Old South offers us the greatest paradox in a subject overflowing with paradox. Here was a regime as clearly capitalist in its origins as any other, but which came closest to perfecting slavery as a distinct mode of production. Since I have outlined my argument on the Old South elsewhere, I shall restrict myself to a few observations on the development of this remarkable slaveholding class.[124] Of the classes under review the slaveholders of the Southern United States most closely resemble those of the Brazilian Northeast. This resemblance is in itself noteworthy, for the two groups differed sharply in background and institutional and ideological inheritance. The Brazilians emerged from a seigneurial society, adhered to a medieval religion, accepted conservative and traditional political principles, and were delightfully free, easy, and Latin in their sexual mores and attitudes toward miscegenation. The American slaveholders emerged from the world's most advanced bourgeois society, adhered to a classically bourgeois religion, accepted liberal and democratic political principles, and were drearily repressed, guilt-ridden, and Anglo-Saxon in their sexual mores and attitudes toward miscegenation. Yet, both groups most closely approximate the standards of paternalism we associate with the patriarchal plantation. Nothing so clearly indicates the enormous social, ideological, and psychological power of the master-slave relationship when embedded in a plantation-based society. With all the encouragement of Church and metropolitan state, and with all their institutional and moral inheritance, it is extremely doubtful that the Brazilian slaveholders exhibited a higher degree of paternalism than those of Virginia or South Carolina, or Mississippi for that matter.

The foundation of a patriarchal and paternalistic ethos ultimately proved to be not the European institutional inheritance, which did play a role, but the plantation regime itself. The confrontation of master and slave, white and black, on a plantation presided over by a resident planter for whom the plantation was a home and the entire population part of his extended family generated that ethos, although where it advanced in harmony with the past, with inherited values, and with received institutions, it had a much easier time. The

most striking feature of the Southern case is that it triumphed, though far from completely, in the face of so many obstacles. One illustration may suffice. As Tannenbaum points out and as is now generally recognized, Luso-Brazilian law recognized the sanctity of the marriage relation among slaves, whereas Anglo-American law did not, but it cannot be demonstrated that a higher proportion of Brazilian slaves enjoyed the protection of a marital status than did American. Many factors would have to be considered in order to qualify properly the Brazilian experience, but we may pass them over and simply note that in the Old South, most slaves probably did have the possibility of marital stability because their masters provided it. They provided it for two complementary reasons: they could more easily control married slaves with families, and their Christian consciences demanded it.

   If the existence of a resident planter class provides the first clue to the nature of the regime, the early suppression of the African slave trade provides the second. In Cuba and Brazil the trade ran well into the nineteenth century and necessarily militated against paternalism; in the Old South, the closing of the trade during 1774–1808 exercised a powerful twofold influence on the maturation of the ruling class. The date is of inestimable importance. The slave trade closed at the very beginning of the cotton boom and at a critical juncture in the history of American slavery. Slavery in the Southeast, even in Virginia, did not, as was once widely believed, totter on the brink of extinction during the Revolutionary and post-Revolutionary period, but clearly the westward march of cotton reinvigorated it in these older areas. Had slavery not expanded geographically, its future would have been problematical, but limits to the expansion of the size and power of the old slaveholding class were in sight, if not already reached. With Virginia and Maryland in the last phase of a secular economic decline and South Carolina at or near a peak, the future of the slaveholders looked bleak and prospects for further internal growth poor. The geographical expansion of

cotton created new opportunities for the expansion and consolidation of the slaveholding class itself and simultaneously
for the maturation of its world view. Until the rise of the
Cotton Kingdom the slaveholders of Virginia and South
Carolina each had gone their own way. The sentiments and
interests of plantation slavery had tied them together, but
specific economic and social interests had left them in at least
partial isolation. The frontier cotton boom, with its derived
demand for slaves, tied the slaveholders of all regions into a
single regional ruling class, notwithstanding all the antagonisms remaining to divide them into different factions and
parties.

Hence the decisive character of the period culminating in
1808. The slave trade closed at precisely the time during
which the slaveholders were undergoing a profound metamorphosis. Two tendencies had existed under the slaveholding regime and were to continue throughout its history: the
patriarchalism of the plantation community, and the commercial and capitalistic exploitation demanded by the exigencies of the world market. With a booming frontier and
the get-rich-quick psychology it engendered, the latter tendency might well have prevailed, but the closing of the slave
trade and its attendant price rise created great counterpressure
within the economic sphere itself. The conflict was not, as it
is usually presented, between "commercial" and "paternalistic" tendencies, for increasingly the commercial side, with
its primary concern for profit maximization, actually reinforced the paternalistic impulse. Without African imports
the planters had to raise a creole slave force and had already
begun to do so well before 1808; the raising of a creole slave
force required adequate standards of humane treatment. Any
evaluation of the Southern slaveholders must begin with an
essential fact about their slaves: the slaves of the Old South
constituted the only plantation slave class in the New World
that successfully reproduced itself. Nothing so clearly demonstrates the relatively good treatment (in the strictly ma-

terial sense of the word) of the slaves and the paternalistic quality of the masters. The initial motivation to provide the slaves with adequate food, shelter, clothing, and leisure was of course economic, and the economic pressures for good treatment if anything grew stronger over time. It is nonetheless naive to leave matters there and to see economic interests and morals as discrete categories. Once extended over a generation or two, the appropriate standards of treatment became internalized and part of the accepted standard of decency for the ruling class. The growth of a creole slave population narrowed the cultural gap between the classes and races and prepared the way for those feelings of affection and intimacy which had to exist if paternalism was to have substance.

The history of the Southern slaveholders had three decisive turning points, only one of which had anything like a counterpart elsewhere. The first was the American Revolution, which, whatever its significance in the North, constituted a reactionary slaveholders' rebellion in the South. If separation from England liberated a national capitalist regime in the North, it simultaneously liberated a plantation slave regime in the South. With the threat of British interference removed and a relatively weak central government to contend with, the road to regional power lay open before the slaveholders, who constituted the only class capable of treading it. This moment had its counterpart in Brazil during a series of political crises from the removal of the Portuguese Crown to Rio de Janeiro to the overthrow of Dom Pedro I.[125] The second decisive turning point was the formulation of the positive-good proslavery argument, which signaled the maturation of the ruling class and its achievement of self-consciousness. Far from being mere apologetics or rationalization, it represented the formulation of a world view that authentically reflected the position, aspirations, and ethos of the slaveholders as a class. The final formulation of that world view, as presented by George Fitzhugh, who argued that slavery was the proper relationship of all labor to capital, had, so far as I know, no counterpart in the Caribbean or in Latin America. Its development would have been especially difficult in Latin America since the Catholic tradition, as reflected for example in *Las Siete Partidas*, recognized slavery but declared it to be unnatural. Paradoxically, it was precisely the most originally bourgeois of the slaveholding countries that produced a coherent defense of slavery as a mode of production in its social, political, ideological, and moral aspects. The paternalism at the core of the slaveholders' ideology rested primarily on the master-slave relationship but extended itself outward to encompass the white lower classes. As the regime developed, the plantations became increasingly self-sufficient and more enclosed as productive-consuming units. In the slave states as a whole, as Fishlow shows, there was considerable progress toward regional self-sufficiency.[126] Locally, this development meant the dependence of yeomen and poorer whites on the plantation market. This problem has been studied inadequately if at all, but scattered evidence does indicate that planters had the option to buy from factors and merchants and could control the local market to their own advantage. Similarly, their ginning and marketing services were indispensable for cotton-producing smallholders. For the most part, these planters do not appear to have exploited their economic opportunities with anything like ruthlessness but to have considered them part of a wider social responsibility. Many of the yeomen and even poor whites (that is, largely declassed freemen) were related to the planters. The local records of Black Belt counties make it clear that members of the same family occupied positions in all classes and income groups within the same county. The distinctly Southern sense of extended family cannot be understood apart from the social structure at the center of which stood the plantation, and it provided a powerful impetus for social cohesion, ruling-class hegemony, and the growth of a paternalistic spirit that far transcended master-slave and white-black relationships. There were undoubtedly powerful counterpressures, especially those associated with the egalitarian ethos, which would have to be given due weight in a full account. It is nonetheless clear that much of the political power of the planters and much of that oft-noted loyalty of the nonslaveholders to the regime derived from these semi-paternalistic relationships. It is not accidental that the plantation systems in Brazil and in the Old South exhibited the strongest tendencies toward autarky among the various slave regimes. The slaveholders of the Old South, however, had inherited no hierarchical political principle to draw upon and had to develop this extended paternalism carefully, with full account of the contrary democratic and egalitarian attitudes residing deep in the lower classes. Southern paternalism developed in a contradictory, sometimes even hypocritical way, but the existence and force of the tendency among so egalitarian-minded a people tells us a great deal about the character and power of the plantation system.

The third decisive turning point in the history of the South was the decision to secede and to stake everything on an uncompromising fight for regional independence. It was at this moment that the slaveholders recognized in other than an abstract way their existence as a ruling class and as the self-appointed guardians of a way of life. The Southerners, among all the New World slaveholders, demonstrated enough strength to bid for full regional autonomy. Elsewhere, in Cuba or Brazil, the insertion of slavery into a thoroughly colonial regime, subject to the great penetration of foreign capital and control, set narrower limits to the power, if not to the pretensions, of the slaveholding class.

The slaveholders of the Old South thereby came closer to forging themselves into a distinct—or if you will, pure—slaveholding class than any others in the New World. Elkins has described the rise of American slavery as having taken place under conditions of uncontrolled capitalism. In the most ironical sense he hits the mark. The liberal bourgeois institutional and intellectual inheritance, which he so suggestively analyzes, provided the perfect framework within which the slave regime could work out its own immanent tendencies, which were antibourgeois in essence. Yet, those tendencies existed side by side with countertendencies generated by the developing world market and by such concomitants as the ideological inheritance of Protestantism, liberalism, and democracy and the peculiar coexistence with a vigorous Northern capitalism within a single nation-state. An account of the struggle between these two sets of tendencies would take us too far afield here, and we shall consider certain features in Part Two. It is enough, for the moment, to observe that even the most powerful slaveholding regime—one holding genuine political power—could not wholly free itself from the ideological effects of the rapid extension of world capitalism and its bourgeois world view. At the base of this ideological dependency lay the economic mechanisms of the world market, which made all slaveholding countries economic satellites of a foreign metropolis.

CHAPTER THREE

Class and Race

I

Modern slavery and the white-black confrontation form part of a single historical process, but it does not follow that slavery can best be understood as a race question. No major problem in the socioeconomic transformation of Western society, apart from the pattern of race relations itself, could possibly be resolved on such grounds. Even the War for Southern Independence, the one major problem that historians have tried to interpret from the point of view of the race question, cannot be satisfactorily dealt with in this way, if for no other reason than that racial hegemony did not require slavery, as many contemporaries clearly understood. To affirm the priority of a class interpretation need not lead us to underestimate the force of racism, much less to expect the automatic or even rapid disappearance of racism in the event of a radical alteration in the class nature of society. As Pierre van den Berghe writes: "Race is only a special case of more general social facts, [and] it follows that there can be no general theory of race and that race relations must be placed within the total institutional and cultural context of the society studied."[1] We have been proceeding in agreement with this line of argument but have also been viewing class formation, confrontation, and struggle as the essential dynamic of that historical context.

The recent work of David Brion Davis and Winthrop D.

Jordan demonstrates that Western European prejudice against black people predated and facilitated African slavery, although neither of these scholars would try to establish a causal link. As Jordan writes:

> It was the case with English confrontation with Negroes, then, that a society in a state of rapid flux, undergoing important changes in religious values, and comprised of men who were energetically on the make and acutely and often uncomfortably self-conscious of being so, came upon a people less technologically advanced, markedly different in appearance and culture. From the first, Englishmen tended to set Negroes over against themselves, to stress what they conceived to be radically contrasting qualities of color, religion, and style of life, as well as animality and a peculiarly potent sexuality. What Englishmen did not at first realize was that Negroes were potentially subjects for a special kind of obedience and subordination which was to arise as adventurous Englishmen sought to possess for themselves and their children one of the most bountiful dominions of the earth. When they came to plant themselves in the New World, they were able to find that they had not entirely left behind the spirit of avarice and insubordination. Nor does it appear, in light of attitudes which developed during their first two centuries in America, that they left behind all the impressions initially gathered of the *Negro* before he became pre-eminently the *slave*.

He adds:

> The concept of Negro slavery there [in Virginia and Maryland] was neither borrowed from foreigners, nor extracted from books, nor invented out of whole cloth, nor extrapolated from servitude, nor generated by English reaction to Negroes as such, nor necessitated by the exigencies of the New World. Not any one of these made the Negro a slave, but all.[2]

Jordan, in his own terms, locates the origins of English racism in the transitional character of society. In our terms, he is locating it within the position of the bourgeoisie, which provided the historical conjuncture for the prevailing social ethos, myths and prejudices, and unfolding economic opportunity.

Once slavery came into being, ethnocentricity and color prejudice passed quickly, although perhaps not immediately, into racism. At that, it required the division of the world among the great Caucasian powers and the attendant vogue of Social Darwinism during the second half of the nineteenth century for a fully developed racist ideology to emerge and conquer the Western world. If scholars like Eric Williams, Marvin Harris, and Herbert Aptheker err in making racism a direct product of slavery, they err less than those who would simply invert the relationship. Previous ideological conditioning made possible a racially based slavery, and the growth of that kind of slavery transformed the conditioning from a loose body of prejudices and superstitions into a virulent moral disorder. Boxer puts it well: "Modern Portuguese writers who claim that their compatriots never had any feelings of colour prejudice or of discrimination against the African Negro, unaccountably ignore the obvious fact that one race cannot systematically enslave members of another for over three centuries without acquiring a conscious or unconscious feeling of racial superiority."[8]

The historical bond which held together the second serfdom in Eastern Europe, the quasi-enserfment of the Amerindians, and the enslavement of the blacks manifested itself culturally, as most clearly illustrated by the passion for the French language and for a cosmopolitan culture among the lords of Eastern Europe, who tried in every way possible to put maximum distance between themselves and the despised lower classes. The social function of racism stands out no matter what kind of causal link one tries to establish between economic exploitation and ideology. In Caio Prado's words:

> Racial differences, particularly when manifested in such clear somatic traits as color, will, if not create—an opinion open

to well-founded doubts, and in my view one which has been incontestably controverted—at least accentuate a discrimination already made on the social level. . . . Racial features give an unmistakeable stamp to existing social differences. They label the individual, helping to raise and strengthen the barriers that separate different classes. Any approach or blending of the classes thus becomes much more difficult, and the domination of one over the other is accentuated.[4]

One might, like Harmannus Hoetink, read the record differently and argue for the centrality of somatic-norm images—for the importance of the aesthetic dimension, as determined by the relative degree of pigmentation in different European peoples.[5] For a class interpretation of the history of slavery, such a reading could be assimilated with one qualification: prejudice, even if seen as deriving from biological and aesthetic factors, would have to be linked to discrimination and the genesis of racist ideology by some such mechanism as Prado describes.

The specific patterns of race relations in the former slaveholding societies of the New World represent the totality of each particular historical and ecological experience. During the slave period three main patterns emerged: that of the Southern United States, that of the Anglo-French Caribbean, and that of Brazil (see chart on facing page). These differences in pattern, presented here schematically and with deliberate simplification in order to dramatize a few main points, can only be accounted for by a combination of historical and ecological influences. Only hopeless romantics think that Brazil is or has ever been free of racial discrimination, but it does present a striking contrast to the United States. Some recent scholars, most forcefully Harris,[6] have pointed out that the position of the Brazilian whites as a small portion of the population forced them to build up a colored middle stratum in society to fill roles that, in the Southern United States, could be filled by nonslaveholding whites. This important insight does not suffice to explain the

	Southern United States	Anglo-French Caribbean	Brazil
CASTE SYSTEM	Two-caste system of whites and Negroes, the latter defined as anyone with some (amounts varied) Negro blood.*	Three-caste system of whites, blacks, and coloreds (those of mixed blood).	Fluid racial system: so many categories of mixture among three races that only the "pure" races were clearly delineated.
CLASS STRUCTURE	Negro = slave. Free Negroes generally a pariah people with limited social functions.	Roughly, coloreds formed a free middle class of traders, artisans, small farmers, etc. In fact, some were slaves and many others planters, bourgeois, and professionals who were divided from whites by caste, not class; others shared class position of poorer whites.	Small producers, artisans, tradesmen, overseers, etc., generally drawn from a wide range of mixed bloods.
RACE RELATIONS	Virulent racism, probably weaker among slaveholders than other sections of the whites.	Strong race prejudice, softened by distinction made by whites between colored and blacks.	Prowhite bias but minimum race prejudice. Acceptance, with qualifications, of blacks and various coloreds according to class position: "Money whitens the skin."

* I use the term "blood," of course, only as a conventional device.

range of responses, for the same might be said of the Anglo-French Caribbean, in which rigid lines were drawn on a three-caste rather than a two-caste basis. The religious, ideological, institutional, and psychological inheritance, stressed excessively by Tannenbaum, Freyre, and Elkins, makes strong claims at this point. This inheritance included Roman Catholic universalism and institutional prerogatives, long contact with Africa and Moorish occupation, and a living slaveholding tradition in law and custom.

The conjunction of historical and immediate socioeconomic factors in the determination of the Brazilian pattern is summed up by Roger Bastide:

> Present-day Brazil offers the world a classic example of racial democracy; but, to understand it, the roots of that democracy must be sought in Brazil's past history as a slave-state. The affective relationships which have grown up between whites and Negroes are the outcome of: (a) the ethos of the Portuguese colonists, who belonged to a population which had already intermingled with the Moors in the home-country, and who came, at least at the outset, without white women . . . ; (b) the colony's social and economic system (rural patriarchy, latifundia and single-crop agriculture) which brought about the dispersal of the whites over vast stretches of territory and, by obliging them to live among slaves, tended to create a certain solidarity, at least between the master and his negro nurse, his servants in the *Casa Grande*, and his coloured mistresses. These two factors, taken together with Portuguese Catholicism . . . provide all the material needed for an understanding of Brazil's racial democracy. But this paternalistic rural solidarity began to change in the second half of the eighteenth century when the masters moved to the coastal towns. These towns, instead of bringing the races together, set them further apart. . . . However, miscegenation had already gone too far, and the influence of Catholicism had become too strong, for the vertical mobility of the mulatto to be ended. . . .[7]

We might file a number of objections immediately. The sig-

nificance of the Portuguese ethos must be evaluated in the
light of the impressive evidence of brutality toward blacks in
Angola and Mozambique, and the significance of the role of
the Church must be evaluated against the undeniable power
of the *senhores de engenho* over the local clergy. Wherever we
find slaveholding classes with bourgeois rather than seigneurial
origins, we generally find a tendency toward more intense
racism. It is a happy coincidence for Hoetink's thesis that
Protestantism and capitalism first emerged in the Anglo-
Saxon countries, in which the somatic-norm image has been
furthest removed from black. Coincidence or no, we need
not deny some validity to the assertion of a biological-
aesthetic dimension to racism to insist on the greater force of
other factors. Even in Brazil a correlation appears between
greater race prejudice and capitalist development: the patriarchal Northeast generally displayed greater racial integration
than the South.[8] During the abolition crisis of the 1880s, the
proslavery party, rooted in the coffee-growing South, unleashed an unprecedented barrage of racist propaganda and
appeals to color prejudice.[9] As capitalist industrialization and
urbanization advance in Brazil, more evidence of racial discrimination appears. Perhaps the uncovering of evidence increases, rather than the discrimination, but there is enough
evidence of deterioration to cause worry.[10]

We therefore find ourselves buffeted between two views.
The first stresses the historical background and institutional-
moral inheritance and interprets Brazilian discrimination as
essentially the result of class rather than racial bias; the other
stresses the economic and demographic setting and considers
discrimination simultaneously and inextricably a matter of
class and race. Undoubtedly, much work needs to be done,
but it ought to be apparent already that both historical and
immediate factors had to be filtered through the institutions
appropriate to specific ruling classes if they were to have force.
Color prejudice, blood pride, and other forms of ethnocentricity preceded slavery and prepared the way for racism,
understood as an ideology of oppression and subordination.

The transition from the former to the latter occurred by means of such institutionalized mechanisms of discrimination as the slave codes, the plantation regime, and the organized caste restrictions against freedmen. But whereas in some societies these discriminations lost some or much of their force after general abolition, in the United States abolition reinforced them. All slave societies displayed racist tendencies, the specific strength of which varied in response to both historical and ecological influences. The strength of the Tannenbaum interpretation, relative to that of Harris, lies in its flexibility, for the former can absorb the latter, whereas the latter rejects historical influences on principle. The extent and depth of racism under slavery depended primarily on the degree to which the slaveholding class acquired a pure or seigneurial character, in contradistinction to a bourgeois character. This character, in turn, grew out of both historical and immediate conditions. The Portuguese background, for example, had its role, but it developed one way in the patriarchal Brazilian Northeast, where it had room to expand, and quite another way in Angola, where a system of capitalist exploitation distorted and limited it from an early date.

During the slave period in all countries intensification of racial antipathy followed commercialization and the ascendancy of bourgeois slaveholding classes. Hubert H. S. Aimes refers to "the time honored policy of Spain which had for its end the assimilation of blacks into the white race,"[11] and we can accept this formulation despite the many qualifications that ought to be introduced. For much of the early colonial period the Crown tried to maintain racial segregation, but largely for reasons of political and social control. This attempted use of segregation ran afoul of religious sentiments and long-standing ethnic attitudes and could never be enforced with a rigor adequate to its purpose. The appearance of anything akin to Anglo-Saxon racism followed commercialization and bourgeois development, notably in Cuba, where it reached epidemic proportions during the sugar boom of the nineteenth century.[12]

The United States made the worst of both possible worlds.
At the very beginning the slave South imported a Protestant,
bourgeois, Anglo-Saxon tradition with strong racist overtones.
The high level of commercialization during the colonial
period reinforced the practices associated with the tradition.
From this point on we might have expected a sharp clash
between this virulent racism and the paternalistic plantation
ethos, and in fact one did develop. Tocqueville pointed out
that racial antipathies were deeper in those parts of the
country where slavery had been abolished than in those where
it had been retained, and recently Eugene H. Berwanger, in
his study of the Western frontier during the secession crisis,
has made a strong case for the contention that they were
deepest in those parts where slavery had never existed.[13] In
the South it was a common observation that the planters had
much less aversion to Negroes than did the nonslaveholders.
When Fitzhugh denounced the abolitionists as enemies of
the blacks and insisted that slavery was not essentially a race
question, he expressed the logic of that side of the Southern
background with which he identified. The softening force of
the plantation ethos, which was inherently racist but much
less so than its bourgeois counterpart, did not prevail owing
to the unique combination of three forces: the historical
legacy, the continued pressure of the world market, and the
exigencies of social control over a population the majority of
which was white. The grim result of this combination was the
sterilization of the countertendencies inherent in the plantation system and the triumph of a racism more insidious than
any other in the New World. At that, one question will always remain open: What would have happened had the
Southern slaveholders survived as a ruling class, for it is possible that the subsequent orgy of extreme racism would have
been avoided. The fall of the slaveocracy opened the way to
new men in the postbellum era and brought to the top exactly
those elements most infected with the racism radiating from
slavery as a system permeating all of society and least influenced by the countertendencies inherent in the master-slave

relation within the plantation community itself. The remnants of the old aristocracy professed to deplore the demagogy and gangsterism of the Tillmans and Vardamans, but they quietly capitulated and sometimes set the pace for racist vituperation. That capitulation is a long and bitter story in itself; for our immediate purposes it is enough that it occurred after a headlong fall from power and reflected defeat, despair, and a frantic attempt to survive in a new and dangerous world. In this sense, too, the triumph of the bourgeoisie in a society that had been originally shaped by slavery spelled the triumph of racist extremism.

I I

By focusing on the nature of the ruling class of each slave-holding regime, we can treat adequately the major problems inherent in comparative historical analysis. We have largely limited ourselves to the question of abolition, as posed by Tannenbaum and Elkins, as a test of the usefulness of a class analysis, but have at least noticed its wider applications. Such an analysis brings us into direct confrontation with the essential duality of the history of slavery in the modern world. The colonization of the New World re-created archaic regimes shaped by the patriarchal plantation, the dominant tendency of which was paternalism. All slave regimes exhibited this tendency, for it was inherent in the master-slave relationship. The strength of this tendency depended primarily on the nature of its particular slaveholding class, which grew up on the spot but was also deeply influenced by its own historic past and relationship to a seigneurial or bourgeois society abroad. Each such class therefore simultaneously displayed general characteristics and yet was unique. Side by side with this process of internal archaic development there continued the far more powerful and ultimately triumphant process of world capitalist expansion—a process that absorbed the independent, internal process within itself and distorted it in decisive ways. The great revolt of the slaveholders of the Old South represented, in this sense, a dramatic reactionary movement to reverse the fundamental thrust of world history. The study of the slave systems of the New World contributes an essential feature to the social and economic history of the wider European world and must progress in a way that renders the subject a coherent whole.

If each slaveholding class was in fact the unique product of a long history on both sides of the ocean, then the strength of Tannenbaum's general argument relative to that of the economic determinists should be obvious. If all slaveholding classes shared other certain fundamental tendencies, arising from their relationship to labor, then the central importance of the mode of production should also be obvious. Yet slavery in the Americas had a racial basis and therefore must be understood, not simply as a class question, but as a class question with a profound racial dimension, which can only be understood as the particular product of each slaveholding regime. A class analysis, in short, is not enough and can only serve as the basis for a much more complex analysis. But then, no one has ever seriously suggested that it could do more.

PART TWO

THE LOGICAL OUTCOME OF THE SLAVEHOLDERS' PHILOSOPHY

AN EXPOSITION, INTERPRETATION, AND
CRITIQUE OF THE SOCIAL THOUGHT OF
GEORGE FITZHUGH
OF PORT ROYAL, VIRGINIA

The coexistence of two world views, often contradictory, one expressed in words and the other shown through actions, is not always due to bad faith. Bad faith may be a true and satisfactory explanation for single individuals, or even small groups, but it is neither true nor satisfactory as an explanation when this contradiction is found in large numbers of people. Then, this contradiction must be the expression of deeper contradictions at a historical and sociological level.

. . . A social class has its own world view but not as yet consciously. The world view is shown only in action, when the class moves as an organic whole, and since this happens only sporadically the world view is manifested only sporadically. This is one reason that the class is not yet conscious of its own world view. However, because of social and intellectual subordination this class borrows a world view from another class and asserts this borrowed world view in words, although in action a contradictory world view in manifested.

Antonio Gramsci,
Il Materialismo storico

CHAPTER ONE

Preliminary Observations on a Man and His World

We deem this peculiar question of negro slavery of very little importance. The issue is made throughout the world on the general subject of slavery in the abstract. The argument has commenced. One set of ideas will govern and control after awhile the civilized world. Slavery will every where be abolished or every where be re-instituted.

GEORGE FITZHUGH,
Sociology for the South

The Old South, having come closest of all the New World slave societies to resurrecting an archaic mode of production, provided the most favorable soil for the growth of an appropriate ideology. The proslavery argument moved from the particular to the general, from a concern with Afro-American labor to a concern with labor in the abstract, from a focus on racial caste to a focus on social class. The social foundations of this unfolding world view lay in the steady formation of a resident planter class and in the effects of the early closing of the African slave trade in promoting consideration of slave welfare and in reducing the cultural distance between the antagonistic races and classes. The successful separation from Britain and the achievement of an adequate compromise during the Constitutional crisis created favorable conditions for the slaveholders to establish their regional power. In this setting they slowly if largely unconsciously forged themselves into a ruling class of a distinct type and with a special character, and even more slowly began to reflect on what the world was making of them and what they chose to make of that part of the world which they increasingly commanded.

George Fitzhugh loomed large in the story of that process of developing class consciousness. Although he generally appears in the historical literature as an eccentric and a curiosity, he appears here, for reasons to be spelled out later, as a central figure. I do not deny some bias, for, as often happens to a historian who dallies with an attractive historical figure for some years, I have come to think of him as an old friend. As my affection and admiration deepened, the task of rescuing him from detractors became something of a private mission. Fitzhugh has been misunderstood even by his most sympathetic and acute interpreters and stands out as a more important and internally consistent thinker than is generally accepted. One charge, however, I do reject—that of using him as a pawn in a game of *épater les bourgeois*. That Fitzhugh's assault on bourgeois hypocrisy should delight any socialist no one need deny, but it ought to be unnecessary to add that the social order and moral standards for which he stood left and leave something to be desired.

If I do not dwell on the evils of slavery and the hypocrisy of its world view, it is for two reasons, the first being an assumption that all ruling-class ideologies are self-serving and that it is enough to point out the worst examples along the way, and the second being that few people any longer seem in need of sermons on the subject. The race question remains with us and properly stirs passions, but the struggle for racial equality needs a cool assessment of the past and of its legacy and does not need the inverted romanticism of the neo-abolitionist viewpoint. To insist, for example, on the reality and centrality of paternalism is to try to account for the development of specific forms of class consciousness and their political consequences; it is not to imply that paternalism was ever a good thing, much less that its current manifestations ought to be tolerated. The essay on Fitzhugh contains editorial comments and value judgments, which the reader can take or leave at his pleasure. I am reasonably certain that Fitzhugh would have raised no procedural objection. The ultimate value of the essay has to rest on its correctness as a statement of what Fitzhugh was driving at and on its estimate of the significance of his argument, not on any ideological uses to which I or anyone else tries to put that argument.

If the interpretation and estimate stand up, then the existence of a major tendency in Southern life and thought has been demonstrated. The preponderance of that tendency relative to others, including its direct antithesis, is certainly not established and would require other kinds of studies. The intention here is to illustrate, not "prove," one of the major theses of the first essay.

I

John Berkeley Grimball of the aristocratic South Carolina low country and Francis Terry Leak of the Mississippi Black Belt come to us as very different men: the one an urbane Charlestonian with that poise and charm to which men must generally be raised from birth; the other a rustic resident planter with that certain awkwardness which betrayed his simple origins and limited horizons. Yet, they had much in common. It was not, after all, Grimball's elegant tastes or the scale of his entertaining that stamped him as a Southern gentleman, nor even the delicacy and deceptive formality of his relationship with the gracious lady who adorned his estate. Grimball was a man of affairs, a public-spirited member of a self-conscious ruling class, and above all, a conscientious and dutiful master of the human beings in his charge. But no more so than was Francis Terry Leak.

When Leak brought his slaves together for the marriage of Moses and Pol in the winter of 1857, he performed the ceremony, as he always did, with a simple dignity and a seriousness worthy of the occasion. The whole plantation family, white and black, attended; the barbecue lived up to its advance notice; and the dancing carried on well into the early hours of the morning. Slave marriages had no status in law in the South as they had in the Catholic slaveholding countries; the marriage relation between Moses and Pol existed on Leak's sufferance. It was no less secure for so doing. The Leaks, who were perhaps two generations removed from the Grimballs in gentility and sophistication, may or may not have constituted the majority of the planter class of Mississippi, but they were its finest representatives and the embodiment of its ideal. The Leaks were Grimballs in the making, and those slave-driving "Southern Yankees," on whom Mrs. Stowe and Daniel R. Hundley poured their wrath, were, for all their barbarism, incipient Leaks.

The South, during the golden age of the slave regime, contained within itself the world of the patriarchal plantation and the antithesis of that world, and the whole content of its life may be discovered in this antagonism, which existed not between the Grimballs and the Leaks but between Grimballs and Grimballs, Leaks and Leaks, and even Southern Yankees and Southern Yankees. The vulgar parvenus of the rough Southwest presented no special problem; time and the pervasive influence of the tidewater tradition would civilize them. So long as the road to power lay through the plantation, the barbarism would be overcome. Yet, who could be sure? The enemy stood within and without; he might be contained but could not be exterminated.

Participation in a mighty middle-class republic had great advantages but also carried great risks. Dependence on a world capitalist market, notwithstanding certain economic advantages to be derived therefrom, proved an almost unmitigated disaster from a moral and ideological point of view. The values of the plantation, its ways of thought and feeling, were antithetical to those of the bourgeois world. The relationship of master to slave, in itself an extension of the relationship of father to perpetual child, could be reconciled to the cash nexus only imperfectly. In the end, the bastard slavery of the commercial South, with its internal slave trade and external participation in the economic struggle in the world market, did preserve and extend the patriarchal tradition. In a pure world, Grimball, Leak, and the Southern Yankee would have ruled self-sufficient plantations unencumbered by debt and fear of bankruptcy or the division of property; in the real world of nineteenth-century America, they had to contend with all the problems and pressures of the capitalist marketplace. The danger arose from the material and ideological opposition of the North American bourgeoisie and its agrarian allies, but it arose also from the inability of the South to build a wall to contain the sentiments and notions that were accompanying the bourgeoisie on its march to world power. Everything suffered contamination—philosophy, religion, economic and political thought, and social values. To defend the material interests of the slaveholders' regime meant also to turn back the assault on its moral sensibilities and its notion of order.

The plebeian origins of the South's ruling class could be lived down and even turned to advantage, for a measure of political and social democracy guaranteed a mobility that constantly invigorated and replenished its ranks. The challenge of liberal bourgeois ideology, rooted firmly in Western European and North American society, was another matter. If the problem had been merely to defend Afro-American slavery as another form of extraeconomic compulsion, it might have been soluble. The planters of the British Caribbean argued their case in London for years and finally, faced with defeat, roared their protests, accepted monetary compensation, transferred investments, and made the best of it. For a capitalist an investment in black bodies could be transformed into an investment in cotton textile machinery anytime, for the transformation was a matter of business. The Grimballs and Leaks were made of other stuff.

The history of the slave South is, in the first place, the history of a process by which the slaveholding class arose, grew, triumphed, and collapsed. Its inner history, understood as the development of class cohesion and consciousness, above all constituted the history of a world view. The defense of Southern slavery need not have consisted of more than two points: that economic interest made it temporarily necessary for the well-being of all sections of the country; and that racial inequality made it temporarily necessary for the safety of all sections of the country. Before long, the argument shifted elsewhere, or rather, it shifted everywhere. The Declaration of Independence and Lockeian political philosophy came under heavy attack from men who had been brought up on them. The hostility to centralization of power, which admittedly also had deep roots in the free states, became an obsession. The easy social democracy, so characteristic of life on the American frontier, gave way steadily before aristocratic pretensions, or perhaps it would be more accurate to say, became overlaid with them. The suspicion of things urban, which had its expression among rural folk in all parts of the country, rose to a tenet of quasi-religious faith in the South. The values of a people underwent inversion; the undercurrent of a seemingly effete tidewater exclusiveness was somehow prevailing over the coarse virility of a democratic people.

Ideas may arise from the minds of isolated geniuses or madmen, but their transformation into world views implies their acceptance by substantial numbers. The slaveholders came to a world view of their own, but the ideas it embraced, especially as they passed through the popular mind, contained all the contradictions of Southern reality: a prebourgeois ruling class with a solidly bourgeois religion; a patriarchal social structure in a market economy; a flesh-peddling chivalry. No wonder so many historians dismiss the Southern mind as schizophrenic. No wonder even so astute a historian as Louis Hartz dismisses the prebourgeois side of the South as an illusion and refuses to take its ideological manifestation seriously, or at least seriously enough. The reality was certainly contradictory, but this affirmation does not relieve us of the responsibility of mastering its uneasy synthesis. This mastery alone can enable us to separate the growing from the receding and the vital from the decaying, for above all, we need to separate the living ideal toward which the material reality was tending from the disappearing ideals which came out of the past and could never wholly be vanquished.

George Fitzhugh, the hero of this piece, and a growing number of his fellow slaveholding intellectuals understood, however imperfectly, those basic assumptions of bourgeois marketplace society which have been astutely summarized by C. B. MacPherson under the name of possessive individualism:

(i) What makes a man human is freedom from dependence on the will of others.

(ii) Freedom from dependence on others means freedom from any relations with others except those relations which the individual enters voluntarily with a view to his own interest.

(iii) The individual is essentially the proprietor of his own person and capacities, for which he owes nothing to society.

(iv) Although the individual cannot alienate the whole of his property in his own person, he may alienate his capacity to labor.

(v) Human society consists of a series of market relations.

(vi) Since freedom from the wills of others is what makes a man human, each individual's freedom can rightfully be limited only by such obligations and rules as are necessary to secure the same freedom for others.

(vii) Political society is a human contrivance for the protection of the individual's property in his person and goods and (therefore) for the maintenance of orderly relations of exchange between individuals regarded as proprietors of themselves.[1]

Fitzhugh and his colleagues also understood that once you insist that a man, to be human, must be the sole proprietor of himself and must be free of all relations save those of the market, then you must reduce all moral values to market values—that once labor power becomes a commodity like any other, then a market society, not merely a market economy, has come into being.

The South had a market economy; it did not have an essentially market society, and the whole point of the defense of slavery in the abstract was to ensure that it did not develop one. The relationship of master to slave was an organic, not a market, relationship. As a slave society, the South had a market in slaves, but master faced master in that market; the relationship to labor existed in another sphere. Being organic, the relationship produced assumptions about the world that were antithetical to those outlined by MacPherson. These might be summarized in juxtaposition to those above:

(i) What makes a man human is his dependence on the wills of others and his existence as a being in society.

(ii) The need to rely on others implies the sacrifice of individual freedom in return for protection and support.

(iii) Being unable to live apart, man owes everything to society.

(iv) The individual can alienate the whole of his property in his own person, not merely his capacity to labor, and must do so if he expects the protection and support of another. The other must have a property in his person to guarantee protection and support, for the necessary sentiment can only arise from interest.

(v) Human society consists of a series of organic relationships in which man holds property in man.

(vi) Since dependence on the wills of others is what makes a man human, each individual's freedom must be limited by his position as the property or propertyholder of another; since the propertyholder acquires a trust and responsibility in this relationship, his freedom must be limited by the general will of propertyholders as a class.

(vii) Political society is a human contrivance for the protection of man's property in man and therefore for the maintenance of orderly relations of production between individuals regarded as owners or owned.

This model of Southern slaveholding thought suggests a good deal more "ought" than "is." The historical position of slave society during the modern epoch made it a hybrid, and therefore this ideological projection represents a one-sided description of a two-sided reality. Its significance lies in its having been the ground on which the advanced slaveholding intelligentsia chose to wage its battle to resolve the contradiction between the cash nexus and the patriarchal plantation implicit in its hybrid quality.

The world view of the slaveholders contained contradictions, as every world view must, but properly understood, it demonstrated adequate coherence and integrity. Like all class ideologies, it infuriated many of those who held it. Slaveholders, like the rest of us, rarely wanted to face the implications of each notion, prejudice, or ingrained commitment. They wished their ideology to be careless, pragmatic, inarticulate, disorganized, lazy; only political fanatics, philosophers, and lunatics can live any other way. How easy, therefore, for us to judge them as cynics who rationalized a system of exploitation or as rustic windbags who talked nonsense, or as thoughtless reactionaries of no account. They were all of these, but none. No matter how guilty they may have been on each count, they did nonetheless stand for a world different from our own that is worthy of our sympathetic attention. The questions they asked are still with us; the inhumanity they condemned must still be condemned; and the values for which they fought still have something to offer.

George Fitzhugh asked a question. If it was true, as proslavery spokesmen confidently asserted, that the Negro slave fared better, materially and spiritually, than the free white workers and peasants of the Western world, then how could capitalism be reconciled with Christian morality? If this assertion was true, did not justice and conscience require that all labor be enslaved for its own happiness and protection?

Historians have dismissed Fitzhugh's argument as propagandistic extravagance, significant primarily as an indication that the slaveholding intellectuals had gone a bit mad. C. Vann Woodward and Louis Hartz, virtually alone, examine the argument with care and respect, and even they finally throw up their hands. They appreciate Fitzhugh as a critic of capitalism and its marketplace values, and Woodward especially sees in him a figure apart from his class and yet one who could speak for an ideal and a moral order with claims to authenticity in Southern society. Hartz pays closer attention to Fitzhugh's social and economic thought but can see in him only a negative critic. Hartz views Southern society as a deformed capitalism, whereas Woodward prefers to leave the question open; as a result both find Fitzhugh caught in a hopeless and contradictory admiration for the capitalism under his attack. In the end Fitzhugh appears, especially in Hartz's reading, as the perverse genius of a social class desperately trying to deny its identity.[2]

The slaveholders' world view grew out of the master-slave relationship as embodied in the plantation community and simultaneously out of and in opposition to the influences of capitalism that surrounded the South and were embedded within it. The slaveholders' mind reflected this world at war with itself. It took over all the notions of the bourgeoisie that spawned it, encircled it, lived within it, and battered it, but its own system of social relations generated alternatives. The slaveholding class, which won political independence in a revolutionary war, matured in opposition to the world view of bourgeoisie, expressed most tenaciously in abolitionism, but it matured positively as well in the process of building plantations as worlds unto themselves.

Slaveholders imbibed the thought and sensibility of the plantation community and the thought and sensibility of the larger bourgeois world. Politically and socially, the South struggled to free itself from that larger world; ideologically, it struggled to perfect its own world view based on its developing social system, adjusted as far as necessary and possible to the modern world. The logic of the plantation ideology led to the repudiation of all bourgeois ideology, but everyman is not a logician, bending his daily life to conform to some philosophical schema. Having been brought up on Mr. Jefferson, equality, democracy, acquisitiveness, and the rest, the mass of the slaveholders retreated slowly. The exact impact of Fitzhugh's message—and the less impressive parallel efforts of Henry Hughes, George Frederick Holmes, and much of the proslavery vanguard intelligentsia—cannot and need not be measured. Fitzhugh was not a "typical" figure, whatever that means, and his argument, considered as a theoretical system, did not sweep the South. It is an open question how many members of the ruling class, let alone the masses, had ever heard of him. Yet, it is significant that J. D. B. De Bow could write in 1857 that although Fitzhugh was the South's "only active working advocate" of the doctrine of slavery in the abstract—a false statement, by the way —"his theory is adopted by many."[3]

The product of a respected planter family in economic decline, George Fitzhugh of Port Royal, Virginia, was a small slaveholder, an indifferent planter, and a man who wrote too much and read too little. He contributed a steady stream of articles to *De Bow's Review*, the *Southern Literary Messenger*, and other publications, but his reputation rests on his two books, *Sociology for the South* (1854) and *Cannibals All!* (1857).[4]

Harvey Wish has summarized the little we know about his life in *George Fitzhugh: Propagandist of the Old South*, which deals mostly with Fitzhugh's ideas and displays such impatience with slave society that it can never move beyond condemnation and abuse.[5] Fitzhugh left virtually no papers, so there is no room for another biography. There is, I hope to show, a good deal of room for a reassessment of his thought, which held a central place in the development of the ideology of the master class. Fitzhugh saw, more clearly than anyone else, the assumptions on which the slaveholders based their social, political, and philosophical positions; he stripped away many of the contradictions and hesitations and brought those assumptions into the open. In so doing, he took a major step toward the formation of a coherent slaveholders' world view. Naturally, he was not always loved for it, even by those for whom he spoke. Social classes, like the individuals who compose them, do not enjoy being made to stand naked before a mirror—being made to face the implications of their thinking without all of the comfortable illusions and contradictions that paper over the unpleasant side of what they are and what they think. The English bourgeoisie did not love Hobbes for telling it what it was and what it believed. As MacPherson says in the concluding paragraph of his brilliant essay, "The English possessing class, however, did not need Hobbes's full prescription. And they had some reason to be displeased with his portrait of themselves: No reader, except the fashionably flippant, could relish such an exposure of himself and his fellows, especially when it was presented as science."[6] Similarly, few slaveholders in the South wanted George Fitzhugh or anyone else to tell them that they could not have the fundamental world view they were in fact developing and at the same time have Mr. Jefferson, the Protestant Reformation, John Locke, and various other favorites. Fitzhugh, in short, was neither typical nor representative; he was a ruthless and critical theorist who spelled out the logical outcome of the slaveholders' philosophy and laid bare its essence.

Whatever his general standing, the Southern intelligentsia certainly appreciated him. Fitzhugh's social theory of slaveholding and his insistence that slavery was fundamentally a class question had deep roots in the unfolding proslavery argument. The core of his position may be found in most writers from Thomas Cooper to John C. Calhoun, from Smith to T. R. Dew, from the suggestions of the early South Carolina school to the vigorous polemics of Hammond and Hughes.

Fitzhugh's own appraisal left much to be desired but did have some merit. "You, and Hughes, and I," he wrote George Frederick Holmes, "in the last year, it seems to me, have revolutionized public opinion at the South on the subject of slavery. Then, not one person vindicated slavery in the abstract—now all endorse my book and thereby endorse slavery in the abstract."[7] He reported himself well satisfied with the sales and thanked Holmes for giving him the support necessary to get *Sociology for the South* a hearing. He praised Holmes as one of the two men who really understood him— the other being Stephen Pearl Andrews—although actually Holmes, an overrated pedant, gave little evidence of having understood Fitzhugh's major contributions. Other men, conversely, probably grasped the point better than Fitzhugh thought, for more and more Southern intellectuals began to speak in Fitzhughian terms. The warm reception given Fitzhugh's writings could be misleading, for almost any anti-Yankee, proslavery tract received approval in the South during those hysterical years. Yet the book was read and did receive sympathetic attention, and, contrary to Fitzhugh's boast, its argument was not so much new as a more rigorous and mature presentation of a line of thought which had been steadily gaining favor for years.

The notion that slavery was a proper social system for all labor, not merely for black labor, did not arise as a last-minute rationalization; it grew steadily as part of the growing self-awareness of the planter class. It is curious that this point is overlooked by so much of recent scholarship, for William Sumner Jenkins demonstrated it conclusively thirty years ago, though with much less emphasis than he might have.[8] In the brief review of the proslavery argument and the extended treatment of the defense of slavery in the abstract, I wish to claim two things for Fitzhugh: that he was the most consistent exponent of the slaveholders' world view and not at all guilty of most of the inconsistencies historians have charged him with; and that he alone saw the necessary last step in the argument, which was that slavery could not survive without the utter destruction of capitalism as a world economic system.

The Old South alone developed a serious positive-good proslavery argument, although hints and patches appeared everywhere that slavery existed. The proslavery argument in the West Indies was almost entirely negative and said no more than that slavery was making essential contributions to the economic life of the colony and metropolis. In the Catholic countries, notably Brazil, slavery was defended as economically necessary and traditionally sanctioned, but no one argued with any discernible conviction that it was a good thing in itself or the proper condition of the laboring classes; such a viewpoint had to have a difficult time in countries where the alternative to slavery was some kind of seigneurial dependency anyway and where paternalism did not depend on the master-slave relation. The Old South came closest of all the New World slaveholding regimes to producing a genuine slave society. Accordingly, it alone could generate a reasonably comprehensive slaveholders' philosophy.

For the most part, the slaveholders accepted the new view but sought to translate it into old terms and to preserve as much of the traditional philosophy as they could. Confronted with the logic and ultimate meaning of the notions they had come to take for granted, they blanched; sometimes, they howled with rage. We ought not to be deceived. However important the howling and blanching may have been—and on the terrain of practical politics they were of enormous importance—the slaveholders were moving along. The plantation ideology grew stronger; the retreat from liberalism quickened. The contradictions in the thought of George Fitzhugh (for there were real ones and not merely those historians have imagined) may be traced to the contradictions in the world that gave it birth. In the end, he more than any other man saw the direction in which his world was moving and perceived what was needed to bring it safely to its destination.

I I

The historical development of the proslavery argument has been ably presented by Jenkins, whose "primary conclusion" is that the Southern mind, as it became absorbed in defending slavery, came to identify it completely with everything distinctive in Southern life. Expressions of proslavery thought appeared immediately after the first appearance of antislavery literature, for, as Jenkins points out, until then the institution was so much a part of custom and circumstance as to require little comment. Both proslavery and antislavery thought became firmly established during the colonial period, and almost all the features of the later, more violent debates were clearly foreshadowed. The American Revolution had made some impact, but not nearly so much as historians once thought. The period 1790–1820 comprised uneasy but restrained years, for the institution was not yet under broadside attack, however much criticism was brought to the surface now and then, and little attention was being paid it in Congress and in the arena of national politics. During this period Southerners often agreed that slavery constituted an evil, by which they rarely meant a sin or a moral blot; the idea that slavery was immoral always had Southern adherents but never came close to general acceptance, even by antislavery elements. Slaveholders during the relatively mild debates of the Constitutional period tended to be apologetic, although Jenkins is probably right in seeing their stance as more a matter of strategy than of deep conviction:

> Throughout the decade [1800–1810] Southern Congressmen, with a polite acquiescence, usually submitted to the charge that slavery was a political evil in contrast to a moral evil. . . . But apology is one form of defense, and so long as there was no danger of federal interference or encroachment, it might have been the most expedient form. Occasionally, however, when excoriation became too severe, the veil

of apology was thrown aside and the true picture of the Southern mind was revealed.[9]

Even Jenkins tends to underestimate the sharpness of Southern reaction, particularly during the tense moments of the debate on the closing of the slave trade.

The foundations of the defense of slavery in the abstract were imperceptibly being laid during these early years, as Southerners increasingly stressed the organic nature of their society and displayed a divergent standard of morality in social relations. John Randolph, that wonderful and impossible man, illustrated an important aspect of the transitional period. Like some other well-known Virginians, he was no friend of slavery, and yet everything he stood for—the particularist theory of liberty, the code of honor, the repudiation of equality, the idea that men were born not free but helpless—reflected the world of the slave plantation. It is not quite fair to see in the posture of those Virginians who expressed doubts about slavery but retained their slaves merely a version of what the Czar said about Maria Theresa at the time of the Polish partition: "She weeps, she weeps, but she takes her share." Personal economic interest, hypocrisy, and the rest no doubt played some role, but these men were in fact wrestling with a profound dilemma. One generation might be able to oppose slavery and favor everything it made possible, but the next had to choose sides.[10]

The period of transition, being especially complex, has been subject to various interpretations, of which William W. Freehling's is easily the most sophisticated and best researched, at least for the state of South Carolina. Freehling's analysis centers on three peak moments—the debate on the Missouri Compromise, the aftermath of the Vesey conspiracy, and the Nullification crisis—and records the evidence of such countercurrents as the admission by some that slavery was a moral evil and the vigorous demand for a positive-good defense.[11] Although one could quarrel with Freehling on particulars in his reading of the literature, his general conclusions deserve the most respectful attention, for they significantly advance our understanding of the period. Summing up, he writes: "The intense fear and guilt which seemed destined to destroy all hope of an effective southern defense of slavery in the 1830's proved to be, in part, the products of the years of transition in southern history."[12] I am not sure that Freehling does not read more guilt and squeamishness into the record than is there. In an exceptionally well-documented book, this point cries out for citations and close examination of texts, and the most impressive evidence for the contention comes from the advocates of the positive-good argument, who might easily have been exaggerating for polemical purposes. These doubts aside, two of Freehling's major findings require comment. He forcefully shows that South Carolina throughout the early nineteenth century reacted to antislavery attacks out of all proportion to their apparent seriousness. The word "apparent" is mine, not his, for he considers the reactions to have been excessive. "A society reveals its deepest anxieties," he argues, "when it responds hysterically to harmless attack. The South Carolina lowcountry's morbid sensitivity to the relatively undeveloped abolitionist crusade in the 1820's is a case in point."[13] Yet Freehling shows, with great skill and care, just how deeply slavery was woven into the fabric of South Carolina's life—in a sense, that is the whole point of his excellent book—and he cannot have it both ways. One is tempted to remind him of the reaction of John Randolph to the "relatively undeveloped" attack on states' rights: Asking a state to surrender part of her sovereignty is like asking a lady to surrender part of her chastity. If slavery occupied the place it did at a time when a moral revulsion against it was rising in Europe and in the North, then no attack could be thought harmless. The continued, if diminishing, strength of a shame-faced attitude toward slavery threatened disaster, for it provided the opening wedge to abolitionism. On another level, the identification of the essential qualities of Southern life with the slave plantation made every attack on slavery an attack on the morality and humanity of the slaveholders, for their self-image rested on the master-slave relationship.[14] In this context South Carolina's reaction may be understood as a rational response to a real threat.

Throughout the period of transition we find evidence of the idea of slavery as a proper social system for certain lower classes, not merely races, and of the division of society into classes of those who worked and those who did not. As John Quincy Adams so shrewdly observed, "The discussion of this Missouri question has betrayed the secret of their souls . . . when probed to the quick upon it, they show at the bottom of their souls pride and vain glory in their condition of master-dom."[15] Jenkins takes the legislative message of Governor Stephen D. Miller of South Carolina in 1829 as probably the first important, clear statement of the positive-good argument, although he recognizes that it came at the culmination of a decade-long discussion. From this point on, the general defense of slavery as a proper social order and the foundation of the social welfare played a major role in the debate. More or less clearly, Miller, Hammond, Holmes, Thornwell, Harper, Simms, Memminger, Hughes, Edmund Ruffin, and a host of others moved step by step toward the defense of slavery in the abstract.

It took Fitzhugh to drive the argument to its final conclusion, but he did not invent it. It was implicit in the beginning and increasingly explicit, if not always consistently so, in the writings of the best minds in the South. The defense of slavery in the abstract presented great difficulties for the politicians, who preferred to deal with it loosely, but it kept slipping out. J. H. Hammond, for example, told Thomas Clarkson and the world that he would not speak to the question since he did not deal in abstractions. So thin was this excuse that the same page on which it appears also says, "You will say that man cannot hold *property in man*. The answer is that he can and *actually does* all the world over, in a variety of forms, and *has always done so*."[16] Intellectuals like Ruffin or William Gilmore Simms could speak more bluntly. "Pity it is," commented Simms, "that the lousy and lounging laz-zaroni of Italy, cannot be made to labor in the fields, under the whip of a severe task-master! They would then be a much freer—certainly a much nobler animal—than we can possibly esteem them now. . . ."[17] The appearance, persistence, and definitive articulation of the argument for slavery in the abstract represented the ideological projection of the master-slave relation; in the end, only it could provide an adequate moral justification for the regime.

The place of John C. Calhoun in the development of the proslavery argument will have to be left aside. In a more appropriate context it could be demonstrated that the image of Calhoun as the "Marx of the Master Class" is wrong in general and in particular, although not so much so as presented in the cautious discussion of Richard Hofstadter, who uses the term, as in that of Richard Current, whom he follows. Calhoun, as a political leader, did not and could not formulate an appropriate social theory, and Hartz properly dismisses him as a much lesser figure than Fitzhugh, so far as this range of problems is concerned. In one respect, however, he has undeniable claims to greatness. The development of the slaveholders as a class necessarily required that their increasing self-consciousness manifest itself politically, and no one saw the need for a slaveholders' Southern party more clearly than Calhoun, nor did more to bring it into being. For the slaveholders, as for any social class that aspires to rule, "the party is the true agent of class unification."[18] A full understanding of the nature of the class consciousness of the slaveholders would require a close examination of the relationship between Fitzhugh's thought, considered as the logical outcome of the slaveholders' philosophy, and Calhoun's, considered as the practical political expression of their position. That complex problem will have to wait for another day and probably another writer. We cannot, however, postpone treating the challenge from a more immediate quarter.

III

Never before or since has an interpretative history, written by a journalist without references or other scholarly trappings, so deeply influenced American historians as has W. J. Cash's *The Mind of the South*. This brilliant and haunting book, so rich in anguish as well as in ruthless probing, has probably done more than any other to set the historical profession against the interpretation of the Old South as other than bourgeois. There is a small irony here, for Cash's argument will serve nicely to refute Cash on this very point.

He begins, appropriately, with the legend of the Old South:

> . . . a sort of stage piece out of the eighteenth century, wherein gesturing gentlemen moved soft-spokenly against a background of rose gardens and dueling grounds, through always gallant deeds, and lovely ladies, in farthingales, never for a moment lost that exquisite remoteness which has been the dream of all men and the possession of none. Its social pattern was manorial, its civilization that of the Cavalier, its ruling class an aristocracy coextensive with the planter group. . . .[19]

Naturally, he immediately reminds us that no informed person any longer believes this cant and that historians have disproved the theory of the Cavalier origins of the Virginia planter class. Yet, the notion still persists that the planters deserve to be considered an aristocracy: "To suppose this, however, is to ignore the frontier and that *sine qua non* of aristocracy everywhere—the dimension of time. And to ignore the frontier and time in setting up a conception of the social state of the Old South is to abandon reality."[20]

Cash admits that colonial Virginia boasted a genuine, if small, aristocracy but properly notes that it did not so much descend from Cavaliers as arise out of two hundred years of American experience. "The test of a gentleman was what the test of a gentleman is likely to be in any rough young society —the possession of a sufficient property. Aristocracy in any real sense did not develop until after the passage of a hundred years—until after 1700."[21] We may pause for a moment before we resume our journey with him: What were these men before 1700? There is only one reasonable answer: They were farmers and planters who were evolving in a particular direction and making particular kinds of men out of themselves. And what direction? What kinds of men? The outcome tells us, and Cash identifies the outcome. Aristocrats.

Cash argues that the advance of the plantation really began in 1800, and only picked up momentum about 1820; we may accept his judgment, if only as a suitable basis for discussion.

> From 1820 to 1860 is but forty years—a little more than the span of a single generation. The whole period from the invention of the cotton gin to the outbreak of the Civil War is less than seventy years—the lifetime of a single man. Yet it was wholly within the longer of these periods, and mainly within the shorter, that the development and growth of the great South took place.[22]

If, Cash suggests, we are to believe the ruling class of the South to have been an aristocracy, we must assume it to have been either a projection of the Virginia aristocracy or the product of a brief forty- or fifty-year period. Following Joseph Baldwin's *Flush Times of Alabama and Mississippi*, he disposes of the Virginians and proceeds to scoff at the idea of a one-generation aristocracy. The ruling class, he concludes, came from among "the strong, the pushing, the ambitious, among the old coon-hunting population of the back-country."[23] In a word, the ruling class of the South consisted mostly of rough and vulgar parvenus. No one doubts it. But one question does occur: Of what aristocratic or other ruling class could not the same be said? It was, as I recall, Saint Jerome who observed that a rich man need not be a thief; he might be the son of a thief. The United States, being a frontier country, produced tough, competitive, acquisitive frontier types, and all frontier parvenus look rather alike

(Cash's description might well be extended to the Brazilian *bandeirantes* and planters of the old Northeast or to the Spanish *conquistadores*). The question remains: What social vision informed these men's dreams? What kind of life did they seek for their children? Parvenus are parvenus, but bourgeois parvenus are not necessarily slaveholding parvenus once one gets beneath appearances. Cash has so far begged the question.

After alleging that the Virginians who went west generally failed miserably, Cash makes a small admission, which like most of his small admissions compromises his argument: "Some of them (some of the completely realized aristocrats and a great many more of those gentlemen farmers who had grown up beside them) did nevertheless succeed. There were few parts of the South, indeed, in which it was not possible to find two or three—occasionally a small colony—of them."[24] Influence, not numbers, is here in question, and Virginia influence need not have meant a recapitulation of the Virginia experience. The questions come to these: Did the rising planters of the Southwest during the 1830s have before them, as an ideal future for themselves and their children, Virginia or Massachusetts? the Cavalier or the financier? Were they, in their economy and social relations, going down a bourgeois or an aristocratic road? Cash at one point scoffs at the idea that the planters had anything essential in common with the English squires, whom he insists had a strong salon flavor about them. It does not occur to him that he might be right and in being right destroy his argument. That the squires were more than half bourgeois is precisely the point; if so, Cash's argument can be turned against him.

Cash again and again returns to his theme that the plantation preserved the frontier aspect of Southern life and that the frontier bred a parvenu ruling class. His viewpoint does occasionally embarrass him, for how, in these terms, does one account for the obvious hegemony exercised by the planters over the yeomen, especially in view of the colonial period's evidence of rebelliousness toward authority? He asks, puzzles, and then offers an astonishing answer: The yeomen had absorbed the aristocratic ideals of those above them.[25]

The men who led the Confederacy were frontier-bred parvenus, but somehow the old aristocracies lingered on and helped shape the new ruling class: "But, by an irony of circumstance, as their power declined, the general influence of these aristocracies was in some fashion increased."[26] No social process within the South accounts for this curiosity, except that which encouraged the Southerners to a fantasy life. Basically, the Yankee did it. His attack on slavery united the South in a romantic pose, separated it from reality, and caused it to look to its old gentlemen to provide a standard. The Yankee created the South, the ideological content of which was a romantic reaction to the outsider's impertinences.

> That conflict, as has been said before me, was inevitable. And not only for the reasons known to every reader of American history, but finally and fundamentally for the reason that it is not the nature of the human animal in the mass willingly to suffer difference—that he sees in it always a challenge to his universal illusion of being the chosen son of heaven, and so an intolerable affront to his ego, to be put down at any cost in treasure and blood.[27]

These pages of *The Mind of the South*, which Stampp calls the best introduction to the Old South,[28] betray a pathetic fascination with the romance of aristocracy. C. Vann Woodward alone seems to have discerned their true character and to have treated them with open contempt.[29] For Cash the planters could not have been an aristocracy because too many of them were not really genteel but acquisitive, vulgar, mean, foul-mouthed, and perhaps even unwashed. But, we may ask, what aristocracy ever arose from any other kind of men? W. E. B. Du Bois, who never suffered from a petty-bourgeois view of the upper classes, had no trouble with the parvenu planters, whom he called the "cursing, whoring, brawling gamblers" who dominated the South's ruling class in the

1850s.[30] Cash is shocked at the pretensions of these men: "In the romantic simplicity of their thought-processes, they seem to have believed for conscious purposes that in acquiring rich lands and Negroes they did somehow automatically become aristocrats."[31] By Cash's standard the patriarchal planters of the Brazilian Northeast do not qualify either. Consider the remarks of Gilberto Freyre on the oldest and most directly aristocratic planter families: "In the words of the people: 'There is not a Wanderley who does not drink, an Albuquerque who does not lie, a Cavalcanti who does not owe. Nor a Sousa Leão or a Carneiro da Cunha who does not like a Negro woman.' "[32] The whole problem comes to this: for Cash an aristocracy is not defined, like any other social class, as a collection of men in the midst of a certain kind of historical process of becoming;[33] it is defined by a particular historical moment and a static ideal. He talks as if he is interested in a social class, but in fact he is merely interested in the idea of aristocracy as an embodiment of a gentlemanly ideal; his criterion has nothing to do with class at all. Instead of seeing that aristocracies, like other ruling classes, rise and maintain themselves on extraeconomic compulsion and labor systems that are naked forms of plunder, he identifies as aristocracies only those classes exhibiting the grace and *noblesse oblige* of fourth- or fifth-generation gentlemen. There is some advantage to this viewpoint, which Cash uses to devastating effect against attempts to romanticize the antebellum planters, but for the most part it represents a secondary line of criticism. All ruling classes have been, by definition, acquisitive, and therefore their origins have been violent and ugly; the first and second generations have naturally borne the marks of origin, and in a frontier country so may have later generations. The juxtaposition of elegance and vulgarity existed in society as a whole and could easily have been reflected within any given family. So, for example, in William Styron's fictional account of the Turner family of Virginia in the 1820s we find two brothers, the one a polished gentleman and the other something less, as one incident in which they were entertaining visiting ministers on the porch of their plantation home will show: "For the minister, in a desperate fidget, was obviously unaccustomed to conversing with anyone who was in the process of taking a piss, which Benjamin did without a flicker of thought and in the most public way whenever he drank in the company of men." In Cash's terms Samuel Turner was an aristocrat and his brother Benjamin a parvenu, not to say a pig. As a rule of thumb for admitting people into the salon, this will do as well as any, but we cannot analyze social classes this way. Berdyaev tells us that real aristocratic breeding is impossible among masters, who are by nature plebeian. Domination, he suggests, is a plebeian affair.[34] The point of view is respectable, for Berdyaev is talking about certain ethical properties, not about class ideology and psychology; he is speaking philosophically, not sociologically. But Cash's treatment is another matter. The dispute over the nature of Southern society concerns the particular, not the general; concerns the end built into the beginning; concerns the world these men were trying to make. Whether or not they ought to be called "aristocrats" is a matter of definition, if not of taste. The essential point is that their acquisitiveness did not make them bourgeois. Much light can be shed on their behavior by reference to their being parvenus, and Cash is at his best on this level of analysis; but if they were parvenu slaveholding planters, rather than parvenu bourgeois, then matters cannot be left on that level.

But let us call W. J. Cash to the witness stand. The cotton planters, he admits, aped those Virginians after all and aspired to their sort of kindliness and good manners:

> The model of the Virginians achieved its happiest effect on the new planters. One must not suppose, surely, that the manner of these planters ever became identical with that of the colonial aristocrats. At its best it was essentially simpler, less formal and highly finished; often the home-spun of the frontier showed through; and yet at its best it

did capture much of the beautiful courtesy and dignity and gesturing grace of its exemplar. . . . In its highest and most favorable aspect, in sum, it was a manner not unworthy of aristocracy—a manner which was perhaps a good deal better than many genuine aristocracies have been able to show.[35]

We began by asking Cash some questions: "Did the rising planters . . . have before them, as an ideal future for themselves and their children, Virginia or Massachusetts? the Cavalier or the financier? Were they, in their economy and social relations, going down a bourgeois or an aristocratic road?" Let him answer: "If the backcountryman turned planter was plainly no aristocrat, he yet had his feet firmly planted on a road that logically led to aristocracy."[36] The defense rests.

We cannot, I fear, ignore the currently fashionable disease, guiltomania, which threatens to reach epidemic proportions among historians. A strange malady, it induces fits of masochistic fantasy and a strong tendency toward self-destruction. All historical problems explain themselves away under its ravages, and if it continues its relentless advance, it will soon render historians obsolete. Nietzsche observed, in Ecce Homo, that were a god to come down to earth, he would do nothing but wrong: "To take upon oneself guilt and not punishment, that alone would be godlike." Some of our infected historians manifest this godlike trait. When they project it onto the slaveholders, however, they take account of the ungodlike and human frailty appropriate to the plantation and mete out fearful punishment at Appomattox. These remarks may well be received with indignation by those who could justly argue that they are *ad hominem* and show rank discourtesy toward colleagues whose views ought to be considered on their merits. Normally, decency would require that we discuss the thesis, not probe the motives behind it. The principle dictated by decency is a fine one, but it entails responsibilities. The slaveholders of Virginia, South Carolina, and Mississippi were and are entitled to the same courtesy, and the sensibilities of living historians call for no greater consideration than that which they extend to their dead subjects. The popular practice is to treat the proslavery advocates and the slaveholders generally as men whose ideas deserve only patronizing dismissal and who are of historical interest only as subjects for amateur psychological analysis. When not simply summed up as a protracted guilt complex, Southern thought is often merely waived. Thus Stampp:

> Slaveholders asked for pity from no one, least of all from abolitionists. Yet, who could withhold it? Who could help but feel compassion for men who found nothing more inspiring than the sterile rhetoric and special pleading of the proslavery argument to justify the institution upon which they lived? The pathos in the life of every master lay in the fact that slavery had no philosophical defense worthy of the name—that it had nothing to commend it to posterity except that it paid.[37]

Who could withhold pity and compassion? The answer, of course, is, anyone prepared to hear what they had to say to the world—to take them seriously.

W. J. Cash bears heavy responsibility for the spread of guiltomania; at least his name is the one most often invoked by the patients. That some historians follow him so uncritically raises questions, for his argument begins with an astonishing assertion. According to Cash, the slaveholders' guilt complex arose from the South's having embraced slavery at the very moment when the Western world was renouncing it. The deductions from this assertion are wonderful to behold, but there is a small problem. Whether one dates the embrace from the early colonial period or the rise of King Cotton, the South embraced the irresistible harlot when all Western Europe was enjoying her company; it confirmed the embrace after the Revolution at a time when no colonial power was abolishing slavery, when abolitionist agitation in London was meeting hot resistance, when Napoleon was

restoring slavery in the islands, when progress toward abolition in the peripheral slaveholding countries of Spanish
America was being more than offset by a sugar boom in
Cuba, and when Brazilian slavery was opening a new period
of expansion. Let Cash continue:

> [The South] had to stand against the whole weight of the
> world's question and even of the world's frown.
>
> And, worst of all, there was the fact that the South itself
> definitely shared in these moral notions—in its secret heart
> always carried a powerful and uneasy sense of the essential
> rightness of the nineteenth century's position on slavery. . . .
>
> This Old South, in short, was a society beset by the
> specters of defeat, of shame, of guilt—a society driven by
> the need to bolster its morale, to nerve its arm against wax-
> ing odds, to justify itself in its own eyes and in those of the
> world.[38]

There is more than enough substance and genuine insight
here; it is the partiality and one-sidedness of the viewpoint
that creates distortions. As Cash implies, slavery was rapidly
becoming disreputable in the Anglo-Saxon world with which
the South was most directly concerned, and the drift of world
sentiment was certainly against slavery. Yet, the antislavery
onslaught came only after the South had had time to set its
course and to consolidate much ground along the way. In its
early period and throughout its history, the morality and world
view of marketplace liberalism remained strong in its midst
and provoked conflict. No one denies that the South remained
at war with itself ideologically. Most modern societies have
faced the same or an analogous problem. What European
nation, for example, avoided splitting into "two nations"
over the social question? One supposes that historians who
wish to could find thousands of scraps of evidence to show
that many capitalists felt awful about their poor, starving,
overworked laborers, and doubtless some did. Yet, no one is
likely to try to interpret the social and intellectual history
of the European bourgeoisie as a reflex of a guilt complex or

to dismiss the whole subject as the mere ideological justification for a particular form of exploitation. If a guilt complex existed as a social force, there would be all the more reason to take the proslavery argument seriously on its own terms, for its evolution in the face of countertendencies would have been decisive for the effort to neutralize the political effects of that complex. Even if we could view the whole argument as an elaborate rationale, we would still have to assess its intellectual strength and power to convince, unless we were prepared to believe that the entire ruling class of the South and everyone under its leadership consisted of corrupt cynics ready to prattle anything to protect their business arrangements.

Did substantial numbers of slaveholders feel guilty about holding slaves? There is no evidence that they did, especially during the nineteenth century, and it is difficult to see why they should have. In a region torn by a struggle of opposing world views and therefore of opposing moral standards, some men doubtless allowed their inner sense of guilt, which probably concerned unconscious wishes about mother or sister or something equivalent, to express itself as a social question, the more easily to avoid its content and implications. If some historians choose to be impressed by the evidence that some planters, accepting the moral standards of bourgeois society, felt guilty about slavery, others may be permitted to be impressed by how many did not, for their failure to display a sense of guilt demonstrates just how far they had advanced toward alternative notions of morality and social order. Unmistakable evidence of guilt feelings exists, but it does get rarer as we approach 1861, for, as we might expect, the victory of the proslavery forces on the ideological plane had to manifest itself psychologically. We are therefore back at the beginning. Even a consideration of the psychological dimension leads us right back to the necessity for a serious assessment of the slaveholders' ideology as ideology.

The denunciations of slavery as an "evil," which abounded

during the late colonial and early national periods and even later, generally made it clear that the issue was one of economic prosperity or social stability and not one of morals. For the late antebellum period the remarks of Orville W. Taylor may be taken as a fair statement for the whole South: "Few people in Arkansas vigorously defended slavery—most of them merely accepted it as a part of the pattern of life. The impression is also received that few people condemned slavery itself, even though they might object, on political or economic grounds, to its spread or continuation."[39] That flat and unquestioning acceptance, in a world of abolitionist criticism, provides the measure of the conquest of the South by the proslavery ideology. How many Americans today would vigorously defend capitalism or even be sure of how to define it? To conclude that in their innermost hearts this apparent indifference spells rejection would be comforting to socialist critics but, to say the least, inaccurate. Unthinking acquiescence and the unconscious supposition that the social system is both natural and permanent ("part of the pattern of life") represent two major marks of a triumphant ideology. There is no reason to believe that for every guilt-stricken, inwardly torn slaveholder there were not many who went about their business reasonably secure in the notion that they did not create the world, that the world existed as it existed, and that their moral worth depended on how well they discharged the duties and responsibilities defined by the world in which they, not someone else, lived.

J. H. Bills, a Tennessee slaveholder, appears to have been a kind and decent master who considered himself a liberal and a democrat. Without a trace of irony he noted in 1843: "My servant woman Lucinda delivered of a male child. Call him *Jefferson* for that great Apostle of liberty."[40] In 1866 he expressed his feelings about emancipation:

> Although the pecuniary loss is great, I feel no regrets that the result is so, for the institution, I never had a fondness, nor could I advocate it on any other grounds than that

slavery was the best state for them. We shall see whether I
was correct in this.

I found the institution here when I came upon the stage
of life. I have bought many & sold few; never bought one
but that I thought I had bettered his or her condition &
most of those I bought I done so at their own request.

May they do better for themselves is the only wish I have,
but fear the result.[41]

Or let us take the Dabneys, as reported by Susan Dabney
Smedes. She tells us, writing long after the war, that many
slaveholders longed to rid themselves of slavery but could not
for reasons of economics and concern for the fate of those
who lived under their protection. Her father, knowing that
the war would bring defeat and disorder, wanted to sell out
and go to England. His wife dissuaded him by pointing out
that to do so would mean to abandon his "people" (that is,
his slaves) and leave them to face the crisis alone, without
his guidance and protection. "My father," she wrote, "was so
well assured of the contentment and well-being of his slaves,
while he owned them, and saw so much of their suffering,
which he was not able to relieve after they were freed, that he
did not, for many years, believe that it was better for them
to be free than held as slaves. But during the last winter of his
life he expressed the opinion that it was well for them to have
their freedom."[42] Implicitly, these men, with all their mis-
givings, doubts, sense of burden, and the rest, accepted direct
social responsibility for others and, in so doing, moved into
adherence to a particular world view. That they did so in a
contradictory and halting way and experienced moments of
self-doubt merely identifies them as human beings. Charles
G. Sellers, who interprets the Old South differently, writes of
the Southerners' deep commitment to liberty and notes that
the extremists themselves did not repudiate the tradition of
the American Revolution but rather "transformed it, sub-
stituting for the old emphasis on the natural rights of all men
a new emphasis on the rights and autonomy of communi-

ties."[43] Since all ruling classes of premodern Western Europe spoke in terms of liberty, we need not be surprised that the slaveholders did so. As for the small adaptation of sentiment of which Sellers writes, within it we may find the whole content of the momentous shift in their world view.[44]

Guilt feelings reside deep in the individual psyche, and for that reason alone we ought to distrust the evidence unearthed by historians who follow Cash. Where a strong sense of guilt exists, as it may well exist in every man, it forms part of an extreme inner tension and necessarily will generally appear in disguised form. If a slaveholder expressed guilt about owning slaves, we have evidence of an ethical and ideological conflict. The rest—the specifically psychological expression of guilt—cannot be evaluated at all; at best, we may assume that his ethical conflict was manifesting itself in the form of feelings that had entirely different roots and that his sense of guilt, which probably arose from deeply personal and early experiences having little to do with the social order, was being given a public face. Hoetink observes that the guilt whites feel toward blacks in our own day may in fact reveal the opposite of what Cash and his followers think:

> Regarding this historical guilt complex, we should note in passing that a collective feeling of guilt might be based on undeniable ethical integrity, although it need not necessarily be so based. Feelings of guilt may be emotions which one can permit oneself only in a position of superiority. True feelings of guilt are not infrequently deeply hidden: a person who speaks about his own guilt feelings may be the practitioner of "philanthropy," in the bad sense of the word: the condescending self-accusation accompanying a gratuity, which one can permit oneself only in a supposedly superior position. The feelings of guilt are then a function of the position of power, and of a doubtful ethical nature. These emotions are bound to be exposed at some later date by those to whom they related.[45]

We are, in short, back with the ideological struggle between two world views and systems of morality, which have to be examined as products of social confrontations and conflicts. The guilt-complex thesis is not necessarily wrong. It is irrelevant.

CHAPTER TWO

The Slaveholders' Philosophy

The philosophy of every man is contained in his politics.
ANTONIO GRAMSCI,
Il Materialismo storico

I

Fitzhugh, in the preface to his biting discussion of classical political economy, disavows any intention of replacing the leading systems of bourgeois philosophy with one of his own. Modesty prompted him to suggest that he had not the ability, but nothing so trivial and subjective as the modesty of George Fitzhugh determined his course. His deep suspicion of all philosophical systems seems ironical since his greatest achievement was to begin to bring order to the incoherent philosophy of the slaveholding class. Yet he intended to do no more than begin, for he insisted that the time had not arrived for a slaveholders' *Summa*. "Philosophy can neither account for the past, comprehend the present, nor foresee and provide for the future. 'I'll none of it!' "[1]

He despised the mechanism of the French and English Enlightenment: Philosophers, he contended, "confounded the moral with the physical world, and this was not strange, because they had begun to doubt whether there was any other than a physical world."[2] Anticipating friendly criticism, he wrote that George Frederick Holmes "would dissent from . . . [my] want of precise definition. The time has not yet arrived, in my opinion, for such precision, nor will it arrive until the present philosophy is seen to be untenable, and we begin to look about us for a loftier and more enlightened substitute."[3] Fitzhugh sounded a note that conservatives had sounded before him and have ever since. Closer to our own day, T. S. Eliot could write that the idea of a Christian society could not be made immediately attractive: "No schema for a change of society can be made to appear immediately palatable, except by falsehood, until society has become so desperate that it will accept any change. A Christian society only becomes acceptable after you have fairly examined the alternatives."[4] Fitzhugh might have written those words.

In taking his stand with the romantic revolt against the rationalism and materialism of the Enlightenment, Fitzhugh betrayed an extraordinary suspicion of science and reason. "No person would employ an overseer who was learned in the natural sciences. Botany, geology, chemistry, mineralogy, and natural history, do very well for the closet philosopher, but would be dangerous attainments in an overseer."[5] A good overseer, and indeed most men, could comfortably rely on their own common sense and practical experience. Agricultural chemistry he denounced as a humbug. What must Edmund Ruffin, the great agricultural reformer who echoed so much Fitzhughism in his own sociological excursions, have thought as he read those sentiments?[6] Fitzhugh did not intend to be unkind to his fellow Virginian, nor to anyone else. Yet despite the honors that eventually fell to Ruffin and the good that he did for Southern agriculture, even he cried out in despair at the hostility to innovation and the distrust of scientific agriculture among the planters and farmers of the South.[7] Fitzhugh, the social theorist, not Ruffin, the planter and agricultural reformer, reflected the feelings of the agricultural classes of the South.

"Had Shakespeare been as learned as Ben Jonson," Fitzhugh declared, "he would have written no better than Ben Jonson. The lofty genius of Milton would have created a glorious English epic, had he not travelled too much abroad, and dwelt too much with the past."[8] These denunciations of science, learning, and history seem extreme and unnecessarily quarrelsome, and must have seemed so even then to much of his slaveholding audience, but he was doing no more than pressing the reactionary romanticism of his class to its logical if exasperating conclusion.

Fitzhugh's comments on Cervantes' *Don Quixote*, a book he apparently loved dearly, are especially instructive. He praised the genius of Cervantes, but with a sad and grave reservation. "His happy ridicule expelled the absurdities of Knight Errantry, but unfortunately expelled, at the same time, the new elements of thought which Christianity and Chivalry had introduced into modern literature."[9] Cervantes, like the Protestants, had gone too far. To criticize the nonsensical trappings of feudalism was one thing; to ridicule them so as to create doubts about feudalism itself was quite another. Fitzhugh's appraisal of the twin heroes of the work sheds some light on his philosophical stance. In 1857 he wrote: "As for Sancho Panza, we think him the wisest man we ever read after, except Solomon. Indeed, in the world of Fiction, all the wisdom issues from the mouths of fools. . . . In the Real world, the philosophers . . . have monopolized all the folly."[10] These words ought to be considered together with their complement, as reflected in his essay "What Shall Be Done with the Free Negroes?" (1850): "Don Quixote mad, is the noblest, because the most chivalrous and disinterested of all the heroes of Epic poetry; he is but a drivelling, penitent dotard when he recovers."[11] Sancho Panza, the practical man of experience, was for Fitzhugh the true philosopher, but it was the mad Quixote, fighting the windmills with the name of the fair Dulcinea on his lips, who won his love. Fitzhugh would have understood the words of George Santayana: "The mass of mankind is divided into two classes, the Sancho Panzas who have a sense for reality, but no ideals, and the Don Quixotes with a sense for ideals, but mad."[12] The mind of George Fitzhugh, of his class, and of his beloved South was that of

Sancho Panza, rejecting the cant of all system builders; but their soul was that of Don Quixote, the madman, defending the old values when no one else cared.

Although Fitzhugh refused to erect a philosophical system, he did try to build a foundation for one on idealist principles. The significance of his "Scriptural Authority for Slavery"[13] lay neither in its theological polemic nor in its biblical exegesis, for these were undistinguished and were being done by others more learned in the relevant subjects; it lay simply in its existence and its insistence upon a religious standpoint in sociology. "Man," he wrote, "is a religious animal. . . . The belief in God and moral accountability . . . is necessitous and involuntary. It is part of our consciousness."[14] Repeatedly, Fitzhugh retreated into an intellectually unimpressive obscurantism that reflected no particular talent for philosophical discourse. When, in *Cannibals All!*, he attacked system building, he defined his position clearly. The only safe and wise course was to develop a "moral pathology" that could take life a step at a time; the ultimate reliance would have to be placed on religion, faith, and Providence. He proposed simply to vindicate the ways of God to man. Fitzhugh's words may be compared with those of Henry Hughes, whose *Treatise on Sociology* appeared the same year as *Sociology for the South*. Hughes, who like Fitzhugh took up the cry for slavery in the abstract (or "warranteeism," as he chose to call it), closed his book by insisting that the philosophy of the good society would have to follow its construction: "When these and more than these, shall be the fulfilment of Warranteeism, then shall this Federation and the World, praise the power, wisdom, and goodness of a system, which may well be deemed divine; then shall Experience aid Philosophy, and VINDICATE THE WAYS OF GOD, TO MAN."[15]

Fitzhugh, Hughes, Holmes, and other serious Southern thinkers had to take the idealist ground, for in no other way could they have justified their society. They found themselves in the position of the political philosophers of the prebourgeois era. We need do little more than consider the implications of C. B. MacPherson's evaluation of Hobbes, as presented in his masterful book *The Political Theory of Possessive Individualism*:

It is not surprising that Hobbes was the first political thinker to break away from the traditional reliance on a supposed will or purpose infusing the universe, and base himself on a supposed mundane equality. Before Hobbes, everything had conspired to make political thinkers rely on standards of value and entitlement imported from outside the observed facts. For one thing, market relations had nowhere penetrated all social relations sufficiently to make it conceivable that values could be established by the operation of objective but not supernatural forces. For another, most political thinkers before Hobbes had worked in markedly class-divided societies in which hierarchical order appeared to be the only alternative to political and moral anarchy. In hierarchical societies the danger of slave or peasant revolts or popular equalitarian movements is never entirely absent. As long as such movements are thought to be anarchical, thinkers who are constructing theories of political obligation must assume some functional or moral inequality between classes of men, for hierarchical society requires unequal rights and obligations. And since the merits of hierarchy and an inequalitarian moral code could not be expected to be made rationally evident to a class which might consider itself oppressed, there was an additional reason to deduce a code of obligation from some divine or transcendent order rather than directly from the capacities and needs of men.

Hobbes also lived in a class-divided society. But he did not find it necessary to impute significantly unequal capacities or needs to different classes of men. For on his reading of the facts of seventeenth-century society, social order was no longer dependent on the maintenance of hierarchy. He thought that the objective market had replaced, or could replace, the inequality of ranks, and had at the same time established an equality of insecurity.[16]

Fitzhugh and his proslavery colleagues stood in a position analogous to that of pre-Hobbesian political theorists, but there was one important difference. The slaveholders had direct contact with both the society of the marketplace and its various intellectual expressions; their aim was to destroy both. For this reason, they could make no fresh contribution to philosophy, sociology, or political theory and could never transcend their negative functions as critics of bourgeois society. Their positive contribution rests elsewhere: in their articulation of the values and direction of the backward-looking society in which they lived.

Yet, Fitzhugh did not shrink from calling for a distinct Southern philosophy, properly understood. In a long article entitled "Southern Thought," he defined his subject as "a Southern philosophy, not excuses, apologies, and palliations." Such a philosophy was to be built up from the Bible, Aristotle, and "our own successful experiment." Little or nothing else would be needed.[17] Fitzhugh contented himself with deliberate ambiguity because he sensed that the slaveholders could put nothing in place of bourgeois liberalism and materialism except a repudiation of reason, which intrinsically could not be made rigorous (although some obscurantists even today insist on maintaining pretenses), and a Burkean appeal to sentiment and tradition, which amounts to the same thing. Burkean traditionalism had the additional disadvantage of lending itself to everything Fitzhugh opposed, for, as Hartz has so forcefully argued, the relevant traditions were those of post-1688 England and post-1776 America.

Fitzhugh's antirationalism and opposition to a market society had counterparts in the romantic movements of the North and of Europe, which sometimes attacked from the left and sometimes from the right. In either case, the difference between them and the proslavery advocates was fundamental. Romantic radicals understood that the greatest boast of liberalism was its assertion of the free rational individual as the criterion of the good society; they also understood that in the real world of the marketplace, where social classes and not merely individuals faced each other as exploiters and exploited, the greater part of the population was sacrificed to the lesser and that therefore individualism passed into selfishness. Consequently, they repudiated not only the marketplace but the rational man at its center. For these radicals, however, the task was to realize the individual freedom promised by liberalism. Transcendence, not destruction, was their goal, and as a result they stood poles apart from Fitzhugh.

European and Northern conservatives also attacked marketplace values, and stood closer to Fitzhugh in doing so. They could never resolve a fundamental dilemma, however, whereas Fitzhugh could and did resolve it. A few ultrareactionaries here and there did call for a new serfdom or slavery and shared Fitzhugh's world view, but these were isolated intellectuals or dispossessed aristocrats who spoke nostalgically and hardly represented any important social force. Mainly, the conservative critique came from men who struggled to restore the old community values within the context of capitalism. They had a hard time and still do. MacPherson comments: "Locke tried to combine traditional and market morality; so did Burke, in a more fundamental and more desperate way, a century later."[18] This link between Locke's liberalism and Burke's conservatism demonstrates the irreversibility of capitalism's conquest even for those who struggled to impose limits on it. Fitzhugh had no such problems. Next to him, Burke, Gentz, Metternich, Brownson, Tocqueville, Müller, and most of the great conservative theorists and men of affairs in Europe and America were mere liberals. He called for the utter destruction of the world capitalist system; he could do so unlike these others, because he spoke from an appropriate social base—from a world in which the fundamental social relations remained nonbourgeois.

Standing on this ground, he could also say frankly that no alternative to bourgeois ideology could develop while the world market pulled everything into its orbit and subjected all ideologies and sentiments to the withering pressure of cosmopolitanism. So long as the South functioned as part of the world capitalist system, it could never wholly establish its moral and intellectual independence. The cash nexus could not be destroyed by moral suasion. The multitude of interests created by the enormous complexity of modern economic life must inevitably compel men to rationalize (in the Freudian sense) their stake in the system and must inevitably overwhelm ideologically the interests of the plantation community. A staggering task confronted the South. To justify her own social system, she had to disprove and refute the whole social, ethical, political, and economic philosophy of the day, which had arisen to support and justify societies based on a wholly different set of social relations.[19]

The struggle was irreconcilable: the bourgeois Carthage must perish; the world-wide system of economic interdependence must be crushed; capitalism, in short, must everywhere be uprooted. Only then could a new philosophy emerge. Fitzhugh thus largely restricted himself to a critique of capitalist social relations and their more direct reflections and to working toward an alternative set of social relations. Sociology, not philosophy, was his main concern. As for a philosophy appropriate to such alternative social relations, he could do no more than suggest a starting point.

I I

The most helpless of animals, thought Fitzhugh, was the isolated, "individualized" man. In *Sociology for the South,* he denounced Locke's theory of social contract and argued that man was naturally a slave of society and had no rights to surrender to it. "Man is born a member of society and does not form society." That is, human beings have no existence apart from their society, for society itself is the being and may make use of the individuals constituting it in any manner necessary for the collective good.[20]

This notion Fitzhugh claimed for his own. When he wrote *Cannibals All!* he acknowledged that Aristotle had developed an acceptable theory of the social nature of man long before him and candidly regretted not having read *Politics* until his trip to the North. Nowhere did he mention Locke's contemporary Robert Filmer; it was only during the war that Fitzhugh invoked his name. He may have read Filmer much earlier, as Woodward suspects, and been influenced by him, but there is no evidence, and the assumption is not necessary. However much he owed to Aristotle, Filmer, or others, his ideas grew out of the slave society he knew firsthand at least as readily as they grew out of any intellectual preconditioning.

Fitzhugh attributed Northern economic advance and Southern economic stability to the association of capital and industry, and he argued further that "all great enterprises owe their success to association of capital and labor."[21] Under the circumstances the laboring classes have the right to demand security against want, hunger, and abandonment to the vicissitudes of the market. Property owners must meet their responsibilities, for property is no inalienable right but a necessary arrangement provided by law; it is a creature of society and must function for the public good. Slave property, like all other, carries with it the duty of public leadership and a sense of responsibility toward the propertyless. Society ultimately retains control of property; individual property owners are the trusted agents of society.

Fitzhugh expressed a deep intellectual debt to the socialists for demonstrating the advantages of the association of labor, and he slighted the contribution of Adam Smith. Smith had "nearly stumbled on the same truth" in his famous discussion of the division of labor, but had failed to see the enormous harm done to the laborer in the process. Without a proper association of labor—presumably he meant a proper, mutually advantageous and responsible relationship between labor and capital—division of labor simultaneously makes labor many times more efficient and less rewarding. "By confining each workman to some simple, monotonous employment, it makes

him a mere automaton, and an easy prey to the capitalist."
Rather than link this alienation firmly to the process of exploitation, he turned the argument around against the socialists. "The association of labor," he maintained, "like all associations, requires a head or ruler, and that head or ruler
will become a cheat and a tyrant, unless his interests are
identified with the interests of the laborer."[22]

How the presence of a head, however sympathetically related to the laborer, could offset the laborer's sense of alienation, which arises from the division of labor, Fitzhugh did
not say. Even if a paternalistic society guaranteed him a secure
place, his estrangement from the fruits of his labor would be
no less. Fitzhugh, here as in so many instances, developed an
argument against the wage-labor system that could effectively
be turned against the slave-labor system. In effect, he could
only argue that exploitation and class stratification were in-
evitable and that slavery, with its principle of responsibility of
one man for another, led to less hardship and despair than
capitalism, with its principle of every man for himself, for at
least the worker had a community to appeal to other than
one based on a cash nexus.

For Fitzhugh, bread and sleep were about all the masses
wanted, and his social system could be made attractive if it
could deliver both. Then might the elite, which alone was
fit to rule, be freed to enjoy liberty. "To secure true progress,
we must unfetter genius, and chain down mediocrity. Liberty
for the few—Slavery, in every form, for the mass!"[23] Fitzhugh
could not trust the masses' quest for security and sleep to
guarantee their submission. Repeatedly, if inadvertently, he
returned to the matter of chaining down. Like Dostoyevsky's
Grand Inquisitor, he saw his fellow slaveholders as guardians
of a mystery: Man wants the security of those chains but does
not know it. Man must be chained down for his own good—to
realize his own inner will. Familiar as it is, the Grand Inquisitor's speech is worth recalling here, for it expresses, with
an eloquence, depth, and candor far greater than Fitzhugh's,
just where his argument finally comes out:

The wise and dread Spirit, the spirit of self-destruction and non-existence . . . the great spirit talked with Thee in the wilderness, and we are told in the books that he "tempted" Thee. Is that so? And could anything truer be said than what he revealed to Thee in three questions and what Thou didst reject, and what in the books is called "the temptation"? And yet if there has ever been on earth a real stupendous miracle, it took place on that day, on the day of the three temptations. The statement of those three questions was itself the miracle. . . . From those questions alone, from the miracle of their statement, we can see that we have here to do not with the fleeting human intelligence, but with the absolute and eternal. For in those three questions the whole subsequent history of mankind is, as it were, brought together into one whole, and foretold, and in them are united all the unsolved historical contradictions of human nature. At the time it could not be so clear, since the future was unknown; but now that fifteen hundred years have passed, we see that everything in those three questions was so justly divined and foretold, and has been so truly fulfilled, that nothing can be added to them or taken from them. . . .

. . . And if for the sake of the bread of Heaven thousands and tens of thousands shall follow Thee, what is to become of the millions and tens of thousands of millions of creatures who will not have the strength to forego the earthly bread for the sake of the heavenly? Or dost Thou care only for the tens of thousands of the great and strong, while the millions, numerous as the sands of the sea, who are weak but love Thee, must exist only for the sake of the great and strong? No, we care for the weak too. They are sinful and rebellious, but in the end they too will become obedient. They will marvel at us and look on us as gods, because we are ready to endure the freedom which they have found so dreadful and to rule over them—so awful it will seem to them to be free. But we shall tell them that we are Thy servants and rule them in Thy name. We shall deceive them again, for we will not let Thee come to us again. That deception will be our suffering, for we shall be forced to lie.[24]

From the grandeur and sense of mission of the Church Militant to the desperate rear-guard action of an anachronistic class of slaveholders, from Christianity's tragic sense of life to the optimistic obscurantism of naive and ignorant rustics, from the tortured genius of a Dostoyevsky to the half-fraudulent, half-earnest shrewdness of a Fitzhugh—admittedly, something less than an equation ought to be made here. Yet, the comparison has its uses and its justification. Plantation slavery generated an ethos, however incoherently expressed, that linked the South to the midstream of the premodern world. Fitzhugh may not deserve to be mentioned in the same breath with Dostoyevsky for brilliance or depth of insight into the nature of human conflict and tragedy, but he nonetheless stands out as a man who saw that the slaveholders' only claims to life rested on their self-recognition as heirs of a great reactionary tradition.

Bryan Edwards, the distinguished historian of the British West Indies and himself a slaveholding planter, wrote at the beginning of the nineteenth century: "In countries where slavery is established, the leading principle on which the government is supported is fear: or a sense of that absolute coercive necessity which, leaving no choice of action, supersedes all questions of right. It is vain to deny that such actually is, and necessarily must be the case in all countries where slavery is allowed."[25] Fitzhugh turned the argument against the bourgeoisie by generalizing it. In a passage reminiscent of Pascal's brilliant comment on the awe surrounding kingship, Fitzhugh wrote:

Physical force, not moral suasion, governs the world. The negro sees the driver's lash, becomes accustomed to obedient cheerful industry, and is not aware that the lash is the force that impels him. The free citizen fulfills *con amore*, his round of social, political, and domestic duties, and never dreams that the Law, with its fines and jails, penitentiaries and halters, or Public Opinion, with its ostracism, its mobs, and its tar and feathers, help to keep him revolving in his orbit. Yet, remove these physical forces, and how many good citizens would shoot, like fiery comets, from their spheres, and disturb society with their eccentricities and their crimes.[26]

Man, then, neither wants nor can afford liberty; even the liberty of the elite must be limited by the collective judgment and power of that elite. If Fitzhugh had been essentially a propagandist, as some historians claim, he would never have written such lines, for they must have upset Southern opinion almost as much as Northern. As a dedicated theorist and intellectual, he spoke out for the hard truth and called upon his class to recognize the logic and foundation of its whole philosophy. "As civilization advances, liberty recedes, and it is fortunate for man that he loses his love for liberty just as fast as he becomes more moral and intellectual."[27] Had he been a mere propagandist, he would have occupied himself with more rewarding tasks than inflaming his opponents, offending the sensibilities of his friends, and risking the generation of confusion in his section.

If we may admire his boldness, we need not ignore the gloominess of his outlook. At its best, it was a humane plea for a system that protects the weak, but at its worst, it was a cynical evaluation of humanity as composed principally of cowards and incompetents.

We conclude that about nineteen out of every twenty individuals have "a natural and inalienable right" to be taken care of and protected, to have guardians, trustees, husbands, or masters; in other words, they have a natural and inalienable right to be slaves. The one in twenty are as clearly born or educated or some way fitted for command and liberty.[28]

Fitzhugh's sociology embarrassed his philosophical standpoint. In repudiating philosophical-system building, he wrote: "When society has worked long enough, under the hand of God and nature, man observing its operations, may discover its laws and constitution."[29] This necessarily had to be his position, but it led him into fresh difficulty. If free society was, as he so stoutly maintained, "a recent and small experiment," then the human race must have had several thousand years of work under the hand of God. If man had proved so far unable to discover the laws and constitution of nature, what hope remained? If tradition, common sense, experience, and a social order of which he approved had not yet led man to knowledge, then there was surely little chance they ever would. In his various discussions of the excesses of the Reformation he suggested that man might ever swing too far in one direction or another. More to the point, he concluded that man's moral and intellectual nature had shown no signs either of improvement or deterioration. "Despite the experience of the past, he re-enacts the same follies now that he acted three thousand years ago. Each individual and each generation has to buy, not borrow, its experience."[30] Thus did the quest for a suitable idealism to bolster absolute values pass dangerously close to cynicism and lead imperceptibly into a repudiation of all human history. This pessimistic turn exposed a deeper antagonism in Fitzhugh's thought. His insistence on man's social nature slid into materialistic doctrine: the origin of sentiments and mores he sought in social relations rather than abstract principles; he saw force rather than ideas as governing the world. These formulations proved indigestible fare for an idealism such as that toward which Fitzhugh groped and had to grope if the master class was ever to arrive at a satisfactory standpoint of its own.

CHAPTER THREE

The Critique of Capitalism

To Carthage I came, where there sang all around me in my ears
a cauldron of unholy loves.

SAINT AUGUSTINE,
The Confessions

I

Fitzhugh began *Sociology for the South* with a massive
attack on "free trade" that puzzled some of his contemporaries and has led historians astray ever since. At first glance,
the issue would seem to be less than essential. If Fitzhugh had
been trying to convert the South to protectionism and
étatisme, even if primarily to fight Northern encroachments
the better, his books would have been and would now be of
only passing interest. Fitzhugh cannot be understood unless
the words "free trade" are read as they were meant to be
read: as "capitalism," defined to mean the private ownership
of the means of production and the freedom of the laborer to
sell his labor power.[1] Fitzhugh was so contemptuous of capitalism's place in history that he referred to it as *"The Little
Experiment* (for it is a very little one, both in time and
space)."[2] And again: "Free society is a recent and small experiment. The English Poor Laws and the English poor constitute its only history."[3]

Unfortunately, Fitzhugh's attack on free trade sometimes
became merely an attack on the policy of free trade, narrowly
considered. The double meaning makes for no important inconsistencies but has led many readers into confusion. The
object of Fitzhugh's attack was the capitalist system and its

principal feature, the competitive world market. His call to the South to abandon free trade was a call to insulate itself from the world market, to strive toward autarky, and ultimately to help overthrow the capitalist system everywhere.

The first chapter of *Sociology for the South* opens with a critique of political economy in general and *laissez faire* in particular:

> Political economy is the science of free society. Its theory and its history alike establish this position. Its fundamental maxims, *Laissez-faire* and *"Pas trop gouverner,"* are at war with all kinds of slavery. . . . It is not, therefore, wonderful that such a science should not have been believed or inculcated whilst slavery was universal. . . .[4]

The identification of political economy and *laissez faire* with industrial capitalism is clear and ordinary; more striking is the implicit identification of Southern slavery with precapitalist systems in general. The latter became explicit when he wrote: "Your [free] world is not one-tenth of the whole world, and all is peace, quiet, and prosperity outside of it. We of the South, and all slave countries, want no new world."[5] Fitzhugh separated European capitalism, which he properly distinguished by its free labor force and competitive world market, from all previous European systems, such as Greek and Roman slavery and medieval serfdom, and he separated it also from the systems of Eastern Europe, Asia, Africa, and Latin America, the dependent labor forces of which led him to group them, however dubiously, as slave societies. The slave South belonged to the mainstream of the past and present; the North to the temporary aberration that had gripped Western Europe. The theme did not originate with Fitzhugh, although he gave it its clearest and fullest expression. As early as 1790, James Jackson had defended slavery by arguing, "On this principle the nations of Europe are associated; it is the basis of the feudal system."[6] Southern reactions to the Crimean War demonstrated their growing sense of solidarity with old regimes everywhere. Czarist Russia, one would think, would have been anathema to any people who considered themselves liberal, and Southerners did at first show sympathy for the Entente. Before long, however, pro-Russian feeling became general. No doubt traditional Southern Anglophobia, resentment at British abolitionism, a concern for the balance of power, and the nature of commercial relations with Britain contributed to anti-British feeling, but the great increase in eulogies of the Russians reflected a sense of common interest in the defense of patriarchal social orders. The war made the Southern intelligentsia realize the strong similarity between the prevalent ideas on slavery and the Russian aristocracy's defense of serfdom.[7]

The attack on capitalism always took moral ground. "Adam Smith's philosophy," Fitzhugh wrote, "is simple and comprehensive. . . . Its leading and almost only doctrine is, that individual well-being and social and national wealth and prosperity will be best promoted by each man's eagerly pursuing his own selfish welfare unfettered and unrestricted by legal regulations, or governmental prohibitions. . . ."[8] Fitzhugh was by no means alone among Southerners in discovering the joys of *étatisme*. Henry Hughes contrasted the free-labor system with warranteeism (his fancy name for Southern slavery) as a system in which the state is sovereign. The state, he insisted, must regulate the economy if progress and order were to be maintained. "A strike in warranteeism is a revolt. It is a rebellion against the State."[9]

When Fitzhugh turned to the origins of political economy, he discovered them in the meanness of its founders. The friends and acquaintances of Adam Smith, he maintained, "were of that class, who, in the war of the wits to which free competition invited, were sure to come off victors." Then, Fitzhugh transformed this seemingly petty, quarrelsome, naive thrust into a telling blow: "His country, too, England and Scotland, in the arts of trade and in manufacturing skill, was an over-match for the rest of the world. International free trade would benefit his country as much as social free trade would benefit his friends." The moral objection to "social free trade"—that is, capitalism within a given nation—was that it ignored the vast majority, which necessarily comprised "the unemployed poor, the weak in mind or body, the simple and unsuspicious, the prodigal, the dissipated, the improvident and the vicious." Some needed support and protection; others, supervision and discipline.[10] The moral objection to "international free trade"—that is, the world capitalist market— was that England, and at best a few other countries, grew rich at the expense of the great majority of the world's peoples. England "was daily growing richer, more powerful and intellectual, by her trade, and the countries with which she traded poorer, weaker, and more ignorant." Thus, whether considered internally or in its world setting, capitalism provided for the ascendancy of the strong over the weak and made the rich richer and the poor poorer.[11]

The moral terms in which the argument was couched should not obscure the lesson we were meant to draw: capitalism as a system, not merely the policy of free trade, produces these grave deformations. Capitalism as a system, embracing free labor, a competitive mechanism, and a world market, is incompatible with a secure and tranquil life for the many. In one of his most brilliant passages Fitzhugh pointed out that the crime committed by the English bourgeoisie against Ireland transcended economic exploitation:

> But far the worst evils of this free trade remain to be told. Irish pursuits depressing education and refinement, England becomes a market for the wealth, the intellect, the talent, energy and enterprise of Ireland. All men possessing any of these advantages or qualities retreat to England to spend their incomes, to enter the church, the navy, or the army, to distinguish themselves as authors, to engage in mechanic or manufacturing pursuits. Thus is Ireland robbed of her very life's blood, and thus do our Northern States rob the Southern.[12]

W. J. Cash, after a review of Southern performance in arts and letters, sums up a powerful indictment: "In general, the intellectual and aesthetic culture of the Old South was a superficial and jejune thing, borrowed from without and worn as a political armor and a badge of rank; and hence (I call the authority of old Matthew Arnold to bear me witness) not a true culture at all."[13] Fitzhugh could have accepted this indictment, although he certainly would have rendered it in different terms, but for him it would only have illustrated the results of the colonial position of the South in the cannibalistic world of the marketplace.

It has been said of Fitzhugh—by George Frederick Holmes in his day and Wish and Woodward in ours—that he was too fond of paradox and constantly contradicted himself. The judgment is not without substance, but it is essentially unfair since the Old South was itself a paradox. Slavery grew in the South to meet the needs of the world market, but it simultaneously extruded a ruling class with economic interests, political ideals, and moral sentiments antagonistic to the bourgeoisie dominating that market. To say, as Hartz does, that the Southern system was an agrarian capitalism based on slave labor is to ignore or decisively underestimate slavery's profound effect in raising to regional power a slaveholding class intent upon reshaping the world (or at least its world) in its own image. Fitzhugh articulated this tendency; his paradoxes and contradictions were those inherent in his class and his society.

> The one the philosophy of free trade and universal liberty— the philosophy adapted to promote the interests of the strong, the wealthy, and the wise. The other, that of socialism, intended to protect the weak, the poor and the ignorant. The latter is almost universal in free society; the former prevails in the slaveholding States of the South. Thus we see each section cherishing theories at war with existing institutions. The people of the North and of Europe are proslavery men in the abstract; those of the South are theoretical abolitionists.[14]

In part the paradoxes such as this one arose from Fitzhugh's peculiar penchant to reach for the startling. He liked to shock and to make statements, at first glance absurd, which compelled reflection and demonstrated life's complexity. He had more admirable reasons for resorting to paradoxical formulations, for the reality under scrutiny was itself paradoxical. Free society, he argued, feels the evils of its way of life and gropes for a solution. The best minds and the most generous spirits tend toward socialism, which as a system of collective responsibility becomes slavery when approached practically. Thus, in various subtle ways, the morals and principles of slavery insinuate themselves into the everyday life of free societies. On the other hand, the South admires free trade because it has no experience with the attendant evils and seeks to attain to the industrial excellence displayed in the capitalist countries.[15] Fitzhugh confused free trade qua capitalism with free trade qua free trade. Had he been more careful, he could have made his argument clearer and stronger by pointing out that the Southern demand for free trade, if acceded to by the North, could only have resulted in exchanging one master for another, whereas the real interests of the South lay in the total destruction of the free-market mechanism on a world scale.

Part of the difficulty arose from his, and his section's, respect for the accomplishments of capitalism, as he himself suggests in the passage quoted above. Fitzhugh readily admitted that the abolition of feudalism and the defeat of Catholicism in Northeastern Europe catapulted "an immense amount of unfettered talent, genius, industry, and capital" into the free market and that the process expanded "the aggregate wealth of society and probably its aggregate intelligence." He noted that scholars and philosophers saw only this liberating side of the capitalist revolution and were blind to its ravages. Still, the admirable effects were, he admitted, due to "unfettering the limbs, the minds and consciences of men."[16] Capitalism, on the one hand, stimulated remarkable advances in mechanical invention and in "great utilitarian operations requiring the wielding of immense capital and much labor"; in this respect, "its progress has been unexampled." Capitalism, on the other hand, represented a decline from the artistic and moral standards of antiquity, when collective organization and slave labor prevailed.[17] He lamented, in particular, the loss of that sense of reciprocal duties and obligations between master and slave, lord and vassal, priest and layman, which was crushed by the force of the free market.[18] He struck hard at the glorification of competition, which, he argued, the Mosaic teachings aimed to suppress. He publicly argued against competition but privately expressed at least one qualification that underscored his anticapitalist moral position. "Again, I like a good deal of free competition," he wrote to Holmes, "but would relieve the weak and the poor and the ignorant from its crushing operations—confine it to the rich, skilful, and professional."[19]

Fitzhugh, like most idealist critics of capitalism, found himself in an unpleasant position. He could not reasonably deny the material advances that had been ushered in by the capitalist era, nor could he repudiate them and call for a return to an earlier standard of living. Such a course might be fine for romantic poets or academic relativists, but it was not open to a man who consciously aspired to speak for a ruling class with responsibilities to meet. His position reminds us, at least superficially, of Marx's praise for capitalism's contributions to mankind, as sung in *The Communist Manifesto*. For Marx, there was no difficulty in hailing the advent of capitalism, for his philosophy of history had room for a revolutionary young capitalism and a reactionary old one, and his sophisticated political economy had no trouble with positive accomplishments even of a moribund capitalism. He looked to a future society built solidly on what the bourgeoisie had created and was not faced with the agonies and perplexities of socialism in one rather backward country. Fitzhugh was not so lucky. Since he looked backward to a restoration of a very old order his praise for capitalism's achievements had to be grudging. He seems to have sensed the danger of admitting too much. He had, in fact, affirmed the following:

1. Precapitalist labor systems were, in general, wholesome, moral, and good.
2. Capitalism freed men's minds and bodies from bondage.
3. Capitalism has produced unparalleled advances in the world economy.
4. Capitalism is an immoral, or better amoral, system, which has condemned the great majority of the world's people to hunger and deprivation.
5. Slavery must, in some form, everywhere be restored in order to restore security, order, and decency to all men of good will.

When Fitzhugh confined himself to the intellectual plane, he could maintain a tolerably consistent position: Medieval thought had become too rigid to satisfy man's spiritual and material needs; the Reformation removed fetters and laid the basis for desirable advances; unfortunately, it went too far and resulted in a revolution that overthrew everything worthwhile in the old regime—just and reasonable authority, responsibility to one's fellow man, and a respect for order and tradition. Once he moved to the material plane—as he had to—he was deep in trouble, for he had to admit that the greatest economic advances occurred during and after the "revolutionary" period. In effect, Fitzhugh embraced the achievements of capitalism as too good to slough off, and in any case too well imbedded, but he also embraced a social order that, by his own account, could do no more than imitate capitalism's achievements; it could not be expected to build on them, for it could never duplicate, much less surpass, the incentives and spirit, nor would it want to.

Fitzhugh's treatment, explicit and implicit, of mercantilism provides essential clues to his anticapitalist stance. Fitzhugh superficially resembled a partisan of mercantilism or at least of neomercantilist national economics; Wish, for one, has insisted that Fitzhugh's economic doctrine resembled that of Carey and List. To relate Fitzhugh's attack on classical economics to that of the protectionist school is to miss the point, for he attacked from a radically different standpoint.

In part the confusion arises from Fitzhugh's casual praise of the mercantilists and the occasional resemblance of his ideas to theirs. Writing of the mercantilist era, he noted that it was distinguished by monopoly, the overthrow of which threw men, naked, back on their own resources. "Men were suddenly called on to walk alone, to act and work for themselves without guide, advice or control from superior authority."[20] On another tack, he drew attention to the salutary features of a favorable balance of trade, owing to which "new pursuits arise," commerce and manufacturing complement each other, and the labor force and population expand.[21]

Yet, Fitzhugh was neither a mercantilist nor some kind of neomercantilist, nor an exponent of a "national" capitalist economy. His ideals were quite different from those of the various types of bourgeois theorists. When, for example, he maintained that trade allowed the North to exploit the South, he saw the possibilities of turnabout: "Trade further South would enrich us [i.e., Virginia] and enlighten us; for we would manufacture for the far South. We should become exploitators, instead of being exploited" [sic].[22] Despite the apparent invitation to Virginia to play the cannibal, he manifestly did not believe that turnabout would be fair play; he did not, for example, want Virginia to exploit the Lower South. We know his sentiments from a letter to Holmes,[23] but we do not need to refer to it, for his whole body of thought points in another direction and recoils at such a notion.

A clue to his fundamental commitment may be found in his discussion of money. All reformers from the days of Plato, he began, have sought to restrict or banish money. He struck a moderate pose: the moderate use of money is essential to civilization and the general good; the excessive use of money is the most potent of factors generating inequality, extreme wealth, effeminacy, corruption, and the oppression of the poor. On balance, he joins the opposition. Free competitive society needs money as a weapon with which skill and capital may oppress labor. Slave society, based on and tending to approximate the family, needs to restrict the use of money to essential transactions. In this way, money plays an essential but strictly limited role in economic life, and the teachings of early Christianity are served.[24]

Fitzhugh envisioned autarky but not the autarky of the mercantilists, who looked toward self-sufficiency at home to promote plunder abroad. Since the mercantilists saw profit as arising from exchange, the policy of beggar-thy-neighbor represented a choice of life over death. Fitzhugh had no need of such a policy. He accepted the labor theory of value as developed by the classical school and deduced from it a crude theory of profit based on production, not exchange. Thus, he referred to Hobbes, who "saw men devouring one another, under their system, two hundred years ago, and we see them similarly engaged now."[25] The mercantilists' war of all against all, to which Hobbes gave political expression, was precisely what Fitzhugh wanted to suppress. Mercantilism, then, ushered in the era of cannibalism, and *laissez faire* perfected it.

I I

Although Fitzhugh denounced classical bourgeois political economy as a fraudulent philosophy of capitalist exploitation, he based his critique and his own economic ideas on the labor theory of value, which he uncritically appropriated from that school. Fitzhugh had a poor understanding of this theory, and his formulation proved much cruder than Ricardo's. Two kinds of difficulties beset him. One kind resulted from his lack of intellectual discipline, which introduced contradictions and distortions that careful work might have avoided; the other and more serious kind arose from his uncritical view of the master-slave relationship, which prevented him from seeing the full implications of his own doctrine. His improper understanding of the theory enabled him to make startlingly effective use of it and to deduce a theory of surplus value that had eluded Ricardo.

In his direct discussions of value and profit Fitzhugh consistently upheld the notion that labor alone lies at their source, although he inadvertently introduced inconsistencies and contradictory elements into his discussions of peripheral issues. (These we may pass over.) "Your capital," he insisted, "will not bring you an income of a cent, nor supply one of your wants, without labor."[26] Repeatedly, he returned to the same point: Labor alone creates value but capital and "wit" expropriate and accumulate it. He never conceded to capital the power of contributing to the formation of value, although he did argue that "skill in the mechanic arts" enables the strong to exploit the weak by forcing unequal exchanges of labor values.

For Fitzhugh, it was enough to say that labor creates value; the difficulties inherent in such a theory escaped him. He worried not at all about the relationship of skilled and unskilled labor, the definition of productive labor, the interpretation of subsistence level, or the implications of considering labor both a commodity and a source of value to all other commodities. Yet despite the confusion that a crude theory of value introduced into his economics, he did derive a theory of surplus value and made brilliant use of it. Ricardo's sophisticated labor theory of value presented a paradox that barred the way to a satisfactory theory of surplus value. Ricardo's commitment to capitalism may have undermined his efforts to resolve the paradox, for a resolution necessarily led to a doctrine of exploitation; Fitzhugh, notwithstanding his lack of economic depth, suffered from no such inhibitions and eagerly explored doctrines critical of capitalism.

Ricardo began with the propositions that labor created commodity value and that labor was itself a commodity. Since commodities must, on the average, exchange at their values in a free market, the wages paid to labor must equal the value of labor. However, if labor is paid in full for the value it imparts to other commodities, how does the capitalist's profit arise? When Ricardo tried to explain profit he had to fall back on a cost-of-production theory that had nothing in common with his original labor theory.[27]

Marx found a way out of Ricardo's difficulty by developing, instead of abandoning, the labor theory of value. He distinguished between the abstract labor that the capitalist buys at its value (labor power) and the physical human effort that produces commodity values but is not itself a commodity (labor). Since labor creates value it cannot itself be a commodity—that is, it cannot itself be the embodiment of value —for there can be no such thing as the value of value. On the strength of this trenchant distinction Marx developed his theory of surplus value, with its account of the origin of profit in the exploitation of labor. A worker may work eight hours and produce eight units of commodity value; he will be paid, not according to his labor, but according to the value of his labor power, which is the cost of his maintenance and reproduction. If the latter is equal to, say, four units of commodity value, then the capitalist has made a profit of four units by appropriating to himself the surplus value—the difference between the value produced by labor and the value of labor power.[28] In this manner Marx demonstrated that there was no logical contradiction between an equal exchange of values and the appearance of surplus value or profit. Fitzhugh never worried about Ricardo's paradox and never dreamed of Marx's solution. His own labor theory of value was crude and based on ignorance of its implications. He passed from a crude theory of value to a crude theory of surplus value. His economic reasoning is not impressive, but his semirational, semi-intuitive insight into his enemy's ideological weakness is impressive indeed.

"Every capitalist," wrote Fitzhugh in summary, "holds property in his fellow man to the extent of the profits of his capital, or income. The only income possibly resulting from capital, is the result of the property which capital bestows on its owners, in the labor of other people."[29] He defined the profit of capitalist production as that amount of labor's output which the employer can command or "exploit." Here he runs into difficulty, for why should not the profits of slavery also be considered the result of exploitation or the appropriation by the master of surplus value?[30] Although he sometimes indulged in evasion. Fitzhugh did admit that the profits of slave labor also represented surplus value. These profits "are that portion of the products of such labor which the power of the master enables him to appropriate." He then slips into nonsense: "These profits are less, because the master allows the slave to retain a larger share of the results of his own labor than do the employers of free labor."[31] The shallowness of this shift from an analysis of objective relationships to one of subjectively determined practice raises grave suspicions of dishonesty, which cannot altogether be dispelled, but a less unpleasant explanation can be found in his confused ideas about wages and subsistence. Apart from the way out provided by his own confusion on these matters, he had to rely on irrelevant chatter about how hard the master had to work to keep his plantation going and to keep his slaves comfortable after their day's work. The cares and responsibilities of the master were contrasted with the freedom of the capitalist, whose responsibilities toward his laborers ended with their day's work.[32] The contrast may have contained some truth, but it had nothing to do with the issue.

Fitzhugh's discomfiture is understandable. After noting that all trades and professions in the South were living off the surplus value extracted from the slaves, he made a bungling attempt to put the master in a more favorable light than the Northern capitalist. The master "has nothing to pay them except what his slaves make. But you Yankees and Englishmen more than divide the profits [with nonproductive groups] —you take the lion's share."[33] Beneath these silly and bullying polemics lay a gnawing awareness that he had gone too far. If he had exposed the profits of capitalism as rooted in the exploitation of labor, he had by the same process exposed the profits of slavery as similarly rooted. "It is remarkable," he wrote in a more confident mood, "that the political economists, who generally assume labor to be the most just and correct measure of value, should not have discovered that the profits of capital represent no labor at all. To be consistent, the political economists should denounce as unjust all interests, rents, dividends, and other profits of capital."[34] These words might easily be turned against Fitzhugh to undermine his defense of slavery.

More plausibly, Fitzhugh defended slavery as the best form of exploitation. Man's nature compelled him to try to raise himself by having others work for him, and civilization could not be built without a leisure class. Slavery was the most humane and mild form of exploitation.[35] To bolster this conclusion he introduced the moral issue of responsibility of master to slave, to which we shall return, and a theory of wages, to which we shall now give attention. If slave labor yielded as great a surplus as free, he began, it would still be the rule in Europe and the North. Competition for jobs guarantees that the wage level remains at subsistence.[36] Fitzhugh projected, in a rough way, the idea of a reserve army of unemployed, which the capitalists could manipulate to depress the wage level.[37] The systematic starvation of a large portion of the working class provided the basis for the ruthless exploitation of the rest. Fitzhugh took the labor conditions of the first half of the nineteenth century to be a distinguishing and permanent characteristic of capitalism. To do so, he had to project an iron law of wages stricter than that attributed to Ricardo. Capitalism, he argued, was creating ever more millionaires and ever more paupers, for the creation of one of the former necessitated the creation of one thousand of the latter.[38] The crudeness of his law of wages enabled him to see capitalism as a static and less formidable system than it was and simultaneously gave him a weapon with which to defend slavery.

Fitzhugh's theory of wages may be summed up in a few propositions: (1) the wages of free labor are depressed by the competitive struggle; (2) on the average, wages must fall to the subsistence level; and therefore, (3) a large portion of the working class receives wages below the average and must suffer hunger and extreme deprivation. He contrasted the view of capitalism flowing from the application of this theory with a much happier view of slavery:

> The wages of the poor diminish as their wants and families increase, for the care and labor of attending to the family leaves them fewer hours for profitable work. With negro slaves, their wages invariably increase with their wants. The master increases the provision for the family as the family increases in number and helplessness. It is a beautiful example of communism, where each one receives not according to his labor, but according to his wants.[99]

This assertion rests on two assumptions: that the level of subsistence is absolute, and that the impoverishment of the working class, engendered by the competitive struggle, must be absolute and must be taken literally.

Fitzhugh's clearest discussion of the level of subsistence appeared in 1850 in his essay "What Shall Be Done with the Free Negroes?" which he later appended to *Sociology for the South*; all his subsequent remarks on wages and profits must be understood in the context of the earlier discussion. "To say that free labor is cheaper than slave labor, is to say that the slave is better off, so far as physical comfort is concerned, than the free laborer."[40] He tried to make the same point in his discussion of taxation. In free society, he began, all taxes come from labor; employers reduce wages to meet tax burdens and continue to live as luxuriously as ever. In slave society, humanity and interest combine to hold the slaves' standard of living firm; the masters have to pay taxes out of their own pockets.[41] He apparently did not see that in order to score a mere propaganda victory, he had contradicted himself. If the wages of free labor were held to a subsistence level, any diminution would impair the survival of the labor force and could only be temporary. On the assumptions of the labor theory of value all taxes, whether in free or slave society, are charged against labor since they form part of its social surplus, but for just that reason they are also charged against capital, which commands that surplus. In any case, Fitzhugh assumed the level of subsistence to be something absolute and biologically determined; he discussed it without reference to productivity. Without these assumptions neither his remarks on relative living standards nor his idea of absolute and literal impoverishment makes sense.

Ricardo and Marx also spoke of wages as tending toward subsistence, but they interpreted subsistence as a shifting, culturally determined "standard of decency," which rose with improvements in technology and the cheapening of the price of necessaries. In their view the subsistence level could not be biologically determined under conditions of a steadily advancing technology. Cursory examination of living standards in different parts of the world should have demonstrated that no one could reasonably retain the subsistence theory of wages and simultaneously interpret subsistence biologically and rigidly. Yet, Fitzhugh tried to retain both the theory and the interpretation.

The liberation of the European serfs, Fitzhugh held, compelled them to work harder than ever before to obtain a livelihood. The bourgeoisie's proud boast that free labor was cheaper than slave had to mean that the conditions of labor had undergone deterioration. This argument is internally consistent only in the sense that, under conditions of subsistence wages, the ever increasing productivity of labor must result in a widening gap between labor and capital—that is, a relative impoverishment of the working class. To be made consistent with the rest of Fitzhugh's economic schema, this awareness of the need to consider labor productivity would have to be introduced into the comparison of free-labor and slave-labor conditions. Had Fitzhugh forced the issue, he could not have smugly concluded that logic proved that slaves were better cared for. In Marxian terms, the steady rise in the productivity of free labor, with its concomitant advance in technology, guaranteed a rising level of subsistence, culturally determined. If we assume the validity of the labor theory of value, we still cannot accept Fitzhugh's conclusion on the relative conditions of slave and free labor, for that conclusion appeals for support primarily to his naive and static notion of a biologically determined subsistence level. Under the circumstances, Fitzhugh's bourgeois opponents could only be puzzled by his critique. Fitzhugh was doubly damned by the labor theory of value to which he looked for an economic rationale for the defense of slavery. It exposed the exploitation inherent in slavery quite as nicely as that inherent in capitalism, and to make matters worse, when properly understood it suggested that the living standards of free labor would normally be higher than those of slave labor, although free labor would normally be the more exploited. Greater exploitation implies a greater gap between labor and capital but is compatible with a rising living standard for all classes.[42]

Henry Hughes grappled with these problems somewhat more successfully than did Fitzhugh. He argued for the moral superiority of slave labor over free labor by invoking the notion of a reserve army of unemployed in a more consistent way. The capitalist seeks to create a surplus of labor, he argued, in order to hold down wages; therefore, the great advantage of slave labor lay in its security. Hughes's remarks on the problem of wages, although hardly adequate, did come closer to a defensible standpoint. Under slave or free labor a subsistence wage is warranted, but under slavery, he insisted, the actual wage tends to rise as productivity rises and the bonds of sentiment grow stronger whereas under wage labor the capitalist has no reason to increase wages along with productivity. Hughes at least glimpsed the cultural dimension, even if he left one or two things, such as unions, out of account.[43]

Fitzhugh's political economy, however shaky and unimpressive in its positive contributions, was therefore his own and reflected the badly compromised position of the slaveholders as a class. Wish is wrong to attribute to him any knowledge of, or influence from, Marx, and it is difficult to understand how virtually every historian who has written on Fitzhugh since could follow his example. It is, of course, rather the fashion these days to link everyone who falls outside the grand liberal consensus with that father of all our woes, and even poor old John C. Calhoun, who bears as much intellectual relationship to Marx as to, say, Saint Francis of Assisi, has been so linked by prominent historians who ought to know better.

Wish writes: "To defend a conservative traditional order, he [Fitzhugh] accepted even the weapons of radicalism, going so far as to rely upon an economic interpretation of history and a pre-Marxian concept of the class struggle."[44] We have looked at his view of history and hardly found either economic determinism, which is in principle anti-Marxist, or a materialist interpretation of history. There is none to be found. Many writers before Marx saw class struggles in history, but most of these were conservatives, not radicals. Fitzhugh's view of history included classes but not class struggles, which he attributed solely to capitalism.

More to the point, Wish writes:

Although Karl Marx's first volume of *Capital* was not published until 1867, certain of his earlier writings were already available in English. Fitzhugh was evidently acquainted with the famous Communist Manifesto of 1848, either directly or indirectly, since he quoted its phraseology in *Cannibals All!* Both Marx and Fitzhugh drew from the common stream of socialist thought, to which, strangely enough, the early classical economists, such as Adam Smith and David Ricardo, contributed no small share, as is evident in the theory of labor as the only cost of production. Marx was indebted in large measure to the despised Utopians for his theories of surplus value and the exploitative nature of interest; Fitzhugh likewise drew from this same source, although through the American school of Socialists. The basic formulation of these ideas appears in the work of the early nineteenth century reformers of Britain, William Thompson and John Gray; and in the American work of J. F. Bray, to mention but a few.

Marx, too, like Fitzhugh and the earlier Socialists, spoke of "labour-time" as a unit of economic value. Certainly he subscribed to the Virginian's conception of "slaves without masters." "In fact," charged Marx in *Capital*, "the veiled slavery of the wage-earners in Europe needed, for its pedestal, slavery pure and simple in the new world." . . . Marx, in keeping with the socialist tradition, which Fitzhugh utilized, did not stress the superiority of free over slave society.[45]

Wish then quotes, out of context, Marx's statement that both slavery and capitalism are systems based on the exploitation of labor.

First, Fitzhugh did not quote the phraseology of *The Communist Manifesto* and almost certainly never read it. There is not a shred of evidence of a "direct" acquaintanceship, and we have his own statement, to which Wish himself elsewhere refers, that he never read a socialist writer, only reviews of their work. As for "indirect" acquaintanceship, there is no evidence that he read reviews of Marx's writings or that he knew anything about him. He did draw his phraseology from the same stream of radical criticism as did Marx. None of Marx's specific phrases—for example, "surplus value"—appear in his work. Wish, in noting that both Marx and Fitzhugh drew on similar sources, overthrows his own argument.

Second, there is nothing at all strange in Smith's and Ricardo's having contributed to the formulation of a labor theory of value. In Ricardo's case especially, this theory formed a part of a political economy that centered on the economic relationship of social classes to each other, rather than, as with the later Marginalist school, on individual units. (The doctrine in question identifies labor as the only source of commodity value, not, as Wish would have it, the only cost of production.)

Third, Fitzhugh did not speak of "labor time," as did Marx; as we have seen, he made no distinction between labor and labor power.

Fourth, Marx did not equate wage slavery with slavery. The quote from Marx is out of context. It is not true that he failed to stress the superiority of the one over the other. On the contrary, during the American war he wrote widely in defense of the North and mobilized the First International in opposition to the Confederacy. *Capital*, which Wish quotes selectively, is full of attacks on slavery and applause for the positive historic role of capitalism. In *The Communist Manifesto* and earlier, Marx and Engels made clear their position that capitalism was superior to all precapitalist class systems.

Fitzhugh, like Marx, was anticapitalist. So have been many spokesmen for noncapitalist classes and societies. Agreement on a negative attitude toward something hardly implies an equation of views. That there were similarities no one need deny. Marx's hatred for slavery, even relative to capitalism, is a matter of record and was at least as deep as Fitzhugh's fear of proletarian socialism.

III

Much of Fitzhugh's economic argument against capitalism cannot be separated from his moral argument. In this respect, too, he worked in the spirit of the predecessors of bourgeois political economy—one thinks of Aristotle and especially of Saint Thomas Aquinas, with whom Fitzhugh does not seem to have been acquainted—and to some extent of its successors. The morality and economics against which he fought were to him inseparable and incapable of discrete analysis. "A beautiful system of ethics this," he commented on the competitive side of the capitalist marketplace, "that places all mankind in antagonistic positions, and puts all society at war.

What can such a war result in but the oppression and ultimate extermination of the weak?"[46] His words, whether so intended or not, struck at both mercantilism and free trade—at the policy of beggar-thy-neighbor and against reliance on the Invisible Hand—for both reflected the world market. He did not deny that man suffered from a "destructive, competitive propensity," but he did insist that God gave man reason to enable him to curb such propensities by erecting political and institutional safeguards to protect the weak and the poor. "To encourage [competition], is to encourage the strong to oppress the weak, and to violate the primary object of all government." Besides, he added, it was hardly the better part of wisdom to encourage a struggle in which the overwhelming majority of mankind would find itself in opposition to society.[47]

And what of the ruling class? What does bourgeois morality have to offer it except a rationale for plunder? "The rich can hardly respect themselves, when they reflect that wealth is the result of avarice, caution, circumspection and hard dealing. These are the virtues which free society in its regular operation brings forth."[48] Under such a system one man's happiness consists in destroying another's.[49]

Fitzhugh softened his critique considerably in *Cannibals All!*, which he wrote after a trip to the Northeast; the softening represented no sacrifice of principle, for it enabled him to advance rather than retreat. He commented favorably on Northeastern philanthropy and humanitarianism but thought them misguided. "The best thing a philanthropist can do is to buy slaves, because then his power of control is greatest— his ability to do practical good most perfect." He then manfully admitted that he had wronged Northerners in his earlier writings: "Benevolence, affection, generosity, and philanthropy are equally common North and South; and only differ in their modes of manifestation. We are one people." He even suggested that in some respects Northerners surpassed Southerners in generosity. "This correction of our error does not affect our theories." And it did not. The great difference between the two sections and the two peoples lay not in any difference in human feeling or decency but in the fundamental difference in social structure and its attendant values. Slavery and the patriarchal tradition made it easy for Southerners to express fully their human feelings for their fellow men, whereas capitalism and the cash nexus made it difficult for Northerners to do so by penalizing them heavily. "The daily and hourly exercise of these qualities is elicited at the South, because it is safe, prudent and expedient so to exercise them. The reverse is true at the North. . . ."[50]

His graceful words on Northern decency qualified only in nonessential respects his earlier, harsher judgments. His estimate of capitalism's basic moral tendency remained the same, but he had come to acknowledge that not all Northerners had succumbed and that few had succumbed totally.

In 1849, in "Slavery Justified," Fitzhugh had charged that the moral effect of free society was the destruction of the Christian principle of love-thy-neighbor:

> The intense struggle to better each one's pecuniary condition, the rivalries, the jealousies, the hostilities which it begets, leave neither time nor inclination to cultivate the heart or the head. Every finer feeling of our nature is chilled and benumbed by its selfish atmosphere; affection is under the ban, because affection makes us less regardful of mere self; hospitality is considered criminal waste, chivalry a stumbling-block, and the code of honor foolishness; taste, sentiment, imagination, are forbidden ground, because no money is to be made by them. . . . What makes money, and what costs money, are alone desired. Temperance, frugality, thrift, attention to business, industry, and skill in making bargains, are virtues in high repute, because they enable us to supplant others and increase our own wealth.[51]

The critique of bourgeois morality passed imperceptibly into the defense of slaveholding morality, with Christianity serving as the bridge. Writing in a Christian country, Fitzhugh asked how the teachings of Christ were supposed to survive in a competitive society. Such doctrines as "Love thy neighbor as thyself" or "Do unto others as you would have them do unto you" would, in a capitalist society, be "acts of suicidal self-sacrifice. Christian morality, however, was not preached to free competitive society, but to slave society, where it is neither very difficult nor unnatural to practice it."[52]

The master embraces Christian morality naturally because his role in life is essentially that of a father and a protector. He may tend toward cruelty or become too much imbued with the spirit of command, but almost always he yields to the softening effects of his slaves' meek submission, much as a despotic husband yields to the helplessness of a submissive wife. The master comes to Christianity because "his whole life is spent in providing for the minutest wants of others."[53] Slavery extends and reinforces the bonds of family life. Accustomed to treat slaves as members of a larger family, the master has his sense of natural family enormously strengthened. No wonder that Southerners cherish ties of kinship even to the fifth degree, whereas Northerners barely acknowledge first cousins. "Love for others is the organic law of our own society, as self-love is of theirs."[54]

Domestic affection, which by its nature cannot be bought, sold, or measured in the marketplace, can only arise from a special relationship of man to man, in which natural tendencies to kindness and the advantages of interest are joined. Fitzhugh saw corporations, associations, socialisms, and communisms as attempts to produce what only slavery could.[55] Only slavery could because only slavery could guarantee that affection and interest complemented and reinforced each other. "Say the Abolitionists—'Man ought not to have property in man!' What a dreary, cold, bleak, inhospitable world this would be with such a doctrine carried into practice. Men living to themselves . . . ? No: 'Love thy neighbor as thyself.' And this can't be done till he has a property in your services as well as a place in your heart."[56] Human law might abolish slavery, but it could never engender between capitalist and laborer, employer and employed, that natural affection binding together master and slave.[57]

Slavery improves the morals of the slave as well as of the master, much as capitalism undermines the morals of the laborer as well as of the capitalist. Fitzhugh denounced as "unfeeling and libellous, unjust and untrue" an article in the *Edinburgh Review* attributing to the English poor an excessive use of alcohol. Great destitution and pauperism preclude the slum population and starving peasants from indulging themselves. He then pointed to the better-paid workers as the ones most prone to drunkenness. "Fatigued, maddened and desperate with the prospect before them, some little charity should be extended to their feelings."[58] To make matters worse, the worker is even shut out from the affection he might normally find with his fellow workers, for the competitive struggle in the labor market sets them against one another. These themes gained great currency in the late antebellum South. The right to subsistence, Henry Hughes cried out, must be guaranteed to all. Toleration of want he denounced as "wrong," "revolting," "horrible," "murder to which every man in the community is accessory." "Existence," Hughes concluded, "is the right of all."[59] It is perhaps an adequate comment on bourgeois society that it had to be told these things, with this degree of passion, by slaveowners.

The alienation and desperation of the working classes, Fitzhugh held, can only be ended by slavery, within which a man may find himself loved and protected. Slavery provides fertile soil for the moral improvement of the enslaved. It separates the laborers from each other, providing plantation-sized units instead of overflowing slums. The master, by example and instruction, teaches his house slaves, who in turn provide examples and instruction for the field slaves.[60] Fitzhugh admitted that under certain circumstances even slavery might fail to protect and instruct the laborers properly. He denounced the latifundia of the Roman Empire as destructive of paternalism. Excessive concentration of landholding and slaveholding generated absentee ownership, an idle ruling class, a lamentable clustering of great numbers of slaves, and nonintercourse between master and slave. His model slavery was that of the Jews, and as we shall see when we turn to his vision of the good society, he sought to guarantee that the South took the Jewish road, not the Roman. The proper instruction of the slaves by contact with a benevolent master remained a foremost concern: "By subjecting them to the constant control and supervision of their superiors, interested in enforcing morality, it becomes the best and most efficient police system. . . ."[61] Police system! For the morality of the masses depends entirely on the quality and quantity of force applied to them.[62]

Fitzhugh related the decline of morals in the bourgeois world to the decline of art and values in general. He declared that an artist of genuine sensitivity, unwilling to prostitute himself before the vulgar moneyed classes, would be ridiculed and cast out.[63] He knew that he had entered upon dangerous ground, for the fate of artists and scientists in an unsympathetic slave South was and is well known. He did not retreat, but rather demonstrated forcibly his understanding of his primary task—to reshape the South in the image of the best of its ruling class. "We have an aristocracy with more of privilege, and less of public spirit, than any that we meet with in history," he wrote in one of his most severely critical passages on the South. "Naturally, Southerners, like all slaveholders, are liberal and public spirited." The problem, then, resulted from the "free trade philosophy" that had corrupted, or perhaps it would be better to say misled, the South.[64]

A passage from his early essay "Slavery Justified" (1849) cleverly demonstrates how certain attacks, apparently aimed at the North, were at least equally aimed at the competitive, "bourgeois" quality of Southern life. Parvenus, he began, have the feelings of decent men, although those feelings become blunted in the race for wealth. They at least normally love their children and would see them grow into cultivated, refined, moral men, such as they themselves could never afford to become. Thus, they rear their children to be gentlemen and thereby risk having them lose out to a new wave of unprincipled upstarts. "In Heaven's name, what is human life worth with such prospects ahead? . . . And yet this is an exact picture of the prospect which universal liberty holds out to its votaries."[65] Fitzhugh knew very well that the Southwestern frontier had already yielded several waves of parvenu slaveholders who rivaled Northern speculators and businessmen in their sharp dealings and vulgarity. He trusted to the long-range stabilizing effects of the plantation system but never ceased to worry about the antithesis buried deep in Southern life.

The remedy ultimately lay in expelling the enemy philosophy from the South. Fitzhugh understood that the South was the battleground for two irreconcilable forces: the one the liberal inheritance and the imported bourgeois values of the world market, reinforced by the acquisitive spirit and social mobility of the frontier and the legacy of political liberalism; the other, the native aristocratic values, firmly rooted in the prevailing social system and indispensable to the survival of the slaveholders as a ruling class. Fitzhugh did not mean merely to encourage needed reforms in the South. He meant to drive the dangerous and contemptible infidels— "these vulgar parvenus, these psalm-singing regicides, these worshippers of mammon"[66]—from the South's City of God.

I V

That the South was Protestant rather than Roman Catholic proved to be unfortunate, as Fitzhugh appreciated in his day and perhaps only Allen Tate has appreciated in ours. As Tate cautiously observes in his penetrating contribution to *I'll Take My Stand*, since the sixteenth century a people might return to an older form of economy but could not develop its own genius unless it blended with the drift of international sentiment:

> The South could blindly return to an older secular polity, but the world was too much with it, and it could not create its appropriate religion.
>
> There were two results of this anomalous position, which may be stated without too much historical argument. The South, as a political atmosphere formed by the eighteenth century, did not realize its genius in time, but continued to defend itself on the political terms of the North; and thus, waiting too long, it let its powerful rival gain the ascendancy. Its religious impulse was inarticulate simply because it tried to encompass its destiny within the terms of Protestantism, in origin, a non-agrarian and trading religion; hardly a religion at all, but a result of secular ambition. The Southern politicians could merely quote Scripture to defend slavery, the while they defended their society as a whole with the catchwords of eighteenth-century politics. And this is why the South separated from the North too late, and so lost its cause.[67]

Fitzhugh did not hide his admiration for Catholicism, nor did many other antebellum Southern intellectuals—there is an important book to be written on this subject—but he could hardly join the Church. Whatever his private thoughts, as a man intent on leading his section to high ideological and political ground, he could not afford to offend its traditional religious sensibilities. Fitzhugh, an admirer and upholder of tradition, had to embrace a traditional Protestantism when he knew very well that the South needed the very Romanism it so instinctively hated.

Fitzhugh avoided sectarian argument and confined himself to the general principle that religion ought to be a social, not merely a private, concern and to a historical critique of religious history from which each could draw his own conclusions. His attitude betrayed ambivalence, as it had to under the circumstances; nowhere did the ambivalence manifest itself more clearly than in his treatment of the Puritans.

Of one thing he remained certain: no government, no society, could long exist without religion. "Society can linger on for centuries without slavery; it cannot exist a day without religion."[68] He called disestablishment and freedom of—that is, freedom from—religion "a bold experiment," for no government had ever done without a state religion.[69] He poured contempt on the reformers, but insisted that despite their intentions Christianity did slip into America society and politics. The prejudice against religion and its role in government was gradually receding. In general, he urged the prudent application of government support to religion, which he likened to fire—dangerous when out of control but nonetheless indispensable.[70] Religious liberty, like all liberty, must be restricted; the masses could not possibly be disciplined without some degree of compulsory instruction in a sound faith.[71]

Fitzhugh admired the manner in which, as he thought, medieval Catholicism had sanctified marriage and the family, which he regarded as the foundation of society. He admired the way in which it had made itself a part of the fabric of society and combined with other feudal institutions to protect the masses. "In the palmy days of royalty, of feudal nobility, and of Catholic rule, there were no poor in Europe."[72] Fitzhugh boldly praised the social discipline, authoritarianism, and respect for hierarchy for which the Catholic Church stood. The Bible, he asserted, remained man's best guide, and next came Aristotle. "But all books written four hundred or more years ago, are apt to yield useful instruction, whilst those written since that time will generally mislead."[73] Thus did he consign the classic works of Protestantism— always leaving room for exceptions—to the rubbish heap.

The enemy of course was not so much Protestantism as capitalism, but long before Max Weber, and like many other important nineteenth-century thinkers, he saw an organic relationship between the two. The Reformation "effected much of practical good"—what else could he say?—but "gave birth to a false philosophy, which has been increasing and ramifying until our day, and now threatens the overthrow of all social institutions."[74] The false prophecy stemmed from the right of private judgment, which passed easily into notions of equality, universal liberty, *laissez faire*, and in a word, all the bourgeois heresies.

He denied that he had a quarrel with the Reformation as such. Catholicism had grown rigid, reactionary, destructive of all individual effort and thought. It had gone too far, and reform had to come. The excesses following reform, however, especially the pernicious right of private judgment, threatened to bring about worse evils than those overthrown. Atheism appeared with the excesses of Protestantism, for both proceeded with the growth of capitalism and the abolition of feudalism and slavery.[75] Fitzhugh took issue with those who thought that the Reformation had increased the liberties of the people. On the contrary, by destroying "the noblest charity fund in the world, the church lands, and abolishing a priesthood, the efficient and zealous friends of the poor," it had diminished the liberties of the masses and impaired their moral and physical well-being. The Church, like the Crown, stood as a natural friend and ally of the poor.[76]

What Fitzhugh admired most in the Reformation was its practicality, its instinctive and intuitive repudiation of Catholic rigidity and decadence, and its distrust of scholasticism and all such compromises with rationalism. The Reformation was not the thought, or even the action, of Luther, Calvin, and other great leaders; it was the response of society, which alone is infallible, to intolerable evils.[77]

The two-sidedness of the Reformation and Fitzhugh's attempt to evaluate it emerge most forcibly in his treatment of Puritanism. When writing of the intolerance of the Puritans, he swings toward approval. "Many tokens of their zeal and affection," he wrote with apparent gratification, "were soon seen pendant from the elms of New England."[78] He would not have been at all unhappy, he admitted, to see intolerance of error restored in New England.[79] Then too, Cromwell had

defended the poor, or so Fitzhugh thought, against the preda-
tory rich. In short, the social discipline, civic spirit, and intolerance of error that marked one side of the Puritan tradition were much to his taste. Alas, for all that the Puritans
were still revolutionaries and bourgeois, and all their work
ultimately went into the worst of causes. Rome remained
safer.

On balance:

> The Reformation was but an effort of Nature . . . throwing off
> what was false, vicious, or superfluous, and retaining what was
> good. . . . The social body is of itself a thinking, acting, sentient
> being. . . . The great error of modern philosophy is the igno-
> rance or forgetfulness of this fact. The first departure from it
> was not the Reformation—for that was preëminently a social
> idea and a social movement—but the doctrine of the right of
> private judgment, which speculative philosophers and vain
> schismatics attempted to engraft upon it, or deduce from it.[80]

He would perhaps have settled for a High Anglicanism, provided it soared very high indeed in its authoritarianism and
institutional discipline. He well knew, one suspects, that the
Reformation, not merely its most radical assertion, had caused
the trouble. Once divide the Church, the Catholics argued
in the sixteenth century and have with justice argued ever
since, and you will never prevent its further division. The
only way out for a society requiring the strict subordination
of one class to another and the promulgation of cheerful
obedience to those of superior intelligence and virtue lay in
the establishment of a religion based on precisely those qualities. In the end, only Catholicism would do; but it was not to
be had in a South that was heir to the religious traditions of
Protestant England.

CHAPTER FOUR

The Defense
of Slavery

If we want things to stay as they are, things will have to change.

GIUSEPPE DI LAMPEDUSA,
The Leopard

Among the subjects considered most important for the development of a slaveholders' philosophy, Fitzhugh placed none higher than marriage and "the sanctity and purity of the family circle." The origin of government, he began, citing the authority of historians and philosophers, lies in the family, which has always been and will always be its simplest and most common form. Perhaps the simplest extension of this viewpoint, which was common to slaveholding intellectuals, came from C. G. Memminger in a lecture delivered in Augusta, Georgia, in 1851: "The Slave Institution at the South increases the tendency to dignify the family. Each planter in fact is a Patriarch—his position compels him to be a ruler in his household. . . . The fifth commandment becomes the foundation of Society."[1]

Fitzhugh began his argument:

Two-thirds of mankind, the women and children, are everywhere the subjects of family government. In all countries where slavery exists, the slaves also are the subjects of this kind of government. Now slaves, wives and children have no other government; they do not come directly in contact with the institutions and rulers of the State. But the family gov-

ernment, from its nature, has ever been despotic. The relations between the parent or master and his family subjects
are too various, minute, and delicate, to be arranged, defined,
and enforced by law. God has in his mercy and wisdom provided a better check, to temper and direct the power of the
master of the family, than any human government has
devised.[2]

References to the slave force as "the black family" abound
in Southern literature, and more impressively, in the private
letters and diaries of slaveholders. Not accidentally, and by
no means as a petty propaganda device, acts of the Confederate Congress referred to the obligations of citizens to their
black and white families. Not infrequently, planters recorded
births and deaths of slaves in their family Bibles. Undoubtedly, the closest approximation to family bonds were established between whites and house servants, but most planters
appear to have made some attempt to get to know their
ordinary field hands, even on the great sugar estates of Louisiana, which were reputedly under parvenu leadership and
impersonal regimes.[3] Fitzhugh linked slavery and the family
in two ways: by suggesting that the majority even in free
society was subject to a despotic power—that is, that it consisted of slaves in all except name—and by showing that
despotic power, when conditioned by ties of affection and a
sense of responsibility, need not be feared. His argument
actually extended much further, at least by implication.

His argument had some strength but greater weakness.
Since women were generally acknowledged to be in some
sense inferior to men, they were analogous to Negroes: sub-
jection to despotic authority was in their interest. Unhappily,
the analogy defended only Negro slavery, which Fitzhugh
admitted was a peripheral issue. His propaganda triumph
revealed his theoretical defeat. Children, like ordinary white
men, if not like women and Negroes, were inferior only
temporarily and could be expected to grow up into responsibility and freedom. At best, Fitzhugh might have argued, as
he here and there hinted, that enslaved whites who demon-

strated their capacity for freedom should be welcomed into the community of free men. The problem obviously was threatening to get out of hand and to lead him down paths he evidenced no desire to tread.

He had, notwithstanding major difficulties with his own position, made his point that the family is a vital institution and must not be undermined by the quest for money; that it must continue to rest on the despotic power of the father, with no nonsense about individual rights; and that its internal justice must be left to the softening effects of women on men and to the natural bond of affection between the master and those in his charge. The weakness of the slaves, like that of women, produces strength. The tendencies toward cruelty and hardheartedness in the master generally yield to the impulse to protect those who, out of weakness, turn to him for comfort and kindness.[4]

The Invisible Hand of Adam Smith's marketplace imperiled the Invisible Hand of Fitzhugh's family. "Within the family," Fitzhugh maintained, "there is little room, opportunity, or temptation to selfishness—and slavery leaves but little of the world without the family."[5] The advance of capitalism, with its cant about liberty and individual rights and its economic pressures against the unity of the household, promised to destroy the institution on which all government and, in fact, all civilization rest. Fitzhugh expressed a widespread Southern fear. Simms, for example, charged that Northern aggression against the South had to be understood, above all, as an attack on the family.

Fitzhugh, in one of his many passages praising the Catholic Church, spoke of its having done much "to preserve the sanctity and purity of the family circle, by making marriage a religious sacrament; the Episcopal Church something in making it a holy ordinance; and in its ritual, which reminded the parties of the solemn and sacred engagements into which they were about to enter." Regrettably, the advance of bourgeois democratic ideas, especially those associated with the French Revolution, had reduced marriage in the North to "a mere civil contract, entered into with no more thought, ceremony or solemnity than the bargain for a horse."[6]

"Marriage," he reiterated, "is too much like slavery not to be involved in its fate. . . . Slavery, marriage, religion, are the pillars of the social fabric [and are in] intimate connexion and dependence. . . ."[7] His blows against liberal bourgeois morality and bourgeois society in general resounded and resound still, but they defended slavery only by deflecting attention elsewhere. The revolt against marriage has, as Fitzhugh expected, turned outward because those celebrated bonds of affection arising from master-slave relationships have never guaranteed justice, harmony, and the well-being and growth of the participants. Such bonds have proved no more reliable than those of the "passional attraction" among all men, which Fitzhugh ridiculed as socialistic humbug.

Fitzhugh forgot, or could not face, the two-sidedness of family life. As George Santayana has observed, on the one hand:

> The family is one of the nature's masterpieces. It would be hard to conceive a system of instincts more nicely adjusted, where the constituents should represent or support one another better. The husband has an interest in protecting the wife, she in serving the husband. . . . So the natural relations subsisting between parents and children become moral when it is not merely derivation that unites them, but community of purpose. The father then represents his children while they are under his tutelage, and afterward they represent him, carrying on his arts and inheriting his mind.[8]

On the other hand:

> Seldom is the private and ideal life of a young son or daughter a matter in which the mother shows particular tact or for which she has instinctive respect. Even rarer is any genuine community in life and feeling between parents and their adult children. Often the parents' influence comes to be felt as a dead constraint, the more cruel that it cannot be thrown off without unkindness; and what makes the parents'

claim at once unjust and pathetic is that it is founded on passionate love for a remembered being, the child wholly theirs, that no longer exists in the man.[9]

Santayana concluded that parental influence, to be rendered permanent, must be bolstered by political and social authority. The ultimate dictatorship of the father arises out of the dependence of the family on an external system of power.

Fitzhugh, Simms, and many other Southerners feared that bourgeois society would destroy the family; they understood that the bourgeois state could recognize only individuals and that, therefore, the authority of the father in the household could not be its concern. The trouble with their proslavery alternative did not lie in the exigencies of lordship, for it covered adequately the master-as-father and the slave-as-child. The master-slave relationship, viewed as a family matter, did not require special kindness or leniency; it required only a strong sense of duty and responsibility. Stampp misses the point when he writes: "One of the inherent tragedies of slavery was that a human master's impulse to be kind to his slaves was severely circumscribed by the inescapable problem of control. He could indulge only the most obsequious of them, and only within the bounds of essential discipline."[10] Paternalism and a patriarchal ethos did not demand kindness, although they may have encouraged it; much less did they demand indulgence. A strong patriarch is not less so for being severe, so long as he accepts responsibility for the welfare of his children, as he and his society define such responsibility. It is on this level that the slaveholder's morality parted company with that of the capitalist who employed wage labor. Ironically, then, the trouble with the proslavery argument lay in its inability to cover the free white family. As Santayana observes, "There is no real instinct to protect those who can already protect themselves; nor have they any profit in obeying nor, in the end, any duty to do so."[11] Fitzhugh's proposal to place a master on the plantation to check the tyranny of husbands and fathers offered only a partial solution, for, at best, it could protect only the wives and children of the slaves. Even if the arrangement fulfilled his expectations, it left untouched the problems besetting the families of the free. The conflict of interests rending the family of adults merely suggested that rending society as a whole. Fitzhugh's identification of the interest of master with that of slave is even more arbitrary and dubious than his identification of the interest of husband with that of wife, or that of parents with those of children.

Southerners generally referred to their slaves as their "people" or their "black family," and within limits they meant it. We need not deny the reality of the sense of responsibility that expressed itself in this way. That reality, however, cannot be taken literally; it was merely a distant approach to genuine family relationships. Let us call, as our witness, Thomas Ruffin, North Carolina's most distinguished Supreme Court Justice. In *State v. Mann* (1829) Ruffin, speaking for the Court, refuted the argument that a master could be charged with committing battery upon a slave in the same way that a parent could be held responsible for the excessive physical punishment of a child. Ruffin, with all the logical force for which he was noted, denied any likeness between the two cases and insisted that they were in opposition to each other. A parent has a duty to train a child to usefulness with a view toward helping him attain the status of a free man. The end of slavery "is the profit of the master"; the task of the slave is "to toil that another may reap the fruits." Such services, he added, can be expected only "from one who has no will of his own; who surrenders his will in implicit obedience to that of another." The power of the master over the slave's body must be absolute. As a moral proposition, he admitted it to be repugnant, but slavery was a fact of life, and there could be no slavery without that power. Fortunately, this harsh doctrine yielded to considerable liberalization, not only in practice but in succeeding decisions of the same court. Those liberalizations, such as

Ruffin's own modifications as expressed in his decision in *State v. Hoover* (1839), which denied a master the right to kill a slave willfully, spoke well for the humanity of slaveholding North Carolina but less well for its adherence to theoretical consistency.[12]

Fitzhugh might have asked: Very well, the family is not perfect internally or ideal as the fundamental social unit; now, what do you propose to put in its place? In his own way he did ask it, confident that the liberals could answer only with such phrases about mutual love and respect as had to prove empty in the competitive world of the cash nexus. Yet, no defender of slavery could easily reply to the terrible taunt of the abolitionist: Your sweet bonds of affection for your virtuous wives, your chivalrous respect for your women, your idyllic family life are inseparable from your power over Negro women; your marriage and your family rest on black brothels.

No doubt they did, no matter how many decent, faithful men graced the planter class, for the abolitionist taunt contained just enough truth to remain unanswerable. Fitzhugh had charged that capitalism reduced women to mere property; his adversaries, in effect, answered that slavery, like feudalism, reduced them to objects of violence. The abolitionist counter-charge did not make the slaveholders' charge less valid, especially since, as Fitzhugh suspected, the "mere property," for all its superficial emancipation, would in time prove lost and, to use his own word, desexed.

The main lamentation, however, was not for the loss of conjugal family—a lamentation that became standard fare in the North—but for the destruction of the extended family outside the sphere of plantation society. In this respect Fitzhugh stood on solid ground, as a glance at Brazil will show. Caio Prado Júnior, in an apparent critique of Gilberto Freyre, insists that slavery, far from promoting the family, undermined it:

> Contrary to what is now usually affirmed, the formation of Brazil was not based on the family unit, save in the limited

and . . . sadly deficient case of the upper class Big House. The mass of the people were not bound by family ties; the newly arrived immigrants and the slaves, as was only to be expected, formed only loose attachments.[13]

Prado scores heavily; yet, the slave regime of the patriarchal Northeast of Brazil has had and has a deserved reputation for being family-based and family-oriented. The sense of family, however, derives principally from the patriarchalism of fundamental socioeconomic relationships, not from any special quality of the nuclear family. So, in the Old South Mrs. Chesnut and the abolitionists made their point, and the Fitzhughs look like hypocrites. But their "hypocrisy" was only a consequence of their retaining too much of the inherited bourgeois ethos; they were hypocrites only to the extent that they proclaimed themselves guardians of an essentially bourgeois notion of family. Their real case lay elsewhere: in the defense of a notion of community within which the traditional family could take on new vigor and bind all individuals and classes together.

I I

Perhaps the most jarring note in Fitzhugh's writings is his polemic against "exclusive agriculture": how strange a note from the ideologist of the planter aristocracy! His views on agriculture and manufacturing and his praise of urban life seem to have set him apart from his class,[14] but in fact they placed him in its ideological vanguard. "We are very sure," he began, "that the wit of man can devise no means so effectual to impoverish a country as exclusive agriculture."[15] Fitzhugh attributed the South's dependence on agriculture and its consequent impoverishment to free trade. Among the concomitant evils he listed a sparse and ignorant population, the ruin of Southern cities, and a crippling emigration.[16] His plea for cities and industry rested on simple and profound notions: "Towns and villages are breaks that arrest and pre-

vent the exhausting drain of agriculture. . . . They consume
the crops of the neighborhood. . . . They afford respectable
occupations . . . for the energetic young men of the neighborhood."[17] He struck hard at commercial expansion without
parallel urban-industrial expansion, pointing out that increased trade without industrial diversification could only
lead to further dependence on foreign markets, increased
exploitation, and the outward flow of capital and population.
He here foreshadowed those twentieth-century students of
economic development who have warned underdeveloped
countries against what Gunnar Myrdal has called "the back-
wash effects of trade." Specifically, Fitzhugh warned that
the prosperous towns and villages of Virginia's back country
would be ruined by improvements in transportation, unless
structural changes occurred in the economy. Their prosperity
rested on local industry, which would be crushed by the influx
of goods from the ports of the tidewater; their prosperity
rested on their isolation.[18]

Fitzhugh pressed his strange notion, with its apparent anti-
Southernism, hard. Virginia needed manufacturing in order
to cut itself off from the parasitic tentacles of the world
market. From autarky would flow the world he wanted:

> A small nationality and dense population, not cursed by free
> trade, necessarily produces an intense civilization, provided
> the nation be of a race that needs and loves civilization. . . .
> But separate nationality is a mere form, not a reality, when
> free trade furnishes what the nation should produce at
> home.[19]

He denounced large cities like New York and London, but
called for the rise of numerous small cities and towns to complement a rich countryside and to keep the wealth generated
by the social division of labor at home. "Each Southern
State may condense within its boundaries all the elements
of separate, independent nationality. Civilization is imper-
fect and incomplete until this state of things arises. Each

State must . . . have within itself . . . every institution and pursuit that pertain to high civilization."[20]

The South, he concluded, must diversify her economy, increase her population, raise cities and towns, promote industry, and decentralize her economic and political life. Yet, he denied any desire to transform the South into an industrial society. In the long run it would be unnecessary and undesirable. In the short run—that is, while the world market remained intact—it would destroy the agricultural surpluses that provided the South's main economic weapon in the competitive marketplace.[21] Fitzhugh saw clearly that if slavery were to survive, it would have to straddle both town and country and make its peace with the technological level of the modern world, and that if the slaveholders wanted things to remain as they were, things would have to change.

Fitzhugh's bold insight here as elsewhere betrayed him and brought him face to face with the agonizing dilemma of Southern slaveholding society. Historically, slave societies had been rooted in the countryside, with towns and cities designed as commercial, intellectual, social, and political meeting places for the ruling class. Even in the decadent phase of Roman history, with its wretched urban *Lumpenproletariat*, political power and social status rested on the latifundia. The "agrarianism" of the Southern planters made sense: slave labor was at its best on the countryside; urban, industrial slaves had to be granted so many privileges as incentives that they were already half free; and the planters had every reason to fear industrialization and urbanization, with its concomitant growth of a subversive bourgeoisie. Yet Fitzhugh understood the arguments of J. H. Hammond, William Gregg, Daniel Pratt, and the other proponents of Southern manufactures, for he realized that without a general industrial advance the political power of the planters would sooner or later be broken by the Northern bourgeoisie.

Turning to the countryside itself, Fitzhugh strove for an aristocracy protected by the restoration of primogeniture and

entail. Property would thus remain within a single family for
generations. The social effect of the ensuing stability would
be to release the younger sons of the aristocracy, in the traditional English manner, to staff the professions, the Church,
and the military. Society would then be guaranteed an Establishment ruled by men tied to the planters. Even a merchant
class—for the total elimination of such a class was unthink-
able—might be so recruited and thereby might acquire a new
dignity.

He saw the dangers. Too great a concentration of wealth
might result. Large estates with uncultivated lands, idle
Negroes, and absentee owners would ruin everything. Unchecked, such concentration would produce a sparse population and a colonial-style plantation decadence. His answer
was to combine the restoration of primogeniture and entail
with effective measures to limit the size of estates and to
guarantee a numerous class of landowners of roughly equal
strength.[22] Small properties in the South, he wrote more as
wish than as description, descend from generation to generation in the same family, and fortunes arise from virtuous
industry rather than from speculation and the tricks of the
marketplace.[23] Southern economy was becoming—he used the
progressive tense—the best form of slavery in history by guaranteeing limits to accumulation and thereby making possible
close relations between master and slave.[24] Following this line
of reasoning, he was able to overcome his contempt for
"agrarianism" long enough to discuss the Agrarian Law of
ancient Rome with sympathy and to note that "attempts
made to revive it seem to have constituted the only crime of
the seditious Gracchi."[25]

Repeating that all government rested on force, he added
that "the governing class should be numerous enough to understand, and so situated as to represent fairly, all interests."[26]
Primogeniture and entail would make possible a society in
which all free men could vote and participate in government
as one great conservative interest. The landless would be

bound to the landed by family ties and general interests. Republican principles could then obtain without threatening the fabric of society.[27]

Fitzhugh here as before tends toward the advocacy of autarky. To reverse the trend toward concentration of land-holding and slaveholding and to guarantee a static system of moderate-sized estates would have required the elimination of the competitive struggle within the slave South itself. That elimination could only follow the drastic reduction of the South's dependence on its export sector and, ultimately, the destruction of the world market.

His solution to the problems of "exclusive agriculture" and the excessive concentration of wealth seems brilliantly to meet all reasonable objections: a limited industrialization based on a small-scale urbanization, tied firmly to a broadly based plantation regime on the countryside by the localization of economic life. All that was needed to transform the theory into practice was the reshaping of the mind of the master class, which was always possible and to which Fitzhugh bent every effort, and the total destruction of the world market—a destruction without which nothing was possible but which itself was a will-o'-the-wisp. The hardheaded Fitzhugh, the realist who smiled condescendingly at the idealistic and impractical schemes of the Utopian Socialists, had to stake all on the wildest of dreams. So much for the socioeconomic side of Fitzhugh's future world. A look at the political side will give us the rest of what we need to see how his vision represented in essence a projection, not a rejection, of the plantation ideology.

Too much government, he repeated endlessly, can never threaten the people, unless it is excessively centralized. The centralization of authority, not the authority itself, should be feared and shunned. "The centralizing effects of free trade alone would be sufficient to condemn it. The decline of civilization under the Roman Empire was owing solely to centralization." Thus did Fitzhugh open his political argument with the bourgeoisie. "Social centralization," he continued, "arises from the *laissez-faire* system just as national centralization."[28] He explained that a small minority possessed of talent and capital could, and invariably would, control the labor market, exploit labor, and crush the independent middle-class proprietors.

Fitzhugh, throughout his writings, stressed the need for more government. Decentralization of political power would guarantee against the evils normally accompanying an expansion of government responsibility.[29] Simultaneously, decentralization would produce a healthy national life. Here as almost everywhere, when Fitzhugh wrote of nationality he meant local attachment. "Narrow and confined territorial limits," he insisted, represent the "only secret of high civilization."[30] In this manner he placed the states'-rights doctrine on the highest ground available and, implicitly, demonstrated his contempt for the constitutional gyrations of the Calhoun school. Fitzhugh, as always, concerned himself primarily with questions of class hegemony and political power and saw clearly that if such questions were to be resolved satisfactorily on a slaveholding basis, they would have to be resolved in the community.

Note the careful phrasing of his dedication of *Cannibals All!* to Henry A. Wise:

> I dedicate this work to you, because I am acquainted with no one who has so zealously, laboriously, and successfully endeavored to Virginianise Virginia, by encouraging, through State legislation, her intellectual and physical growth and development; no one who has seen so clearly the evils of centralization from without, and worked so earnestly to cure or avert those evils, by building up centralization within.

Much of Fitzhugh's social thought and much of the slaveholders' philosophy, in logical extension, may be found in that dedication: political decentralization with the vigorous exercise of power and no nonsense about the best government governing least.

The demand for state nationality (the Virginianizing of Virginia) might seem arbitrary. Why not Fauquierize Fauquier County? The answer is simply that Fitzhugh, as a practical man, understood the political limits of decentralization and the need to protect the smaller community through combination. The extent of the combination and the optimum size of the "nation" he left to the judgment and good sense of the ruling strata to determine locally. He carried his glorification of the community to its logical extreme and assailed all cosmopolitan tendencies. He appealed for local dress, local opinions, local manners, and local speech. "Mr. Calhoun . . . talked South Carolina dialect in the Senate. But for all that, it was the best English of the day. Its smack of provincialism gave it a higher flavor."[31] (Fitzhugh even claimed to prefer local wines to the French, but neither courtesy nor charity compels us to believe him.) The federal union, he concluded, has neither territory, nor subjects, nor the force to impose its will. Its future—if, as he hoped, it had one—lay in its being considered a league of separate "States or Nations."[32]

One last problem remained: what to do with the Southern nonslaveholders. To call for their enslavement would have marked him mad and perhaps even earned him a lynching. Yet to be consistent he would have had to urge precisely that. His solution had the usual elements of opportunism and evasion but was essentially a reasonable development of his main ideas. Once again, the first principle was destruction of the world market, without which nothing could be done.

We need no white slaves in the South because we have black ones—thus did he echo countless Southern propagandists. He did not stop there, however. He proposed educating and raising all the white poor for employment as skilled factory workers and as professionals. If there were to be industrial growth, let the slaves be the unskilled laborers, the whites the skilled. Let white labor be privileged and imbued with caste pride; let it benefit from the more lowly labor of the Negro.

The trouble with this happy ending lay in the beginning. White labor, skilled or no, would, on Fitzhugh's showing, be exploited labor. Where would be its security in sickness and old age? His answer was to provide a paternalistic, welfare industrialism: let society guarantee the white workers their rights. This side of Fitzhugh's argument appears to veer toward an equation of *étatisme* and slavery and has led Wish and others to see in him a forerunner of fascism. This interpretation is dubious, but we shall return later to his thinking on the future of European labor and to his relationship to fascism. For the moment, let us note that his proposal for Southern whites was in fact an exceptional one made possible by the presence of black slaves.

In effect, he proposed a mild, disguised slavery for the Southern whites. They would be legally free and civically responsible but would be economically wholly dependent on the slaveholders. I say "slavery" here because Fitzhugh would have defined it as such. Obviously, the same solution could not work in Europe, for a genuinely slave base would have to support an equivalent stratum of privileged workers of this type. Hence, Southern exceptionalism.

Fitzhugh did try to relate Negro slavery to the world scene; his effort failed, but the failure is instructive.

The population of Western Europe, sustained and stimulated [by colonial slave labor], was trebled, and that of the North increased tenfold. The products of slave labor became scarce and dear, and famines frequent. Now, it is obvious, that to emancipate all the negroes would be to starve Western Europe and our North. Not to extend and increase negro slavery, *pari passu*, with the extension and multiplication of free society, will produce much suffering. If all South America, Mexico, the West Indies, and our Union south of Mason and Dixon's line, of the Ohio and the Missouri, were slaveholding, slave products would be abundant and cheap in free society. . . . Free white laborers might live in comfort and luxury on light work, but for the exacting and greedy landlords, bosses, and other capitalists.[33]

Fitzhugh almost betrayed his entire theoretical position by this thinly veiled and demagogic appeal to European labor to support Negro slavery, which was, after all, supposed to be merely a peripheral question. First, he advocated "a people's colonialism" similar to the "people's imperialism" that certain socialist writers have seen developing in our own day. Then, he tied this collective exploitation of colonial Negroes to a European labor whose security has been assured. That assurance, in his own terms, could only come about through some kind of stewardship. This pleasing arrangement brought him back to his starting point, for if European labor were under stewardship—that is, modified slavery—its welfare need not depend on colonialism. If it were to remain free, then it would necessarily continue to be exploited, even if less than without colonialism. The only way in which the world could be set right would be through general slavery. That implied autarky. Autarky implied an end to colonialism. The appeal to European labor to support Negro slavery was, therefore, demagogic and contradicted his theoretical scheme. No wonder he let it go and returned to higher ground. No matter how he tried to arrange politically viable compromises, his schema brought him back to the necessity of destroying the world market and replacing it with virtual provincial self-sufficiency, supported by only a modest amount of trade.

Fitzhugh's thinking on these economic and political matters was only superficially at variance with that of his class and section. If he denounced the Southern canon of free trade, it was to warn against all trade; if he demanded cities and industry, it was to break the dependence on outside cities and industry; if he ignored the Constitutional case for states' rights, it was to demonstrate that the only meaningful case for states' rights arose from the exigencies of community solidarity; if he ridiculed those Jeffersonian notions of weak government which were still so strong in the official political ideology of the South, it was to arouse the slaveholders to take strong measures to protect their interests. His ideal, then, however curious it might seem, was that of an insulated slave-holding community, self-sufficient, family-based, and glorying in its very provincialism—the ideal of the patriarchal slave plantation recapitulated in the large.

III

Fitzhugh holds no claims as a political theorist, although his works do contain some penetrating observations here and there on political power. During the War for Southern Independence he wrote about Locke's contemporary adversary Filmer, whom both Dew and Calhoun had denounced, and used him to support his long-standing anti-Lockeian position. Accordingly, he proclaimed a new saint for the Pantheon of the Chivalry. Fitzhugh's view, however, had long been in print and represented merely a simple defense of class rule; political theory as such had apparently bored him. If Fitzhugh wanted to bring down the world of capitalism and establish provincial autarky, he clearly needed only one principle of government: the ruling class must be able to rule and must therefore have clear responsibilities to those ruled. The specifics he could leave to the collective judgment of the rulers of each locality; the intellectualization of the specifics he could leave to professors and theologians.

Government is force, and the only question is who rules whom: therein lies all that is essential to Fitzhugh's political outlook. "The very term, government, implies that it is carried on against the consent of the governed." He then added a sentence that General de Gaulle has given us new reason to appreciate: "The governments of Europe could not exist a week without the positive force of standing armies."[34] Fitzhugh was echoing a theme increasingly heard in Southern political and intellectual circles. Hammond had proclaimed in the 1840s that no country on earth would stand a month "but for its standing armies, maintained at an enormous and destructive cost to those whom they were destined to overawe."[35] Simms used the same argument to particularly good effect when, in 1837, he replied to the abolitionist taunt that Southerners lived in fear of slave revolts: "Suppose we grant it, and in what then does our condition as a community and our relation with our slaves differ from that of any European people? Why are there standing armies in all the states of Europe?"[36] Fitzhugh, replying to those liberal theorists who looked to government to protect liberty, insisted, "Liberty is an evil which government is intended to correct."[37] Since liberty and the competitive marketplace were deemed inseparable, the absence or weakness of government merely guaranteed the strong absolute power over the weak, whereas proper government, defined as the collective force of the strong, protected the weak against individual lapses from a sense of duty by those in whose charge they are placed. Government suppressed class war by controlling the lower classes while forcing the upper classes to meet their responsibilities as guardians.

The Declaration of Independence and the Virginia Bill of Rights naturally came under fire. "Men are not created or born equal, and circumstances, and education, and association, tend to increase and aggravate inequalities among them, from generation to generation."[38] Fitzhugh could make this observation because he assumed, with the liberals, that private property must prevail and with it those who do and do not own it—that is, social classes. He supposed that Jefferson meant, by the Declaration of Independence, to give all men an equal title to property. "Carry out such a doctrine, and it would subvert every government on earth."[39]

The weak-minded or weak-bodied who make up the inferior masses deserve to be cared for, and no wise, just, humane ruling class would ignore so well founded a claim. The masses too have their rights: "They have a natural right to guardians, committees, teachers or masters. Nature has made them slaves; all that law and government can do, is to regulate, modify and mitigate their slavery."[40] Property is a trust. If private property fails to meet its responsibilities, it ought to be abolished.[41] Government, the force that maintains private property, ought also to compel those who own it to use it properly. In other words, the collective conscience of the ruling class must prevail over the individual interests constituting that class.

With this general stance, Fitzhugh dismissed the rise of parliamentarianism in England and the Glorious Revolution as respectively the dawn and high noon of the conquest of society by the money power. As for the American Revolution, he had no trouble defending it from the slaveholders' point of view. He had already taken a stand against centralization. The Revolution had established home rule; it was merely a necessary and grand reform.

> Our revolution, so wise in its conception and so glorious in its execution, was the mere assertion by adults of the rights of adults, and had nothing more to do with philosophy than the weaning of a calf. It was the act of a people seeking national independence, not the Utopian scheme of speculative philosophers, seeking to establish human equality and social perfection.[42]

He may have missed much of its impact for the country as a whole, but for the South he grasped the essential point. Whatever else it did, the separation from England had freed the strongest local elements to make their own world in their own image.

Fitzhugh's attitude toward war in general and a war for secession in particular must be evaluated in the context of his view of political power, for despite some extravagant statements he fully understood that war, as well as lesser degrees of force, ought never to be considered apart from the policies they are designed to implement. He did not glorify war in the abstract, as Wish and others have charged; his reluctance to join the secessionists ought to put us on our guard against such quick judgments.[43]

When war broke out, Fitzhugh denounced pacifism and

found the most wonderful virtues in militarism and war. Wish entitles his chapter on this period "War Elevates the Sentiments," the expression being Fitzhugh's. Fitzhugh was primarily a theorist, only secondarily and of minor importance a propagandist. He told the truth too directly to be a good propagandist for any cause. During the War for Southern Independence, like many Southern and Northern intellectuals, he became a propagandist first and a theorist only incidentally. He wrote a great deal—too much—and much of it drivel. He had a simple job to do, that of stiffening morale at home, and he did it as best he could. "War elevates the sentiments . . ." Certainly. "Frequent wars of invasion are necessary to keep nations progressive."[44] Of course. What else should he have told the citizens of a Virginia that was preparing for war?

Wish observes that Emerson said some similar things under similar conditions; he ought not to stop there. Let the reader consult the writings of our finest liberal intellectuals, those glorious champions of peace, prosperity, and the moral equivalents of war, to see what they had to say in 1917. The truth is that Fitzhugh and those liberal intellectuals were guilty, but not quite as charged. Having spent their lives defending social systems that have never been able to exist without periodic bloodletting, they could do no other than defend this or that manifestation of it. We nonetheless have a responsibility to separate militarists and warmongers from those who try their best to defend their social system without making a general virtue of every military necessity. Fitzhugh showed no interest in building a permanent war machine into his world. He and most slaveholders respected the stance, discipline, and chain of command of the military life. They had their own moral equivalent of war—slavery itself, spiced with an army large enough to maintain internal order and provide an honorable diversion for the younger men of the ruling class. Beyond that, it was not war they sought but what war might bring. In this respect, how much worse were they than their enemies?

As a matter of fact, Fitzhugh bent all his efforts toward avoiding secession precisely because it would mean war and threaten social institutions. He always displayed an awareness that war could trigger social upheaval. If the South were to separate itself from Christendom, he argued, it would in effect challenge the world to a test of strength which it did not need and for which it was unprepared.[45] "A world at war with her institutions," Fitzhugh concluded with deliberate understatement, "might not respect her rights."[46]

Earlier, in *Sociology for the South* (1854), he took a hopeful if worried view of the sectional clash, and not until *Cannibals All!* (1857) did he begin to resign himself to a secession he knew would mean war. The abolitionists, he wrote with apparent regret, will probably succeed in bringing about a "civil and fratricidal war."[47] He feared both secession and war, for Virginia, as a border state, could not happily look forward to separation; it properly intended "to cling" to the Union so long as honor would permit. Yet seeing the dangers and probabilities, he wisely refused to attack the fire-eaters. He indicated his disagreements with them but added that he "would not shoot down the sentinels of our camp. If not the wisest, most far-seeing, and most prudent, they are the most zealous friends of the South."[48]

He moved toward secession reluctantly, would have preferred it to have been peaceful, and showed no special fondness for military adventures abroad. The war he sought was primarily ideological, although, like Lincoln and a few others, he was always ready to look to his arms when argument was exhausted.

> 'Tis not possible that our two forms of society can long co-exist. All Christendom is one republic, has one religion, belongs to one race, and is governed by one public opinion. Social systems, formed on opposite principles cannot co-endure.[49]

When a Seward, a Lincoln, or a John F. Kennedy utters such sentiments, we are called upon to applaud his moral courage and profound grasp of reality; when a Fitzhugh, a Goldwater, or a Mao Tse-tung says the same thing, we are expected to deplore his extremism, inhumanity, and lack of moral sensibility. Fitzhugh, like many who hold the same view today on both sides of the Cold War, preferred the struggle to take place on the level of ideological argument and the material performance of the rival social systems. The South, he said hopefully, "is ready for philosophical argument and discussion, and for historical and statistical comparison."[50] If he knew in his heart that it would end in war, that the system sinking into defeat would stake all on a *coup de main* of some kind, so do we all know as much. Who believes for a moment that anything but the threat of nuclear annihilation has prevented the re-enactment on a world scale of a very old story?

Like most reactionaries, Fitzhugh, while deprecating the mental and moral capacity of the masses, overestimated their ability to perceive their own exploitation. Any good liberal could have lectured him, or could lecture us now, on the importance of ideology and the possibilities for maintaining class rule by avoiding instead of promoting rigid stratification, and thereby creating a class society capable of denying that it has classes at all. The only point they really score—and Hartz scores it well—is that he underestimated American capitalism's staying power. For Fitzhugh the propagandist, the fault was grievous; for Fitzhugh the theorist, it was minor. The questions, especially the moral questions, that he raised about bourgeois society recur. What, even now, do you propose to do about the

Lonely men in shirt-sleeves, leaning out of windows . . .[51]

besides put them in front of television sets?

Half of Europe and Asia in our time have given a rude answer, and the other half may yet. Fitzhugh's miscalculation on the staying power of American capitalism, which as we shall see was only a partial miscalculation, was in itself a minor slip, but it was related to another, more fundamental one. He overestimated the ability of slavery to survive long enough to pick up the pieces. Fitzhugh's work provides a wonderful, if inverted, example of one of the slogans that the revolutionary students painted on the walls of Paris during the anti-Gaullist crisis of 1968: "*Soyez réalistes, demandez l'impossible!*" It was the only realism open to him; any other course would have led to the "realism" of capitulation. On his desperate estimate of slavery's prospects for survival hung the life or death of his world, and it is therefore less than charitable to chide him now for having dared to work for its realization.

I V

Fitzhugh's appraisal of the future of free—that is, bourgeois —society appropriately began with an assertion of its historical tendency to impoverish wage labor. Not even Marx, in his controversial and generally misunderstood theory of impoverishment, took so gloomy a view. The peasants of feudal England, according to Fitzhugh, were brave, virtuous, and secure. Capitalism, by freeing them from the land, transformed them into dissolute vagabonds. The halcyon days of this vagabond liberty soon passed into the stern era of industrial discipline. "A bloody code, a standing army and efficient police keep them quiet enough now."[52] Long hours of debilitating work under the most inhumane conditions, slum living quarters, a future without hope, and the whip of economic law, supported by naked force, have restored order and simultaneously broken the body and much of the spirit of the masses. Hunger, fear, and desperation have bred new disorder or at least the constant threat of it, and the bourgeoisie trembles with foreboding. Socialism, which is merely a new and pretty name for various forms of slavery, has made its appearance, and both workers and capitalists, although for opposite reasons, rush to embrace it. Thus, Louis Napoleon, a "socialist," comes to power in France and taxes the rich to feed the poor. He is trying to institute a "great economy." Thus, the

High Tories in England understand the disease and struggle to cure it with large doses of social welfare. "Towards slavery the North and all Western Europe are unconsciously marching."[53]

At first glance, Fitzhugh was never sillier than in his appraisal of Louis Napoleon, never less convincing, never more self-contradictory. In what way, after all, did Napoleon's—or the Tories'—alleged welfare programs do away with those fundamental evils of capitalism against which Fitzhugh had so uncompromisingly argued? Did they destroy the competitive marketplace? Did they overthrow bourgeois morality? Did they promise to restore small nationalities, do away with cosmopolitanism, or establish the rural-urban balance he so eloquently expounded? None of these. In the most charitable reading, they proposed, as Disraeli was to make clear, to throw enough sops to the discontented workers at home to support a national effort to extend abroad the same system of exploitation on a scale greater than anything previously dreamed of. Was this, then, what all of Fitzhugh's polemics came to—the proposal that the bourgeoisie should learn from the slaveholders and give their own workers old-age insurance so that millions of foreign workers could be murdered, starved, and plundered? Such a reading cannot be tolerated except on the assumption that he was a cynical scoundrel without a shred of principle and that the class for which he spoke had no object but to guarantee itself a place at the table in the developing world-wide imperialist barbecue. Such a reading is possible but arbitrary and, I think, essentially false.

There were at least three reasons for Fitzhugh's puzzling presentation. First and least, he was lazy (or rather, was a product of a regional atmosphere that discouraged intellectual rigor) and had hardly studied European developments with sufficient care to make a considered judgment on such questions as the nature of Napoleon's regime. Second, his predisposition to see capitalism as a system in a state of collapse betrayed him into misreading events, especially since upon the reality of his wishes hung the fate of his own society. Third, he chose to see the developments in Europe as a series of half steps or false steps that would either lead direct to a new seigneurialism or by their failure force society to try again on a sounder basis. All civilized governments, he noted, were abandoning *laissez faire* for some program to protect the poor. This trend represented the beginnings of a march back to slavery, for "it is domestic slavery alone that can establish a safe, efficient and humane community of property."[54] The extreme proslavery men of the South did not yet see where the world was heading and therefore thought that abolitionist sentiment was increasing. On the contrary, the rise of the Republican Party, he believed, reflected not an increase in abolitionism but a misguided sectional fear of growing Southern power. The North felt itself becoming isolated because Southern proslavery thought was making great strides toward the conquest of Western Europe. The South "leads public opinion everywhere because she is in advance of that new counter-current of opinion that has set in everywhere about slavery." Nature wins out in the long run, and nature was on the side of the South.[55]

Had he considered the issue more closely, he might have seen that a successful welfare state, especially in an imperialist setting, would extend the life of the bourgeoisie and of its world view. Instead, he naively interpreted England's development of the coolie trade as the first step toward the reinstitution of slavery in the islands. Colonialism, he thought, would force a return first to *de facto* and then to *de jure* slavery. If the South could remain in the Union, it would in time get the upper hand as the North became increasingly isolated from world opinion.[56] The same process that he welcomed as marking the crisis of the system could, if not properly controlled, ruin all his hopes. Well might he have said with William Morris:

> Ill would be the Change at Whiles,
> Were it not for the Change beyond the change.

To understand fully the nature of these hopes we must turn to his appraisal of Northern society, which presented the slaveholders, as well as capitalism's enemies on the left, with their greatest challenge.

Fitzhugh began:

> But the restraints of Law and Public Opinion are less at the North than in Europe. The Isms on each side of the Atlantic are equally busy with "assiduous wedges," in "loosening in every joint the whole fabric of social existence" [Carlyle]; but whilst they dare invoke Anarchy in Europe, they dare not inaugurate New York Free Love and Oneida Incest, and Mormon Polygamy. The moral, religious, and social heresies of the North are more monstrous than those of Europe. The pupil has surpassed the master, unaided by the stimulants of poverty, hunger, and nakedness which urge the master forward.
>
> Society need not fail in the Northeast until the whole West is settled, and a refluent population, or excess of immigration, overstocks permanently the labor market on the Atlantic board. Till then, the despotism of skill and capital, in forcing emigration to the West, makes proprietors of those emigrants, benefits them, peoples the West, and by their return trade, enriches the East.[57]

The passage contains two ideas, both of which are necessary to the general point of view. First, the socioeconomic crisis of Northern capitalism was not yet; for the moment, and perhaps for a long time, American capitalism had room to grow and prosper. Second, American capitalism nonetheless contained in embryo the same elements of failure that were plaguing European capitalism, and therefore it was generating a moral crisis, expressed in a plethora of radical isms, which threatened the South with abolition and the North with class war. The origin of this paradox lay in the lack of traditions and authoritative institutions in Northern society. "The competitive system . . . is carried out with less exception or restriction in America than in Europe. . . . And this begets more

Socialists in the higher classes, and more mobs, riots, and trade-unions, with the laborers than in Europe."[58] Fitzhugh began, at this point, to edge toward a call for a slaveholder-bourgeois alliance. So long as the class war could be held in check by the presence of virgin land, he could not delude himself into expecting the momentary collapse of his chief enemy. In this sense, contrary to what recent critics aver, he did not underestimate the staying power of American capitalism. While Northern society, without crumbling in crisis, continued to generate frustration and radicalism, these were certain to be turned against outside enemies, especially against the slaveholders. If Fitzhugh could convince the bourgeoisie that the abolitionists and socialists posed a single threat to class society in general, he could have his defensive alliance and all would be well. Yet, by proposing to defend Northern capitalism against imaginary enemies, did not Fitzhugh cynically repudiate his whole moral attack on bourgeois society and its ethics? I think not, for his proposal was in fact a strategic retreat aimed at isolating and disarming the Northern bourgeoisie. To demonstrate this contention we need first to consider his polemical identification of socialism and abolition and then his proposal for a conservative alliance.

George Frederick Holmes, who admired and praised Fitzhugh's work, reacted with noticeable irritation to his treatment of socialism. Why on earth should a conservative man of property, a defender of authority and order, have to go out of his way to express sympathy with so subversive and obnoxious a doctrine? It may have seemed to Holmes a frivolous and dangerous course, but Fitzhugh persisted firmly and was not alone in doing so. Notwithstanding Holmes's qualms, Grayson, Edmund Ruffin, Hammond, and many others pointed to the socialist critique of bourgeois property to bolster their position. Ruffin, for example, agreed with Fitzhugh that only slavery could realize the goals of socialist philanthropy, and Jefferson Davis told the Senate: "And the current suggestion, that slave property exists but by the local law, is no more true of this than it is of all other property. In fact, the European Socialists, who in wild radicalism . . . are the correspondents of the American abolitionists, maintain the same doctrine as to all property, that the abolitionists do as to slave property."[59]

Fitzhugh's applause for the socialists was just, for their critical insights into the origin of capitalist profit provided him with the starting point for his own analysis. Just as Marx drew on Utopian Socialism's critique of capitalism but had no patience with its arbitrary schemes to remake the world by education and example, so Fitzhugh appreciated its exposure of the ills of the marketplace but dismissed its proposed cures.

Socialism proposed to do away with competition, to protect the laboring classes and the poor, and to bring about a community of property and associated labor. "All these purposes, slavery fully and perfectly attains."[60] Every Southern slave had a guarantee of livelihood, protection, and support. If a master could not provide these, he would be forced by circumstances to sell to another who could. "Slaves, too, have a valuable property in their masters."[61] As children, sick, helpless, aged, or infirm, they formed a charge on their master. To speak of his property in such persons would be absurd; in these cases, they had property in him. If only the socialists could realize these truths, they would link their correct critique of the political economy and morality of capitalism to a correct solution: the world-wide affirmation of a system based frankly on man's property in man.

This identification with the critical side of socialism went hand in hand with a harsh attack on its positive programs, which he related to the abolitionist movement. Viewed negatively, socialism reflected the failure of free society and the desperate attempts of honest and humane men to transcend it. The danger, as he saw it, was that the reaction against capitalism was sputtering wildly in all directions and was producing a reform psychology determined to overthrow everything in civilized life—religion, family, government, law, and of course slavery. Slavery first and foremost: first because here was an institution outside the immediate circle of frustrations, seemingly vulnerable, and on the defensive; foremost because hatred for capitalism had bred pseudophilanthropic cant about the rights of man in general and of the laboring man in particular. The socialists, especially the socialist-abolitionists, undermined their own war on capitalism and defeated their own hopes. "Yet those people who confess that their situation is desperate, insist that we shall imitate their institutions, starve our laborers, multiply crime, riots and pauperism, in order, we suppose, to try the experiment of Mormonism Socialism or Communism. Try it first, yourselves!"[62]

Fitzhugh could have followed Holmes's advice and left socialism out of the discussion, but he was wise not to. However much his two-sided evaluation of socialism must have confused readers, it did enable him to restate his main theme in a richer, bolder way. "Every one of them concurs in deprecating free competition, and in the wish and purpose to destroy it. To destroy it is to destroy Liberty, and where liberty is destroyed, slavery is established."[63] He saw in socialism the destruction, rather than the transcendence, of the world market, and he knew that such a development would pave the way for some kind of seigneurial reaction.

> St. Simon would govern his social establishments by savants, more despotic than masters. . . . He would have a despot without the feelings and the interests of a master to temper his authority. . . . All human experience proves that society must be ruled not by mere abstractions, but by men of flesh and blood. To attain large industrial results, it must be vigorously and severely ruled. Socialism is already slavery in all save the master. It had as well adopt that feature at once, as come to that it must to make its schemes at once humane and efficient.[64]

Fitzhugh treated the paper republics of the Utopians with happy disdain. Some socialists, such as Fourier, he thought honest enough to see that they would have to reconstruct human nature in order to succeed. Their promise to build a new world in order to change human nature, when the coming into being of that new world required precisely a changed human nature, he thought to be great sport. In a few generations they would be able to expel human nature and run their system admirably. Wonderful! "Until then, we would advise them to procure good practical overseers from Virginia. . . ."[65] Once they tried the overseers they would be sure to keep them. Fitzhugh came down hard on the side of an unchangeable human nature. Reactionary that he was, it was the rock on which he built.

The same reasoning that made a man an abolitionist made him a socialist and ultimately a nihilist—or so he thought. Everywhere the abolitionist turned he found slavery in some form. He found it in the relationship of wife to husband and so converted to free love; he found it in the relationship of man to church and so converted to free thought; he found it in the relationship of citizen to government and so converted to anarchism. The abolitionists were, to Fitzhugh, all socialists or socialists-without-knowing-it. No wonder Garrison found difficulty in understanding what he was talking about. Garrison could hardly have recognized himself.

Fitzhugh confused three "socialisms," or only dimly perceived their distinctions. First, there was proletarian socialism, which terrified him but which he could dismiss easily since he saw only its feeble beginnings in the work of the Utopians. Second, there was the feudal socialism for which he stood. Third, there was the bourgeois socialism of the Northern crusaders, which in fact was either a perfectly respectable reformism or a harmlessly disreputable bohemianism; in either case it had little to do with socialization of the means of production, whatever the rhetorical pretenses. To some extent his confusion may have been deliberate, for the identification of abolition with socialism must have seemed a marvelous bogy to float in front of the solid property owners of the North. If so, it was a hopeless gambit. Bourgeois reformism, however much shopkeeper "socialism" there may have been in it, proved a staunch ally of Fitzhugh's enemies, and no amount of demagogy could obscure the real nature of the contending forces. Abolition made war on the slave-holders, the main rivals of the bourgeoisie. And they were the main rivals: Fitzhugh never tired of saying so. When Garrison burned a copy of the Constitution of the United States, he was not burning its liberalism or its defense of property, but only its acquiescence in property in man. Fitz-hugh could never have frightened the North with the specter of an allegedly socialist abolitionism, the bourgeois soul of which was so apparent.

And so Fitzhugh, the beneficent, worrying to grief over an impending anarchy destined to bring down society in the North, offered the bourgeoisie free advice and a deal. "We think that by a kind of alliance, offensive and defensive, with the South, Northern Conservatism may now arrest and turn back the tide of Radicalism and Agrarianism."[66] That this Northern Conservatism was none other than the same army of cannibals against whom he had been warring did not seem to trouble him. Both North and South, he continued as in-nocently as ever, face a common enemy in Abolitionism, which is the natural child of Political Economy. "With in-exorable sequence Let Alone is made to usher in No-Govern-ment."[67] He did not ask the North to surrender capitalism, only to control it. Welfare-state protection for the masses, together with a strict discipline and the suppression of agi-tators, would put down the isms. The South generously stood ready to assist in every way possible. Besides, both sections needed Negro slavery to survive. Without it, the South would reproduce the North's social system, and the two sections would develop rival instead of complementary economies.[68] This from Fitzhugh! He had taken up an old Southern cry but hardly in good faith. What kind of a proposal was this from a man who had built his whole theoretical schema on the need to destroy capitalism, not merely to control it?

Beneath this demagogy lay an awareness that he might turn

the bourgeoisie's nightmares of socialist revolution to his own advantage. The trouble, to begin with, was that there were no such nightmares in the United States, however many there were in Europe. His confusion, deliberate or not, of the radical rhetoric of a few of the abolitionists with a genuine threat from the left hardly frightened a North that knew solid bourgeois, even fuzzy-headed, mischievous ones, when it saw them. At the very beginning of *Cannibals All!* he took a different view:

> Society will work out erroneous doctrines to their logical consequences, and detect error only by the experience of mischief. The world will only fall back on domestic slavery when all other social forms have failed and been exhausted. That hour may not be far off.[69]

No call for a conservative alliance here: Carthage must perish!

Conditions did not exist for such a coalition of Southern planters and Northern capitalists. As Barrington Moore points out, the Northern bourgeoisie had no strong, radical working class at home to fear and no powerful immediate enemies abroad; it had no need to compromise its ideas and ideals in order to win the support of a reactionary landowning class.[70] Had conditions been more favorable, the resulting coalition might have profoundly altered the politics and ideology of both sections. In the North it certainly would have generated a tendency toward authoritarianism and compromised the democratic commitments of the bourgeoisie. In the South it would have had an even more profound effect, since it would have strengthened those who stood merely for the protection of property against those who were imbibing a radically different social philosophy from their plantation milieu. If such a coalition had come into being and triumphed, it would, as Moore and others have recognized, have seriously compromised the moral and political principles of the North, but—what is generally overlooked—it would have destroyed or revolutionized much of the developing moral and political principles of the South. It would have provided favorable conditions for the triumph of an authoritarian bourgeois ideology over an authoritarian paternalistic ideology, and might well have sealed the fate of the slaveholders as a class by reducing them in time to the status of an appendage of their more powerful allies.

This question appears in the historical literature at many points, notably in those speculations about the fate of a victorious Confederacy in which it is assumed that slavery could not have long survived. This assumption is a magnificent tribute to the ubiquitousness of economic determinism especially among those historians most likely to be appalled at the label. Weaknesses inherent in the slave economy did create insoluble problems but by no means determined a change in the basis of society. Other methods for dealing with crises existed, the most attractive, historically tested, and ideologically acceptable of which was territorial expansion. More sophisticated historians have argued for the probability of the voluntary abandonment of slavery in an independent Confederacy on a more reasonable combination of economic and moral grounds. They point out that a quiet but important campaign had long been under way to reform the slave codes and that the groundwork for a conversion to a system of at least half-free labor was being laid. We ought to be warned by the identity of the reformers, including such men as Fitzhugh, Holmes, Hughes, and Thomas Ruffin, that the evidence of a substantial reform movement could and should be read differently. With exceptions, those who advocated reform strongly advocated retention and consolidation of the slave regime. Their proposals for guaranteeing certain rights for slaves, including the right to marry at law, were designed to humanize and secure existing social relationships; they went hand in hand with the steps toward sealing off slaves from manumission. The twofold strategy called for confirming the slaves as slaves while rendering them more comfortable in their condition. As such, it illustrated the forward thrust of paternalist ideology, which ought not to be confused with personal indulgence toward slaves, much less with a tendency toward antislavery.[71]

The argument for the probable peaceful abolition of slavery in the Confederacy assumes that the slaveholders would have wanted to take the South down the Prussian road to capitalism or, alternatively, that events would have compelled them to take that road. The first assumes too much, for the most that could be said is that a struggle was bound to break out between those who favored industrialization and regarded slavery as a matter of convenience and those who stood by a primitive agrarianism and regarded slavery as sacrosanct. The latter group seem to me to have been by far the stronger; in any case, their existence and determination cannot seriously be challenged. As for events, they cannot be relied upon to take the course historians think they should. All that could safely be said is that an independent Confederacy based on slave labor would certainly have been regarded as something of a moral leper by the peoples of Western Europe, that the establishment of an economy strong enough to guarantee an adequate military posture would have been difficult while slavery existed, and that well-documented Southern expansionist ambitions in the West Indies would have caused tension and probably war with England and other powers. So long as military adventures and expansionism provided an alternative to abolition, all speculation about a voluntary Southern adjustment reduces to wishful thinking. There is no evidence of important sections of Southern opinion having been prepared to raise the issue; it is important that the moral objection to slavery had been successfully equated with anti-Southernism, for without a strong, if small, morally driven vanguard to spur discussion, confrontation, and polarization, peaceful evolution had poor prospects. The examples of Brazil, the Caribbean, and the United States as a whole speak for this generalization, at least as a probability.

Countries like Germany and Japan, which did take the Prussian road to capitalism—that is, the road of authoritarian-

ism based on a coalition of industrialists and great aristocratic
landowners—have much to say to this question. The Junkers
provided the key to the German solution; an aristocracy
effectively crossed over into the ranks of the capitalist class,
bringing with them much of their old notions of order, status,
and leadership. What is too often forgotten is that great
disasters and external pressure forced aristocracies like the
Junkers to do as they did. Western pressure on Japan and the
attendant humiliation brought latent tensions to the surface
in Japanese society and generated an explosion. Whether or
not one regards the period of the Meiji Restoration as the
core of a bourgeois revolution—and the debate has been
vigorous—the awareness by substantial sections of the old
ruling class that it faced impending disaster is not in question.[72] The Junkers, to whom the slaveholders were once
compared by William E. Dodd, did agree to the abolition of
serfdom in 1807 and to other reforms carried out under the
ministries of Frederick William III, whose reluctance to
change is well known. It is enough to note that 1807 came a
year after the crushing defeat at Jena. "Jena had put them on
their mettle. As happened so often in their history the threat
of destruction taught them how to avoid destruction."[73] The
years following Napoleon's march to the east no doubt did
as much to generate a socioeconomic transformation as to
bring to fruition one that had long been under way. The fact
remains that a political crisis has generally been necessary to
prevent the absorption of such processes into the framework
of the old regimes. As for the transformation itself, Max
Weber puts it well, if too schematically: "The old economic
order asked: How can I give, on this piece of land, work and
sustenance to the greatest possible number of men? Capitalism asks: From this given piece of land how can I produce as
many crops as possible for the market with as few men as
possible?"[74]

Although the peasant revolts and popular ferment had
spent their force by the end of 1807, their combination with
the Napoleonic impact and the unavoidable lessons of the

military catastrophe generated an internal reform within the ruling class. At that, the resistance was great, and it required a tough, experienced, and entrenched bureaucratic apparatus to split the ruling class and to provide for an orderly transition.[75] That this familiar record may be read differently no one denies, but the simultaneity of political crisis and economic transition cannot be denied either. Those who simply assume that the South would have opted for a Prussian course unwittingly also assume some imminent political catastrophe, the nature and consequences of which, had it occurred, are beyond reach.

The German case provides some clues to the totality of the South's defeat and to that disappearance of so much of its ideology which has misled historians into questioning the depth and genuineness of proslavery thought. The bureaucracy provided the political mechanism by which the Prussian aristocracy transformed itself into a capitalist class. The bureaucracy's origins in dynastic absolutism and its secure place in the old regime permitted it to lead the fight for change from within and, in effect, to isolate those old-guard aristocrats who resisted all change. Whether one regards the bureaucracy as a semi-autonomous stratum of the ruling class or as an emerging new class is irrelevant for our purposes; it is enough that a transition occurring under these conditions had to build in much of the older ethos. For the Old South, without a complicated state machine, traditional officer corps, and bureaucracy, there were no institutional mechanisms for shaping the new regime in the mold of the old. When the planters went down, their way of life and its attendant ideology went down also. For the adherents of the old regime Appomattox literally marked "when the world ended."

From this point of view we may reassess Fitzhugh's argument for a conservative coalition. Notwithstanding his occasional lapses into political opportunism, we may grant his fundamental honesty of purpose. Capitalism stands condemned as an enemy of the human race because it produces

economic exploitation, degradation, alienation, and hopelessness. Wherever capitalism has triumphed, the family has
been undermined and all community has perished. Virtually
alone, the cash nexus rules the bourgeois world. The vehicle
carrying the bourgeoisie to power has been the world market
which it brought into being. Within the marketplace the
strong crush the weak, the gifted rob the simple, and all are
degraded in the process. Only slavery offers a way out. Necessarily, slavery can offer a way out only if its own tendencies
can flourish uninhibited by the corrupting influence of the
world market. Fortunately, most of the world is slaveholding, or at least noncapitalist, and capitalist society is only
"a small and recent experiment." It can be undone, and is
almost everywhere breaking under the strains produced by
its own barbarism. Almost everywhere. The exception, unhappily, rests snugly within the same national state as the
most virile of the West's slaveholding systems. The problems,
then, are how to transform Europe, how to avoid civil war
in the United States, and how to transform the North. Fitzhugh's call for a conservative alliance should be understood
in this context.

Fitzhugh's hopes rested on the collapse of European capitalism; he knew and candidly admitted that American
capitalism had a long life ahead of it. Suppose civil war
could be avoided at home; suppose the South could put up
with Northern corruption and even support its main bene-
ficiaries in return for being left alone. If so, time would
be bought—the time needed for European capitalism to
crumble and with it the world market. If Northern capitalism could stand alone in a slaveholding and seigneurial
world that would certainly unite to prevent the American
bourgeoisie from exploiting any part of it, very well. If the
exceptional conditions of American life permitted an isolated
national capitalism to exist in the North, no one would be
badly hurt. If not, then the North would follow Europe in a
voluntary conversion to slavery.

Let us waste no more time poking fun at Fitzhugh for the grandest miscalculations imaginable. What else could he have thought? His wisdom led him to see what few others could. Slavery could not exist much longer as a social system, in contradistinction to an occasional or peripheral labor system, in a bourgeois world. Either everything had to be gambled on the annihilation of the bourgeoisie as a class, and with it the whole structure it had built, or the world would succumb to the barbarians. His call for an alliance with Northern conservatives constituted a strategic holding operation, not a principled reversal of ground. The stakes were far too high for that.

If I am correct in this interpretation, then Wish and others are profoundly mistaken in regarding Fitzhugh as a forerunner of fascist doctrine. Wish writes:

> However much his own native kindliness would have compelled him to stop short of the modern implications of his thought, there is little doubt that his "system" belongs within the ideological orbit of contemporary Fascism. From Fitzhugh to Mussolini the step is startlingly brief.[76]

And again, in greater detail:

> The context of his middle-class radicalism is best suggested in the anticapitalistic vocabulary used by modern Fascist states despite their own retention of capitalistic modes of production. Fitzhugh's emphasis on the ethical weaknesses of the capitalistic spirit did not deny the need for a large competitive element within an ideal society, and here his distinction has much in common with the "good" and "bad" capitalism, recognized in the economic theory of National Socialism. Although the ante-bellum South never completely accepted Fitzhugh's entire framework of pre-Fascist ideas, these doctrines are indicative of the fact that the necessities of social domination may produce startlingly similar reactions at various times despite sharp differences in the environmental setting.[77]

Fascism does bear a formal resemblance to Fitzhugh's slave world. Both demand strict submission by the masses to authority, repudiate cosmopolitanism, abhor all compromises with liberalism, stress traditional values of one kind or another, and more. Certainly, Fitzhugh's world approached much closer to fascism than to socialism, if only because of its class stratification. Wish would have been on firmer ground had he gone to Henry Hughes, for although the *Treatise on Sociology* expresses in an immature and rather pompous way an argument similar to Fitzhugh's, it contains certain possibilities for Prussianization and fascism. Hughes also saw capitalism in transition toward a form of social organization like that of the South. He praised the trade unions as potential agents of transition and stressed their discipline and corporativism. Perceiving a tendency toward disequilibrium in free-market economies, Hughes viewed the state as the proper agent for guaranteeing a proper relationship between the quantity of labor and of capital.[78] These views, which take quite a different turn from Fitzhugh's, strongly resemble the arguments of the so-called left-wing fascists and those of American labor leaders, such as Samuel Gompers, who momentarily saw Mussolini's corporate state as labor's deliverance.[79] To the extent that the proslavery argument betrayed such tendencies, hints of which appear even in Fitzhugh, some justification for linking it to fascism exists; both can be said to form part of a continuing reactionary tradition, the later phases of which recapitulate as much of the earlier as circumstances permit and demand.

The resemblance between Fitzhugh's views and those of the fascists is largely formal. It is ahistorical to posit a direct link, especially since the fascists have always been good at claiming every previous reactionary as a precursor—one thinks of their use of Nietzsche. Fascism's rhetoric has generally been anticapitalist; its content, as Wish himself notes, has been nothing if not capitalist. It has not striven to overthrow or transcend the world market, but to conquer it. The foreign economic policies of Nazi Germany, for example, often termed with some justification neomercantilist, were predicated on the fiercest kind of war of all against all. The vaunted Nazi autarky was nothing more than the resurrection of the mercantilist demand for a degree of self-sufficiency adequate to the purposes of foreign economic aggression. Fascism, in short, was the culmination of the bourgeois barbarism against which Fitzhugh had struggled.

Southern slavery and the world-wide slavery Fitzhugh sought were genuinely prebourgeois and antibourgeois: "We want no new world!" Their vision of a society recapitulating a patriarchal plantation stood poles apart from fascist centralization. Their ideals represented the legitimate outcome of the prevailing system of social relationships, not, like fascism, the demagogic inversion of the social relationships on which it was predicated. Slavery did constitute a community, however unjustly ordered; fascism never could.

Fitzhugh did not try to appeal to the North, as Hartz assumes, except in a narrow political way. He appealed to the South to understand that it was different, that it had more than an institution, peculiar or not, setting it apart, that it was rebuilding a lost civilization. The defeat was indeed total. Its civilization was put to the torch, together with those ways of thought which reflected the ways of life constituting its essence. General Sherman, not the indomitable ideology of liberalism, marched through Georgia. The notion that America has always united on liberal principles breaks down here. The slave South stood for something else. We should not forget that our liberal, confident, tolerant, and good-natured bourgeoisie, when for once confronted with a determined and powerful internal foe, forgot its commitment to reason together and reached for its revolver.

CHAPTER FIVE

Last Thoughts

Genius never anticipates his time, but always merely divines its
substance and meaning, which are invisible to everyone else.

V. G. BELINSKY,
"On Pushkin's Eugene Onegin,"
Selected Philosophical Works

I

Fitzhugh, after spending the better part of his life denouncing Negrophobia as un-Christian and inhuman and insisting that slavery had to be understood entirely as a class question, ended as a Negrophobe. After the war he described the black man in terms that would have revolted him a few years earlier. He did not repudiate his long-held general viewpoint; he merely tacked an extreme racism onto it. He stopped writing a few years after the war, and his last years were forlorn. Penniless and going blind, he had to leave his beloved Tidewater for the Southwest and the protection of children who were having their own difficulties. There can be no doubt that the war years shattered him. His small postwar literary output contains so much bitterness, harshness, and evidence of growing despair that it is difficult to believe it was written by the same good-humored, confident, humane man who wrote the slashing but delightful polemics of the fifties. The Negrophobia may be traced to the traumas of defeat and Reconstruction, but his flirtation with the "types of mankind" theories, which he had once scorned, came too early to be dismissed so easily.

Historians, most particularly Wish, say that Fitzhugh

became a convert to racism between the publication of *Cannibals All!* and the outbreak of the war. In fact, he had always been a racist; only the quality of his racism changed. For years he, like so many other Southerners, had insisted that the slaveholders were the only friends the blacks had in the United States and were all that stood between them and annihilation. He had denounced abolitionists, free-soilers, and Northerners generally as enemies of the blacks, bent on genocide. The charge rested on a simple observation of Northern behavior, but Fitzhugh had something else in mind as well. Abolition, he believed, would throw the blacks into market relations for which they were not suited either as laborers or as Negroes. Faced with unequal competition, they would starve and disappear. Fitzhugh here followed earlier writers like William Harper in warning that the master-slave relation alone created a class of whites whose position combined interest and sentiment in such a way as to produce a frame of mind capable of transcending racial antipathies. Those who would dismiss such remarks as mere proslavery propaganda have antislavery Southerners to contend with. Hinton Helper made the same point, but disapproved. When speaking of his enemies, he intended no irony by his references to "pro-slavery, pro-Negro" mobs. When Fitzhugh put forward this interpretation, he also put forward, from his earliest writings onward, the idea of Negro inferiority. The Negroes provided a special case of the general problem of class division. All labor, white and black, ought to be enslaved for its own good, but whereas some whites could be masters, few if any blacks could.

Henry Hughes took up the question more directly. After explaining his theory of warranteeism, he described the social system of the Old South as warranteeism with an ethnic qualification and proceeded to a straight defense of the two-caste system. Most Southerners who accepted, however hesitantly and inconsistently, the defense of slavery in the abstract simply argued that the presence of large numbers of Negroes permitted all whites to be masters—an argument that ignored every serious question and reeked of bad faith.

Hence, we come to our final paradox in the paradoxical history of the Old South. The slaveholders, on the strength of a particular Anglo-Saxon inheritance and a particular set of socioeconomic conditions, emerged as the closest thing to a "pure" slaveholding class to be found in the New World, but this same combination of inherited and acquired characteristics produced an especially virulent racism manifesting itself in a rigid two-caste system. Thus, the same circumstances and events that drove the slaveholders to develop an ideology appropriate to a slave mode of production —that is, the defense of slavery in the abstract—prevented them from perfecting it. The meaning of Fitzhugh's collapse into Negrophobia is to be located in this contradiction in his world. All New World slaveholders and all those affected directly or indirectly by the existence of slavery had to be touched by racism, but the Southern slaveholders most of all. The necessity to defend simultaneously a system of class rule and one of caste privilege created enormous difficulties, which could only be hidden so long as no attempt was made to bring rigor to the ideological defense of either.

Fitzhugh's work laid bare the class essence of the regime, but no one could fail to recognize that race played a major role in the thinking and action of the Southern ruling class, as well as of other classes. Stanley M. Elkins, in a critique of a paper I delivered on Ulrich Bonnell Phillips, chided me for attempting to subsume the race question under the general rubric of class rule:

Which is to be called the tail and which the dog, and which wags what? I am quite willing to grant that race was functional for maintaining the stability of the class system within the white community. But to stop with that is to prevent us from examining the power of race itself and from seeing that the whole notion of race—with its complex of fears, phobias, and tensions rooted in a century and a half of Southern experience—had taken on a life of its own by the 1840's and 1850's. We should be free to see that it was not subsumed under "class" or any other term![1]

There is little to disagree with here, if we clear up one point of definition. To say that the race question has to be sub-sumed under the class question is not to make it a mere façade for class exploitation, nor to deny it a life of its own. Rather, it is a matter of arguing that racism restricted the options open to those charged with guarding class interests; that it forced the defense of class power into some channels rather than others; and that it helped form the ideology of the ruling class in such a way as to render it much more rigid than would have been the case without it. It is to argue that race gave shape to class hegemony, not vice versa.

Fitzhugh and his colleagues did not ultimately retreat into Negrophobia because they had become racists; they had never been anything else. They retreated because they could not master the class question. They could not press the logic of their position to include an open call for the enslavement of lower-class Southern whites, because those whites had evolved into an independent class with an *élan*, tradition, and power at least sufficient to kill those who tried it. This in-sistence on the priority of class simply affirms that the equa-tion of slavery and white supremacy was a fraud. During the war certain sections of the South defected to the Union side and were bombarded by propaganda that warned of Negro rule, racial equality, and sleeping-with-baby-sister. The gam-bit did not work. Why should it have? Why should anyone in the South have thought that slavery was necessary to the maintenance of white supremacy? One did not have to be a Hinton Helper to realize that the proposition was nonsense. (Racism no doubt contributed to the failure of Helperism, but much, much more was at work, including the influence of culture in the widest sense and a variety of social and economic ties among the whites.) We ought indeed to take

the autonomy of racism seriously, but we ought to do it for
the North as well as the South. Had the Southern leaders
been willing to convert to another labor system while guaranteeing white supremacy, who in the North, apart from a
handful of abolitionist extremists, would have raised objections? The class nature of the slaveholders' ideology, not the
commitment to racism, provided the great stumbling block
to the evolution of the Southern social and economic system.
The defense of slavery in the abstract and the whole body
of Fitzhughian thought represented the logical end of that
line of thought, rather than a cross section of it. Therein
lies its significance, for it lays bare the fundamental nature
of Southern society as something to be understood, not as a
form of capitalism, much less as a form of feudalism, but as
a slave society deformed by internal and external ties to the
capitalist world and profoundly flawed by racial caste.

II

Hartz unfairly taunts Fitzhugh and the slave South with the
totality of their failure. He is right, of course, in saying that
they sank into oblivion after 1865 and that no later American conservative has built on their work. They could not do
so. American conservatism accepts and has always accepted
capitalism as a proper social order—if that makes it "liberal,"
very well—whereas Fitzhugh explicitly, and the slaveholders
as a class implicitly, stood in opposition to capitalism and its
values.

American conservatism has always displayed two contradictory tendencies: on the one hand, it has espoused the
nineteenth-century liberalism of *laissez faire*, as we were
reminded by the decision of the Republican Party in 1964 to
enter the lists to defend the honor of Dulcinea del Toboso;
on the other hand, it has spoken for a return to an organic
society, although as Allen Guttmann points out in *The
Conservative Tradition in America*, this tendency is largely

to be found in literary circles.[2] Since it would be presumptuous for a Marxist to try to settle the family quarrels of those who today rally to the conservative standard, I shall restrict myself to the observation that whatever right Goldwater, Buckley, and Hayek have or do not have to call themselves conservative, their theoretical position in general and their espousal of neoclassical economics in particular clearly separate them from anything of importance in Fitzhugh. The second group requires closer attention, especially since Southern literary conservatism, as formulated most sharply in *I'll Take My Stand*, has generally been of this kind.

Guttmann, following Robert Gorham Davis, who follows De Maistre and Maurras, offers us a list of terms of honor and rejection-contempt as a rough guide to conservative sensibility:[3]

HONOR	REJECTION & CONTEMPT
Authority	Liberalism
Hierarchy	Individualism
Catholicism	Protestantism
Aristocracy	Equalitarianism
Tradition	Naturalism
Absolutes	Pragmatism
Dogma	Progress
Truths	Personality
	Scientism

Fitzhugh qualifies splendidly and so do Gentz, Adam Müller, T. S. Eliot, and the Twelve Southerners who wrote *I'll Take My Stand*. The trouble is, so too do Mussolini, Gentile, Franco, Salazar, and a host of fascists. And, although everyone on the right has something in common with everyone else—namely, being on the right—for our immediate purposes the tossing of all these chaps into one ideological pot does not prove helpful.

If we turn to Russell Kirk's *The Conservative Mind*, we find six canons of conservatism according to Saint Edmund:

A universal constitution of civilized peoples is implied in
Burke's writings and speeches, and these are its chief articles:
reverence for the divine origin of social disposition; reliance
upon tradition and prejudice for public and private guidance;
conviction that men are equal in the sight of God, but equal
only so; devotion to personal freedom and private property;
opposition to doctrinaire alteration.[4]

Kirk ought to be embarrassed at how many honest and
socially conscious fascists would leap to his standard—even
to the element of personal freedom, for Ugo Spirito long
ago explained that, after all, corporate fascism was, among
others things, "absolute liberalism." We may leave Kirk to
worry about his embarrassments; those on the left have
enough of their own. No one should be surprised that Kirk
finds much space for Randolph and Calhoun but none for
Fitzhugh in a book of 566 pages, or that no other important
conservative writer seems to think Fitzhugh worthy of
notice.

Let us grant that Fitzhugh's contention that the solid
values of community and tradition are incompatible with a
system of bourgeois social relations may not be indispensable
to a conservative viewpoint. It nevertheless does raise fair
questions, which one would think would compel reply. The
brutal fact remains that when conservatives are not extreme
laissez-faire liberals, or apolitical literary men who dabble in
political abstractions (like T. S. Eliot, whose greatness as a
poet and usefulness as a social critic I certainly do not mean
to deny), they have difficulty in not ending as fascists. And
when they do, they embrace the final hypocrisy, for fascism
has nowhere been other than the dictatorship of big capital
over labor, no matter how much radical rhetoric and pre-
tense has gone into the making. Anticapitalist rhetoric has
always come cheap, but no collectivism has been possible in
the modern industrial world except socialist collectivism.
The rest has been demagogy, as with Hitler; pedantic
chatter, as with Sombart; petty-bourgeois nihilism, as with

Röhm; or tragedy and bitter betrayal, as with the idealistic National Socialists who filled the Hitler Jugend.

There is no secret to the silence of modern conservatism on Fitzhugh. When he called for the destruction of the world market, he put himself beyond the pale, for American conservatism has, for better or worse, always been bourgeois. The Agrarians of *I'll Take My Stand* came closest to his standpoint but could not take up, much less answer, his main point: If you will the world to be thus, then you must will the social relations that alone can make it thus. In fact, they spent most of their time in pretending that slavery had been only a trivial feature of Southern life. And so, Fitzhugh and the slaveholders remain an embarrassment to people who want capitalists without capitalism. Fitzhugh's message came to one simple point that few if any conservatives still want to hear: To have a world without marketplace values you must have a world without a marketplace at its center. Go backward or go forward, but if you are in earnest, then go!

I I I

Modern conservatives have not treated Fitzhugh with proper respect and have therefore lost sight of a powerful criticism of their own position, but they have tried to make use of Randolph and Calhoun, with indifferent results. At best, men like Randolph and Calhoun offered some interesting variations on well-developed conservative themes; we would be hard pressed to think of a single special contribution that either made to political philosophy. But then, Fitzhugh contributed nothing original or permanent to social thought either. His great achievement lay in the negative insight that slavery as a system of society, not merely as an occasional or peripheral economic device, was incompatible with capitalism and that the two could not long coexist. For the rest, he summed up the social side of the proslavery argument and pressed it to its logical conclusions. These were the formidable tasks to which he addressed himself, and he acquitted himself well.

But his achievement lay in ashes in 1865, for he had given us only half—by far the more frail half—of what we expect from a major thinker. He had properly explained and interpreted his world, but had failed utterly to do so in a manner that permitted its transcendence. The failure was implied in and was inseparable from the achievement. By taking up the defense of slavery with an uncritical eye he had condemned himself to remain on the level of ideologue. In so doing he penetrated deep into the nature of his society, the quality of its values and sentiments, and the roots of its confrontation with a hostile exterior world. This outstanding success destroyed his chance to contribute something worthy of his talent to future generations. So tied was his thought to his world that the total defeat of that world spelled the total defeat of his thought, even if the old questions do remain in our own day to haunt those whom he called cannibals.

Yet he had the last word: he did make an important contribution to the understanding of his world and of the historical process in general by accounting for his own failure. He knew, and told us the reason, that no flowering would be possible so long as the South simultaneously retained slavery and paid moral, intellectual, and economic tribute to the capitalist world. Ancient slave regimes might raise a great culture, but modern slave regimes were necessarily colonies and as such suffered both from the export of intelligence and material resources and, more important, from a fundamental inability to establish ground on which its intelligentsia could stand. We can, if we wish, merely dismiss the struggle of the slaveholding intellectuals to solve this problem as evidence that slavery could produce nothing of philosophical value and that the proslavery argument was merely a rationalization for a system of plunder. Propaganda victories over dead opponents are always easy to score. The real problem lay elsewhere. Slavery did create a body of sensibilities, a way of judging human relationships, a notion of social order, and a good deal more, but it could not in the world of the nineteenth century produce a science or an art of its own. Representing as it did an archaic regime, it had to repudiate much of the stunning scientific progress of the age, for it could not assimilate its methods, its spirit, or more than a fraction of its technical achievement. To produce an impressive and authentic art under such conditions would have been a formidable task even without the many other, obvious complications. So long as the South stood for an archaic social order that had been spawned by a more dynamic, antithetical order and so long as it could never free itself from the influence, internal and external, of that antithetical order, it had to remain suspended and sterile. Only in this sense could it be said that the slave South produced "no philosophical defense worthy of the name," but this is a sense quite different from that of neo-abolitionist criticism. Fitzhugh's great merit was to have seen this problem clearly, to have brought it to the surface, and to have tried to deal with it in a manner appropriate to his class. His failure reflected the failure of a class, its world, and its world view. And it exposed the limits of all modern reaction: The reconstruction and consolidation of an archaic world order being an impossibility, all attempts at a prebourgeois restoration can only end as the counter-revolution of the bourgeoisie itself.

NOTES

Part One
The American Slave Systems in World Perspective

Chapter 1. Preliminary Observations on Afro-American Slavery and the Rise of Capitalism

1. Among American historians David M. Potter has been the most sensitive to this contradiction and has used it to excellent effect in evaluating the work of historians of the slave South, who have tended to see only one side or the other. A volume of his essays, *The South and the Sectional Conflict*, has now appeared (Baton Rouge, La., 1969).

2. Fernando Henrique Cardoso, *Capitalismo e escravidao no Brasil meridional* (São Paulo, 1962), p. 231.

3. Ralph Ellison, *Shadow & Act* (New York, 1964), p. xviii.

4. Cf. David Brion Davis, *The Problem of Slavery in Western Culture* (Ithaca, N.Y., 1966), Ch. 8. I have discussed this problem more fully in a critique of Elkins' work, "Rebelliousness and Docility in the Negro Slave: A Critique of the Elkins Thesis," *Civil War History*, XIII (December 1967), 293–314.

5. Styron has been savagely attacked for this part of his novel *The Confessions of Nat Turner* (New York, 1967) by certain black militants, who accuse him of racism, of being a proslavery apologist, and of various other crimes against humanity. See John Henrik Clarke, ed., *William Styron's Nat Turner: Ten Black Writers Respond* (Boston, 1968). Actually the novel, by means of this sexual confrontation, provides a profound examination of the American racial experience. For a fuller discussion see my review essay in *The New York Review of Books*, XI (September 12, 1968), 34–37.

6. Frantz Fanon, *Black Skin, White Masks*, trans. C. L. Markmann (New York, 1967), p. 220, n. 8.

7. Sidney W. Mintz, review of Elkins' *Slavery*, *American Anthropologist*, LXIII (June 1961), 583. This review, which is an interesting and provocative essay in its own right, may be found reprinted with another, related contribution by Mintz in Laura Foner and Eugene D. Genovese, eds., *Slavery in the New World: A Reader in Comparative History* (Englewood Cliffs, N.J., 1969).

8. Eric Wolf, "Specific Aspects of Plantation Systems in the New World: Community Sub-Cultures and Social Classes," Pan American Union, *Plantation Systems of the New World* (Washington, 1959), p. 138.

9. Frank Tannenbaum. *Slave and Citizen: The Negro in the Americas* (New York, 1947), pp. viii–ix.

10. Eugene D. Genovese, "Materialism and Idealism in the History of Negro Slavery in the Americas," *Journal of Social History*, I (Summer 1968), 371–94 reprinted in Foner and Genovese, *Slavery in the New World.*

11. Eugene D. Genovese, "The Treatment of Slaves in Different Countries: Problems in the Applications of the Comparative Method," in Foner and Genovese, *Slavery in the New World.*

12. Cf. Raimondo Luraghi, *Storia della guerra civile americana* (Turin, 1966), pp. 69 ff.

13. Maurice Dobb's extraordinary *Studies in the Development of Capitalism* (New York, 1947), which develops Marx's work with considerable force and originality, has served as the starting point for all serious Marxist work in economic history since its appearance. See also the symposium on its leading theses, which first appeared in *Science & Society* and was then issued in convenient pamphlet form by that journal: Maurice Dobb, ed., *The Transition from Feudalism to Capitalism* (New York, 1954).

14. For dogmatists such definitions quickly take on mysterious properties, but when used by serious Marxists they are intended as starting points. Eric Hobsbawm, for example, has even suggested that all precapitalist forms of class society might conveniently be grouped together, but clearly he means only to highlight certain important similarities and would be the last to play the game of constructing broad definitions in order to substitute sterile models for particular historical investigations. See his introduction to Karl Marx, *Pre-Capitalist Economic Formations* (New York, 1955), pp. 9–65. Hobsbawm's introduction is, by the way, immeasurably more valuable than the book it introduces.

15. Richard Pares, "The Economic Factor in the History of Empire," *Economic History Review*, VII (1937), 119–44.

16. Eric J. Hobsbawm, "The Crisis of the Seventeenth Century," Trevor Aston, ed., *Crisis in Europe, 1560–1660* (Anchor paperback ed.; Garden City, N.Y., 1967), pp. 5–62.

17. H. K. Takahashi, "A Contribution to the Discussion," in Dobb, ed., *Transition*, p. 48, n. 56. The failure of Marxists to pay adequate attention to the ideological and psychological side of the process has left them open to attacks like that of H. R. Trevor-Roper, who attempts to replace Hobsbawm's thesis of a general crisis in the seventeenth-century European social system with one that argues for the existence of "a crisis in the relations between society and the state." A critique of Trevor-Roper's argument would be out of place here, but it should suffice to note J. H. Elliott's simple but damaging observation that all revolutionary periods, by definition, involve a crisis in the relations of society and state, and Roland Mousnier's analysis of the political crisis in France, which leads right back to the economic questions. Closer to our range of problems, Trevor-Roper insists that Marxists err in connecting their notion of a crisis in the system of production with the Puritan Revolution. To demonstrate that the revolution was "bourgeois," it would, he argues, be necessary to show at least one of three things: that the men who made the revolution had such an aim; that those who wished the result forwarded the revolution; or that the result would not have occurred without the revolution. None of these, he insists, could be demonstrated. In Trevor-Roper's view, Dobb makes only three connections: agricultural capitalists favored the revolution whereas "feudal" landlords opposed it; industrially rooted sections of the bourgeoisie supported the revolution; and the industrial towns took a radical position. The third he accepts while trying to explain it away; the other two he denies on the grounds that each class split politically. Trevor-Roper reads Dobb narrowly and reduces what was meant to be a suggestive discussion, necessarily somewhat schematic since it was an initial appraisal, to vulgar Marxism. No serious Marxist would make such direct connections between economic and political forces, although Dobb does leave himself open by excessive attention to the purely

economic side of the formation of the capitalist class. It would have been enough if the antagonism between the developing forces of production and the state had provoked a revolutionary crisis into which the new elements could successfully intrude themselves. All classes should be expected to split: Hobsbawm's remarks on the big industrialists and Dobb's analysis of the big merchants adequately explain the main lines of division within the bourgeoisie. As for the landowners, Dobb's analysis is a rough approximation; no doubt other factors, not the least of which were family ties, personal loyalties, and the like, would introduce major qualifications. The real question is whether, objectively, the revolution swept away remaining obstacles to the emergence of capitalism and provided greater opportunities for the new men to work in the political arena. Capitalism might have prevailed without the revolution, provided that the political obstacles to its growth could have been removed some other way. By having Marxists believe the revolution to be both fated and indispensable, Trevor-Roper gratuitously attributes to them a simple-mindedness from which at least the best of them do not suffer. His strictures ought, however, to warn against attempts to account for the emergence of capitalism in strictly economic terms.

Chapter 2. The Slave Systems and Their European Antecedents

1. Traian Stoianovich, *A Study in Balkan Civilization* (New York, 1967), p. 161.

2. See, e.g., the analysis of J. H. Parry, *The Spanish Seaborne Empire* (New York, 1966), pp. 215-28.

3. Rolando Mellafe, *Le Esclavitud en Hispano-América* (Buenos Aires, 1964), pp. 42-43.

4. Cf. Mellafe, *Esclavitud*, p. 60, for a summary of the data from such well-known studies as those of H. and P. Chaunu and F. Mauro.

5. V. T. Harlow, *A History of Barbados, 1625-1685* (London, 1925); but see also Ramiro Guerra y Sánchez, *Sugar and Society in the Caribbean*, trans. Marjory M. Urquidi (New Haven, Conn., 1964), which links the Barbadian experience to that of Cuba and the Caribbean generally.

6. Eric Williams, *Capitalism & Slavery* (Chapel Hill, N.C., 1944), p. 54; Noel Deerr, *The History of Sugar* (2 vols.; London, 1949), I, 158-74.

7. Elsa V. Goveia, *Slave Society in the British Leeward Islands at the End of the Eighteenth Century* (New Haven, Conn., 1965), p. 53.

8. *Pace* Perry Anderson *et al.!* Anderson attacks E. P. Thompson for calling the English agrarian upper class a bourgeoisie: "A bourgeoisie, if the term is to mean anything at all, is a class based on *towns*; that is what the word means. It is ludicrous to call a landowning class a 'bourgeoisie'—one might as well call artisans a peasantry." "Socialism and Pseudo-Empiricism," *New Left Review*, No. 35 (January–February 1966), p. 8. Anderson, a talented Marxist, ought to have better things to do with his time than to ape the philistinism of the bourgeois intelligentsia and should not have to be told the advantages of this characterization, even if it does create some semantic difficulties.

9. D. A. G. Waddell, *The West Indies & the Guianas* (Englewood Cliffs, N.J., 1967), p. 58. On absenteeism see esp. the excellent discussions

in Lowell Joseph Ragatz, *The Fall of the Planter Class in the British Carib-*
bean, 1763–1833 (New York, 1928), Chs. 1 and 2; Williams, *Capitalism &*
Slavery, pp. 85–104; and H. Orlando Patterson, *The Sociology of Slavery*
(London, 1967).

10. Patterson, *Sociology of Slavery,* p. 33; Philip D. Curtin, *Two*
Jamaicas: The Role of Ideas in a Tropical Colony, 1830–1865 (Cambridge,
Mass., 1955), p. 15.

11. Winthrop D. Jordan, "American Chiaroscuro: The Status and
Definition of Mulattoes in the British Colonies," *William & Mary Quarterly,*
3rd Ser., XIX (April 1962), 196.

12. Ulrich Bonnell Phillips, *American Negro Slavery* (New York, 1918),
p. 52. Phillips' two articles on Caribbean slavery still command the respect
of specialists: "A Jamaica Slave Plantation," *American Historical Review,*
XIX (April 1914); "An Antigua Plantation, 1769–1818," *North Carolina*
Historical Review, III (July 1926); both have been conveniently reprinted
in Ulrich Bonnell Phillips, *The Slave Economy of the Old South* (Baton
Rouge, La., 1968).

13. J. Harry Bennett, *Bondsmen and Bishops* (Berkeley, Cal., 1958).

14. Davis, *Problem of Slavery,* p. 158. See the comparison of Jamaica and
Cuba in Hubert H. S. Aimes, *A History of Slavery in Cuba, 1511–1868* (New
York, 1907), pp. 142–43.

15. Goveia, *Slave Society,* pp. 260–66.

16. *Ibid.,* p. 329.

17. See the evaluations of two leading Caribbean scholars: Arthur Percival
Newton, *A Hundred Years of the British Empire* (London, 1940), p. 48; and
Sir Alan Burns, *A History of the British West Indies* (2nd ed., rev.; London,
1965), p. 624.

18. Burns, *British West Indies,* p. 623.

19. Trevor-Roper, in Aston, *Crisis in Europe,* p. 64.

20. Pieter Geyl, *The Netherlands Divided, 1609–1648* (London, 1936),
p. 162. I have relied heavily on Geyl's books, as well as on Violet Barbour,
Capitalism in Amsterdam in the Seventeenth Century (Baltimore, 1950)
esp. Ch. 3, and B. H. Slicher van Bath, *The Agrarian History of Western*
Europe, A.D. 500–1850, trans. Olive Ordish (London 1963).

21. Barbour, *Capitalism in Amsterdam,* p. 71.

22. Trevor-Roper, in Aston, *Crisis in Europe,* p. 94.

23. C. R. Boxer, *The Dutch Seaborne Empire, 1600–1800* (New York,
1965), p. 58. Ch. 3 gives an excellent account of industrial conditions.

24 Barbour, *Capitalism in Amsterdam,* p. 60.

25. Edgar J. McManus, *A History of Negro Slavery in New York*
(Syracuse, N.Y., 1966), Ch. 1; Charles de Lannoy, *A History of Swedish*
Colonial Expansion, trans. G. E. Brinton and H. C. Reed (Newark, Del.,
1938), pp. 38–39; and H. Hoetink, "Diferencias en relaciones raciales
entre Curazao y Surinam," *Revista de Ciencias Sociales,* V (December,
1961), 499–514.

26. Cf. C. R. Boxer, *The Dutch in Brazil, 1624–1654* (New York, 1957).

27. The words are Boxer's, *Dutch Seaborne Empire,* p. 151; cf. Deerr,
Sugar, I, 210; Arthur Percival Newton, *The European Nations in the West*
Indies, 1493–1688 (London, 1933), pp. 135–36; Willemina Kloosterboer,
Involuntary Labour Since the Abolition of Slavery (Leiden, 1960), pp.
32–33.

28. In 1730, according to Deerr, 115 of the 400 sugar estates were owned
by Jews. *Sugar,* I, 210.

29. Waldemar Westergaard, *The Danish West Indies under Company Rule* (1671–1754) (New York, 1917), p. 158. This section relies heavily on Westergaard's book.

30. Frank Wesley Pitman, "Slavery on the British West India Plantations in the Eighteenth Century," *Journal of Negro History*, XI (1926), 662.

31. Cf. Westergaard, *Danish West Indies, passim.*

32. Eli F. Heckscher, *Mercantilism*, ed. E. F. Söderlund, trans. Mendel Shapiro (2 vols.; 2nd ed., rev.; London, 1955), I, 97.

33. *Ibid.*, I, 84, 102–9, 349–51.

34. E. P. Thompson, "The Peculiarities of the English," *The Socialist Register*, 1965, p. 321.

35. Henri Carré, *La Noblesse de France et l'opinion publique au XVIIIe siècle* (Paris, 1920), pp. 152–53.

36. Gabriel Debien, *Les Engagés pour les Antilles, 1634–1715* (Paris, 1952), esp. Chs. 4, 5, 12, 13.

37. C. L. R. James, *Black Jacobins: Toussaint L'Ouverture and the San Domingo Revolution* (2nd ed., rev.; New York, 1963), p. 29.

38. The inability of the French to export seigneurialism should not surprise us in view of the advanced capitalist development of their economy. The objection might be raised that seigneurialism was in fact exported to Quebec. See, for example, Louis Hartz *et al.*, *The Founding of New Societies* (New York, 1964). Recent work, notably Cameron Nish, *Les Bourgeois-Gentilshommes de la Nouvelle-France, 1729–1748* (Montreal, 1968), seriously undermines this argument and demonstrates essentially bourgeois relations even in agriculture despite the persistence of certain minor seigneurial obligations.

39. On the stake of the commercial bourgeoisie in the West Indian economy see Gaston Martin, *L'Ère des Négriers, 1714–1774* (Paris, 1931), esp. p. 424; on the rapid generation of plantation profits see Richard Pares, *Merchants and Planters* (Cambridge, 1960), pp. 46–47; for an excellent overarching sketch, which discusses the social as well as economic consequences of the sugar boom, see James, *Black Jacobins*, especially Chs. 2 and 3; for a general introduction to slavery in the French islands see Gaston Martin, *Histoire de l'esclavage dans les colonies françaises* (Paris, 1948).

40. The following discussion is based on an unpublished paper by Elizabeth Fox Genovese, "The Girondins and the Moderate Revolution in Bordeaux."

41. Cf. Stewart L. Mims, *Colbert's West Indian Policy* (New Haven, Conn., 1912).

42. Elsa V. Goveia, Comment on Elena Padilla's paper in Pan American Union, *Plantation Systems*, p. 60.

43. The phrase is T. Lothrop Stoddard's *The French Revolution in San Domingo* (Boston, 1914), p. 13. See also Georges Lefebvre, *The French Revolution from Its Origins to 1793*, trans. Elizabeth M. Evanson (London, 1962), p. 11.

44. Gordon Wright, *France in Modern Times: 1760 to the Present* (London, 1962), p. 256.

45. Cf. Marc Bloch, *Feudal Society*, trans. L. A. Lanyon (2 vols.; Chicago, 1964), I, 186–87, 266; Elena Lourie, "A Society Organized for War: Medieval Spain," *Past & Present*, No. 35 (December 1966), especially pp. 54–55.

46. For these relationships and much of what follows, see J. H. Elliott, *Imperial Spain, 1469–1716* (New York, 1964), pp. 52–69, 102–12, 184–99.

47. *Ibid.*, p. 102.

48. Cf. Karl A Wittfogel, *Oriental Despotism: A Comparative Study of Total Power* (New Haven, Conn., 1957), pp. 215–19; Parry, *Spanish Seaborne Empire*, pp. 29–30.

49. Arthur Helps, *The Spanish Conquest in America and Its Relation to the History of Slavery and the Government of Colonies* (4 vols.; London, 1855–61), I, 32. For slavery's survival in medieval Europe, see Charles Verlinden, *L'esclavage dans l'Europe médiévale* (Bruges, 1955).

50. Raymond Carr, "Spain," pp. 43–59 of Albert Goodwin, ed., *The European Nobility in the Eighteenth Century* (2nd ed.; London, 1967), p. 48; Jean Hippolyte Mariéjol, *The Spain of Ferdinand and Isabella* (New Brunswick, N.J., 1961), p. 234.

51. Rodney Hilton, "Comment," in Dobb, ed., *Transition from Feudalism to Capitalism*, p. 69.

52. Christopher Hill, "Comment," in Dobb, ed., *Transition from Feudalism to Capitalism*, p. 75.

53. Richard Pares, *The Historian's Business and Other Essays*, ed. R. A. and E. Humphreys (London, 1961), Ch. 1.

54. Lefebvre, *French Revolution . . . to 1793*, p. 35, n. 1.

55. Heckscher, *Mercantilism*, I, 21–22.

56. Cf. *ibid.*, I, 345; R. Trevor Davies, *The Golden Century of Spain, 1501–1621* (London, 1964), p. 22.

57. "As successful development of overseas enterprises resulted in an increase in princely power, so the princely power had to be there before the first overseas expansion could take place." Robert L. Reynolds, *Europe Emerges: Transition Toward an Industrial World-Wide Society, 600–1750* (Madison, Wis., 1961), p. 438.

58. Carr, "Spain," in Goodwin, ed., *European Nobility*, pp. 46, 49–50.

59. R. Trevor Davies, *Spain in Decline, 1621–1700* (London, 1966), p. 93.

60. *Ibid.*, p. 95.

61. Richard Herr, *The Eighteenth-Century Revolution in Spain* (Princeton, N.J., 1958), p. 118.

62. For a suggestive discussion of these historically determined Spanish attitudes see Ramón Menéndez Pidal, *The Spaniards in Their History*, trans. Walter Starkie (New York, 1950), pp. 20, 26, and *passim*.

63. Good general treatments of the constraints on industry may be found in the works previously cited of Elliott and Davies, but see also Karl Marx and Frederick Engels, *Revolution in Spain* (New York, 1939), esp. Marx's essay "Revolutionary Spain"; and Sergio Bagú, *Economía de la sociedad colonial: Ensayo de história comparada de América Latina* (Buenos Aires, 1949), pp. 36–53.

64. J. H. Plumb, Introduction to Parry, *Spanish Seaborne Empire*, pp. 23, 25.

65. On developments in eighteenth-century Spain, see esp. Herr, *Eighteenth-Century Revolution*, Ch. 5.

66. Josué de Castro, *Death in the Northeast: Poverty and Revolution in the Northeast of Brazil* (New York, 1966).

67. Cf. Mellafe, *Esclavitud*, p. 71. This book is a useful summary of Spanish American slavery and contains a good bibliography.

68. *Coartación*, the elaborate arrangement for self-purchase of freedom by slaves, has been subjected to a protracted discussion about its effectiveness and extent. For contrasting views see the discussions in Herbert S. Klein, *Slavery in the Americas: A Comparative Study of Virginia and Cuba* (Chicago, 1967), pp. 196–200; Davis, *Problem of Slavery*, pp. 266–67.

69. When, at the end of the nineteenth century, the ruling class needed more forced labor, it had no trouble obtaining it from the Indian population, long accustomed to seigneurial obligations. See Kloosterboer, *Involuntary Labour*, p. 79.

70. Allan Nevins, *Ordeal of the Union* (2 vols.; New York, 1947), II, 63.

71. Cf. Klein, *Slavery in the Americas*, and Franklin W. Knight, "Cuban Slavery on the Eve of Abolition," unpublished doctoral dissertation, University of Wisconsin, 1968. I obtained a copy of Dr. Knight's excellent dissertation after this essay had been finished but in time to take some account of it. Fortunately, if I have understood him correctly, his analysis supports the main lines of my argument. Generally useful are Guerra y Sánchez, *Sugar and Society*, and Philip S. Foner, *A History of Cuba and Its Relations with the United States* (2 vols. so far; New York, 1962–1963), esp. Vol. I. On matters of central importance to this essay Foner followed Arthur F. Corwin's doctoral dissertation, which I had overlooked. I did, however, obtain a copy of the book that grew out of it: *Spain and the Abolition of Slavery in Cuba, 1817–1886* (Austin, Tex., 1967). It was too late to give Corwin's book the close attention it deserves, but once again I was fortunate in that it seems to support rather than contradict the main argument of this essay. On the general problem of Cuban slave society I found four other studies especially valuable: H. E. Friedländer, *Historia económica de Cuba* (Havana, 1944); Roland T. Ely, *Cuando reinaba su majested el azúcar* (Buenos Aires, 1963); Leland H. Jenks, *Our Cuban Colony: A Study in Sugar* (New York, 1928); and Manuel Moreno Fraginals, *El Ingenio* (Havana, 1967).

72. Guerra y Sánchez, *Sugar and Society*, p. 35.

73. For an unusual treatment of the significance of tobacco and sugar in Cuban economy and culture see Fernando Ortiz, *Cuban Counterpoint: Tobacco and Sugar*, trans. Harriet de Onís (New York, 1947).

74. Deerr, *Sugar*, I, 130.

75. Ortiz, *Cuban Counterpoint*, p. 61.

76. Ely, *Cuando reinaba*, pp. 106–7. On this and most other important and directly relevant matters, see Knight, "Cuban Slavery."

77. Cf. Corwin, *Spain and Cuba*, and Foner, *Cuba*, Vol. II. Cf. also Raúl Cepero Bonilla, *Obras históricas* (Havana, 1963), pp. 93 ff., 285 ff.

78. Gilberto Freyre, *The Masters and the Slaves*, trans. Samuel Putnam (2nd English ed.; New York, 1956), p. 247. For the argument that Portugal in 1500 was fundamentally a capitalist society see Roberto C. Simonsen, *História econômica do Brasil, 1500–1820* (2 vols.; São Paulo, 1937), esp. Vol. I. Simonsen appears to have been influenced by Sombart and perhaps by Bento Carqueja, who tried with unfortunate results to interpret Portuguese economic history in Sombartian terms. See Werner Sombart, *The Quintessence of Capitalism: A Study of the History and Psychology of the Modern Business Man* (New York, 1967), pp. 134–36, in which Sombart discovers his own version of the capitalist spirit—which is a far cry from Weber's—in fourteenth-century Spain, only to have to have it disappear in order to account for the specific features of the

seventeenth-century decline. See also Carqueja, *O Capitalismo moderno e as suas origens em Portugal* (Oporto, 1908). Simonsen generally sees capitalism wherever he finds monopolies, trade, and exploration, and equates seigneurialism with natural economy—a common way of defining the problem out of existence. See the critical appraisal of Bagú, *Economía de la sociedad colonial*, p. 54.

79. Davies, *Golden Century*, p. 189; *Decline*, p. 34.

80. H. V. Livermore, "Portuguese History," in Livermore, ed., *Portugal and Brazil: An Introduction* (Oxford, 1953), p. 60; see C. R. Boxer's essay in the same volume, "The Portuguese in the East, 1500–1800," pp. 185–247, in which he discusses the aristocratic stance of the Portuguese military in contradistinction to the bourgeois attitudes of the Dutch.

81. H. V. Livermore, *A New History of Portugal* (Cambridge, 1966), p. 107.

82. Bailey W. Diffie, *Prelude to Empire: Portugal Overseas Before Henry the Navigator* (Lincoln, Neb., 1960), pp. 33–35, 60–68.

83. See Heckscher, *Mercantilism*, I, 342; II, 272–85, esp. p. 283.

84. Celso Furtado, *The Economic Growth of Brazil*, trans. R. W. Aguiar and E. C. Drysdale (Berkeley, Cal., 1963), p. 8.

85. *Ibid.*, p. 89; Alan K. Manchester, *British Preëminence in Brazil: Its Rise and Decline* (Chapel Hill, N.C., 1933), p. 18; Simonsen, *História econômica*, II, 45–49.

86. Cf. Octávio Ianni, *As Metamorfoses do escravo* (São Paulo, 1962); Cardoso, *Capitalismo e escravidão*; Caio Prado Júnior, *The Colonial Background of Modern Brazil*, trans. Suzette Macedo (Berkeley, Cal., 1967); C. R. Boxer, *The Golden Age of Brazil, 1695–1750* (Berkeley, Cal., 1962); Emília Viotti da Costa, *Da Senzala à colonia* (São Paulo, 1966); and Stanley J. Stein, *Vassouras: A Brazilian Coffee County, 1850–1900* (Cambridge, Mass., 1957).

87. Gilberto Freyre, *New World in the Tropics: The Culture of Modern Brazil* (Vintage paperback ed.; New York, 1963), p. 54. Freyre follows the decline of this patriarchalism in the postslavery, postimperial period in *Ordem e progresso* (2 vols; Rio de Janeiro, 1962).

88. Prado, *Colonial Background*, p. 334.

89. For an excellent account of the role of the Church see *ibid.*, pp. 327, 335, 386, 395–97, 411, and *passim*.

90. Alexander Marchant, "Colonial Brazil," in Livermore, ed. *Portugal and Brazil*, p. 297.

91. Cf. Deerr, *Sugar*, I, 105; C. R. Boxer, *Portuguese Society in the Tropics: The Municipal Councils of Goa, Macao, Bahia, and Luanda, 1510–1800* (Madison, Wis., 1965), p. 100.

92. Cf. F. J. Oliveira Vianna, *O Povo brasileiro e sua evolução* (Rio de Janeiro, 1922), pp. 66–67.

93. Furtado, *Economic Growth*, p. 57.

94. This is strange in view of Furtado's stated concern with class forces in history. See his *Diagnosis of the Brazilian Crisis*, trans. Suzette Macedo (Berkeley, Cal., 1965), which in its historical sections also displays the weakness of economism.

95. Furtado, *Economic Growth*, p. 59.

96. *Ibid.*, pp. 105–6.

97. The following sections contain material on Brazilian economic history from a number of sources. There are, however, three outstanding

general works, those of Simonsen and Furtado, already cited, and Caio Prado Júnior, *História econômica do Brasil* (7th. ed.; São Paulo, 1962). For general purposes I have referred, wherever possible, to Furtado's book, since it is the only one available in English and is in a convenient paperback edition.

98. For a description of these types see Manuel Diégues Júnior, "Land Tenure and Use in the Brazilian Plantation System," in Pan American Union, *Plantation Systems of the New World*, p. 107.

99. Prado, *Colonial Background*, p. 169.

100. De Castro, *Death in the Northeast*, p. 9.

101. Viotti da Costa, *Da Senzala à colonia*, p. 458.

102. The following section leans heavily on two interpretive essays: Richard Graham, "Causes for the Abolition of Negro Slavery in Brazil: An Interpretive Essay," *Hispanic American Historical Review*, XLVI (May 1966), 123–37; and Robert Brent Toplin, "The Movement for the Abolition of Slavery in Brazil, 1880–1888," unpublished doctoral dissertation, Rutgers University, 1968. Dr. Graham's essay broke new ground despite a certain eclecticism; Dr. Toplin's represents a substantial advance over Graham's both in analysis and in wealth of data, although it was of course able to build on it. An older article by Percy Alvin Martin, "Slavery and Abolition in Brazil," *Hispanic American Historical Review*, XIII (May 1933), 172–96, although weak in analysis, is still useful. Of special theoretical importance is the work of Octávio Ianni, especially his short, tight argument, "Capitalismo e escravidão," *Raças e classes sociais no Brasil* (Rio de Janeiro, 1966), pp. 75–85. Senhora da Costa's *Da Senzala à colonia* clearly influenced Toplin's essay and presents the fullest picture of the transition in the Brazilian South.

103. Perry Anderson, "Socialism and Pseudo-Empiricism," *New Left Review*, No. 35 (January–February 1966), p. 9.

104. As Manoel de Oliveira Lima says, the emancipation of the slaves in the United States undermined the moral defense of slavery throughout the hemisphere and placed it on the road to rapid extinction. See *The Evolution of Brazil Compared with That of Spanish and Anglo-Saxon America*, ed. P. A. Martin (Stanford, Cal., 1914), p. 44.

105. Prado, *Colonial Background*, p. 76.

106. The best published introduction to the Paraíba Valley is Stein, *Vassouras*. I have also drawn heavily on Toplin's unpublished dissertation and the work of Furtado and Senhora da Costa.

107. Stanley J. Stein, *The Brazilian Cotton Manufacture* (Cambridge, Mass., 1957), Ch. 1; Viotti da Costa, *Da Senzala à colonia*, pp. 185–86.

108. Stein, *Vassouras*, p. 6.

109. See esp. Warren Dean, "The Planter as Entrepreneur: The Case of São Paulo," *Hispanic American Historical Review*, XLVI (May 1966), p. 163.

110. Cf. Cardoso, *Capitalismo e escravidão*, pp. 232–35; Viotti da Costa, *Da Senzala à colonia*, pp. 154, 173–74.

111. European immigration to São Paulo:

1870s: 13,000
1880s: 184,000
1890s: 609,000

The great majority came from Italy. Figures from Furtado, *Economic Growth*, p. 140.

112. Dean, *Hispanic American Historical Review*, XLVI (May 1966), p. 145.

113. Cf Cardoso, *Capitalismo e escravidao*, pp. 216, 233–35.

114. J. F. Normano, *Brazil: A Study of Economic Types* (Chapel Hill, N.C., 1935), pp. 24–49.

115. Furtado, *Economic Growth*, p. 160.

116. Roy Nash, *The Conquest of Brazil* (New York, 1926), p. 239.

117. Caio Prado Júnior, *Evolução política do Brasil e outros estudos* (4th ed.; São Paulo, n.d.), Ch. 3.

118. Cf. Arthur Ramos, *The Negro in Brazil* (Washington, 1933), pp. 66–67.

119. João Pandiá Calogeras, *History of Brazil*, trans. and ed. Percy Alvin Martin (New York, 1939), p. 255; Graham, *Hispanic American Historical Review*, XLVI (May 1966), 133.

120. José María Bello, *A History of Modern Brazil*, 1889–1964, trans. J. L. Taylor (Stanford, Cal., 1966), pp. 27 ff.

121. R. A. Humphreys, "Monarchy and Empire," in Livermore, ed. *Portugal and Brazil*, p. 315.

122. Furtado, *Economic Growth*, p. 154.

123. Ianni, "Capitalismo e escravidão," in *Raças e classes sociais*.

124. Eugene D. Genovese, *The Political Economy of Slavery: Studies in the Economy and Society of the Slave South* (New York, 1965), and "Marxian Interpretations of the Slave South," in Barton J. Bernstein, ed., *Towards a New Past: Dissenting Essays in American History* (New York, 1968), pp. 90–125.

125. Quite properly, it required a Brazilian to glimpse the implications of the American Revolution for the South: "This independence of the ruling class vis-à-vis the metropolis was to be a basic factor in the development of the North American colonies, since it meant that they could rely on political organizations which could be true interpreters of their own interests rather than being mere sounding boards for events in some dominating but distant economic center." Furtado, *Economic Growth*, p. 33.

126. Albert Fishlow, *American Railroads and the Transformation of the Ante-Bellum Economy* (Cambridge, Mass., 1965), Ch. 7.

Chapter 3. Class and Race

1. Pierre L. van den Berghe, *Race and Racism: A Comparative Perspective* (New York, 1967), p. 6. This little book is an important contribution to the vast literature on race relations and has influenced this discussion. Among recent works mention should be made of three of special relevance: Harmannus Hoetink, *The Two Variants in Caribbean Race Relations: A Contribution to the Sociology of Segmented Societies*, trans. Eva M. Hooykaas (New York, 1967); Magnus Mörner, *Race Mixture in the History of Latin America* (Boston, 1967); and Winthrop D. Jordan, *White over Black: American Attitudes Toward the Negro, 1550–1812* (Chapel Hill, N.C., 1968).

2. Jordan, *White over Black*, pp. 43, 72. Emphasis in original.

3. C. R. Boxer, *Race Relations in the Portuguese Colonial Empire, 1415–1825* (Oxford, 1963), p. 56.

4. Prado, *Colonial Background*, p. 319.

5. Hoetink, *Two Variants*, pp. 88–89 and *passim*.

6. Marvin Harris, *Patterns of Race in the Americas* (New York, 1964).

7. Roger Bastide, "Race Relations in Brazil," *International Social Science Bulletin*, IX, No. 4 (1957), 495–96.

8. Cf. Harley Ross Hammond, "Race, Social Mobility and Politics in Brazil," *Race*, IV (May 1963), 3–13. These data are subject to other interpretations. See, e.g., Oracy Nogueira, "Skin Color and Social Class," in Pan American Union, *Plantation Systems of the New World*, pp. 169–74.

9. Toplin, "Abolitionist Movement in Brazil," Ch. 6.

10. On the recent racial situation see esp. Thales de Azevedo, *Cultura e situação racial no Brasil* (Rio de Janeiro, 1966); Roger Bastide and Florestan Fernandes, *Brancos e negros em São Paulo* (2nd ed., rev.; São Paulo, 1969); Fernando Henrique Cardoso and Octávio Ianni, *Côr e mobilidade social em Florianópolis* (São Paulo, 1960), and Roger Bastide, "The Development of Race Relations in Brazil," Ch. 1 of Guy Hunter, ed., *Industrialisation and Race Relations: A Symposium* (London, 1965).

11. Aimes, *Slavery in Cuba*, p. 216.

12. Cepero Bonilla, *Obras históricas*, p. 21.

13. Alexis de Tocqueville, *Democracy in America* (2 vols.; New York, 1961), I, 427; Eugene H. Berwanger, *The Frontier Against Slavery: Western Anti-Negro Prejudice and the Slavery Extension Controversy* (Urbana, Ill., 1967).

Part Two
The Logical Outcome of the Slaveholders' Philosophy

Chapter 1. Preliminary Observations on a Man and His World

1. C. B. MacPherson, *The Political Theory of Possessive Individualism: Hobbes to Locke* (Oxford, 1962), pp. 263–64.

2. Louis Hartz, *The Liberal Tradition in America* (New York, 1955), Chs. 6–7; C. Vann Woodward, "George Fitzhugh, *Sui Generis*," Introduction to George Fitzhugh, *Cannibals All! Or, Slaves Without Masters* (Cambridge, Mass., 1960; first published in 1857). See also Professor Woodward's recent witty and combative essay, "The Southern Ethic in a Puritan World," *William and Mary Quarterly*, XXV (July 1968), 343–70.

3. J. D. B. De Bow, in *De Bow's Review*, XXII (1957), 449. This journal is hereafter abbreviated DBR.

4. George Fitzhugh, *Sociology for the South: or, The Failure of Free Society* (Richmond, Va., 1854); *Cannibals All!*, see note 2 above. These titles are hereafter cited respectively as *Sociology* and *Cannibals* without mention of author. All references to articles in journals that have no author listed are by Fitzhugh.

5. Harvey Wish, *George Fitzhugh: Propagandist of the Old South* (Baton Rouge, La., 1943).

6. MacPherson, *Possessive Individualism*, p. 106.

7. Fitzhugh to Holmes, March 27, 1855; also April [?], 1855, in Holmes Letterbook, Duke University Library.

8. William Sumner Jenkins, *Pro-Slavery Thought in the Old South* (Chapel Hill, N.C., 1935).

9. *Ibid.*, p. 55; for an account of how the religious defense of slavery yielded to the defense of slavery in the abstract, see pp. 215–16.

10. The literature on Randolph and John Taylor is large, but for a useful introduction to some central problems see Richard Beale Davis, *Intellectual Life in Jefferson's Virginia, 1790–1830* (Chapel Hill, N.C., 1964), pp. 415–16.

11. William W. Freehling, *Prelude to Civil War: The Nullification Controversy in South Carolina, 1816–1836* (New York, 1966), esp. pp. 258, 306–9, 328–39, 355–60.

12. *Ibid.*, p. 360.

13. *Ibid.*, p. 49.

14. Cf. Genovese, *Political Economy of Slavery*, pp. 31–34.

15. Quoted in Jenkins, *Pro-Slavery Thought*, p. 66.

16. J. H. Hammond, "Letters on Slavery," in *The Pro-Slavery Argument, as Maintained by the Most Distinguished Writers of the Southern States* (Charleston, S.C., 1852), p. 104. Emphasis in original.

17. William Gilmore Simms, "The Morals of Slavery," in *Pro-Slavery Argument*, p. 265.

18. Augusto Illuminati, *Sociologia e classi sociali* (Turin, 1967), p. 119. See pp. 119–24 for a suggestive discussion of this question. I do not of

course mean that the Old South was ever a political monolith with a single, disciplined party. The general unification of the slaveholders and their allies in the Democratic Party in the 1850s came close enough.

19. W. J. Cash, *The Mind of the South* (Vintage paperback ed.; New York, 1960), p. ix.

20. *Ibid.*, p. 4.

21. *Ibid.*, p. 8.

22. *Ibid.*, p. 10.

23. *Ibid.*, p. 14.

24. *Ibid.*, p. 21.

25. *Ibid.*, pp. 61–72.

26. *Ibid.*, p. 61.

27. *Ibid.*, p. 62.

28. Kenneth M. Stampp, "Reconsidering U. B. Phillips: A Comment," *Agricultural History*, XLI (October 1967), 368.

29. C. Vann Woodward, in *The New Republic*, December 9, 1967, pp. 28–30.

30. W. E. B. Du Bois, *Black Reconstruction in America* (Meridian paperback ed.; New York, 1962), p. 43.

31. Cash, *Mind of the South*, p. 66.

32. Freyre, *Masters and Slaves*, p. 268.

33. Cf. E. P. Thompson, *The Making of the English Working Class* (New York, 1963), p. 11: "If we stop history at a given point, then there are no classes but simply a multitude of individuals with a multitude of experiences. But if we watch these men over an adequate period of social change, we observe patterns in their relationships, their ideas, and their institutions. Class is defined by men as they live their own history, and, in the end, this is its only definition."

34. Nikolai Berdyaev, *Slavery and Freedom*, trans. R. M. French (New York, 1944), p. 180.

35. Cash, *Mind of the South*, pp. 70–71.

36. *Ibid.*, p. 62.

37. Stampp, *Peculiar Institution*, p. 422. The guilt theme is presented most forcefully in Charles G. Sellers, "The Travail of Slavery," pp. 40–71 of Sellers, ed., *The Southerner as American* (New York, 1966).

38. Cash, *Mind of the South*, p. 63.

39. Orville W. Taylor, *Negro Slavery in Arkansas* (Durham, N.C., 1958), p. 37, n. 21.

40. J. H. Bills Diary, December 16, 1843. Ms. in Southern Historical Collection, University of North Carolina.

41. *Ibid.*, January 1, 1866.

42. Susan Dabney Smedes, *A Southern Planter* (London, 1889), pp. iv–v, also esp. pp. 141, 149.

43. Sellers, "Travail of Slavery," *Southerner as American*, p. 42.

44. Charles B. Dew, reviewing the various signs of guiltomania among historians of the Old South, asks a good question: "One wonders . . . how many Southerners living in the Deep South in the 1950's and 1960's experienced a subconscious sense of guilt over segregation and lashed out verbally and sometimes physically at the federal government because of their anxiety and frustration. My guess is not many." See "Two Approaches to Southern History: Psychology and Quantification," *South Atlantic Quarterly*, LXVI (Summer, 1967), 322.

45. Hoetink, *Two Variants*, p. 77.

Chapter 2. The Slaveholders' Philosophy

1. *Cannibals*, p. 56.
2. *Sociology*, p. 175.
3. *Cannibals*, p. 6.
4. T. S. Eliot, "The Idea of a Christian Society," in *Christianity and Culture* (New York, 1949), p. 18; cf. *Cannibals*, p. 6.
5. *Sociology*, p. 155.
6. See, e.g., Edmund Ruffin, *Address to the Virginia State Agricultural Society* (Richmond, Va., 1853).
7. Cf. Genovese, *Political Economy of Slavery*, esp. Chs. 4 and 6.
8. *Cannibals*, pp. 63–64; cf. pp. 66–67.
9. *Ibid.*, p. 62.
10. *Ibid.*, p. 252.
11. "What Shall Be Done with the Free Negroes?" Appendix to *Sociology*, p. 288.
12. George Santayana, *Interpretations of Poetry and Religion* (New York, 1900), pp. vi–vii.
13. *Sociology*, Ch. 6, p. 96.
14. *Ibid.*, p. 116.
15. Henry Hughes, *Treatise on Sociology, Theoretical and Practical* (Philadelphia, 1854), p. 292.
16. MacPherson, *Possessive Individualism*, pp. 89–90.
17. "Southern Thought," *DBR*, XXIII (1857), 339.
18. MacPherson, *Possessive Individualism*, p. 86.
19. Fitzhugh expressed this idea repeatedly in both his books and in numerous shorter writings.
20. *Sociology for the South*, p. 25.
21. *Ibid.*, p. 27.
22. *Ibid.*, p. 161.
23. *Cannibals*, p. 63.
24. Fyodor Dostoyevsky, *The Brothers Karamazov*, trans. Constance Garnett (Modern Library ed.; New York, 1950), pp. 298–99, 300–301.
25. Bryan Edwards, *The History, Civil and Commercial of the British Colonies in the West Indies* (5 vols.; 4th ed.; London, 1807), III, 36.
26. *Cannibals*, pp. 248–49.
27. *Sociology*, p. 30.
28. *Cannibals*, p. 69.
29. *Sociology*, p. 176.
30. "Black Republicanism in Athens," *DBR*, XXIII (1857), 20.

Chapter 3. The Critique of Capitalism

1. "Liberty and free trade . . . are convertible terms; two names for the same thing." *Sociology*, p. 169.
2. *Cannibals*, p. 102. Original emphasis.
3. *Ibid.*, p. 118.

4. *Sociology*, p. 7.
5. *Cannibals*, p. 106.
6. Quoted in Jenkins, *Pro-Slavery Thought*, p. 52.
7. Cf. Horace Perry Jones, "Southern Opinion on the Crimean War," *Journal of Mississippi History*, XXIX (May 1967), 95–117.
8. *Sociology*, p. 11.
9. Hughes, *Treatise*, pp. 110, 125, 158.
10. *Sociology*, p. 12.
11. *Ibid.*, p. 13.
12. *Ibid.*, p. 14.
13. Cash, *Mind of the South*, p. 97.
14. *Sociology*, p. 80.
15. *Ibid.*, pp. 80–81.
16. *Ibid.*, p. 8.
17. *Ibid.*, p. 90.
18. *Ibid.*, p. 9.
19. *Cannibals*, p. 26; Fitzhugh to Holmes, April [?] 1855, Holmes Letterbooks, Duke University Library. Fitzhugh once privately insisted, in a letter soliciting political favors, that he was "no friend of slavery or the slave trade." He suggested that if he had been writing in the North he would have put matters differently and would have argued for a society based on "a series of subordinations." In effect, all he meant—apart from a dose of dishonesty to disarm criticism—was that Southern slavery should be considered only one possible form of a properly stratified society. In fact, he specifically added that in his usage "the terms ["slavery" and "a series of subordinations"] mean the same." His published writings always insist on the same point, without the disingenuous gambit, and it is only necessary to recall that for him proper stratification required property in man if it was not to become inhumane and vicious. See Fitzhugh to Jeremiah Black, May 6, 1857, Black Papers in the Library of Congress. I am indebted to Professor William Freehling for drawing my attention to this letter.
20. *Sociology*, pp. 9–10.
21. *Ibid.*, p. 121; also p. 118.
22. *Cannibals*, p. 50.
23. "All North of the Chesapeake cheats us. I don't wish we should cheat, plunder, and fillibuster [sic] South of the Chesapeake." Fitzhugh to Holmes, April [?], 1855.
24. *Cannibals*, p. 51.
25. *Ibid.*, p. 215.
26. *Ibid.*, pp. 19–20.
27. David Ricardo, *The Principles of Political Economy and Taxation* (Everyman ed.; New York, 1955), Chs. 1, 6.
28. Karl Marx, *Capital* (3 vols.; Moscow, n.d.), Vol. I, esp. Chs. 6–9.
29. *Cannibals*, p. 236.
30. Technically, value is commodity value and surplus value the result of the exploitation of labor in a system of commodity production. Historically, the latter has been essentially the system of capitalism. Therefore, slavery as practiced in the largely nonmarket economies of the ancient world generated a surplus, but not surplus value. Since modern slavery was part of the world-wide system of commodity production, the distinction becomes useless.

31. *Cannibals*, p. 15.
32. *Ibid.*, p. 16.
33. *Ibid.*, p. 221.
34. *Ibid.*, p. 23.
35. *Ibid.*, p. 27.
36. "What Shall Be Done with the Free Negroes?" Appendix to *Sociology*, p. 278.
37. *Sociology*, pp. 22, 78.
38. "Private and Public Luxury," *DBR*, XXIV (1858), 49–50.
39. *Sociology*, p. 29.
40. "What Shall Be Done with the Free Negroes?" Appendix to *Sociology*, p. 279. This was a familiar theme in the South. See, for example, the writings of Edmund Ruffin.
41. "Southern Thought," *DBR*, XXIII (1857), 344.
42. This relationship may be expressed most simply in Marxian formulas. Let v equal value and s surplus value. The rate of exploitation may then be expressed as s/v. If the numerator increases faster than the denominator, then exploitation has increased. But v is necessarily also equivalent to wages. Therefore, any increase in v suggests an improvement in wages and is compatible with an improvement in living conditions. The workers may be absolutely better off while they steadily become more exploited.
43. Hughes, *Treatise*, pp. 156–57.
44. Wish, *George Fitzhugh*, p. 192.
45. *Ibid.*, pp. 182–83.
46. *Sociology*, p. 23.
47. *Ibid.*, p. 32.
48. *Ibid.*, pp. 38–39.
49. *Ibid.*, p. 180.
50. *Cannibals*, p. 188.
51. "Slavery Justified," Appendix to *Sociology*, p. 235.
52. *Cannibals*, p. 30.
53. "Slavery Justified," Appendix to *Sociology*, p. 247.
54. *Ibid.*, p. 248.
55. *Sociology*, p. 68; *Cannibals*, p. 65.
56. *Sociology*, p. 69; cf. *Cannibals*, p. 28.
57. *Cannibals*, pp. 205–6.
58. *Sociology*, p. 79.
59. Hughes, *Treatise*, p. 81.
60. *Cannibals*, p. 29.
61. *Ibid.*, p. 29.
62. *Sociology*, p. 77.
63. *Ibid.*, p. 92.
64. *Ibid.*, p. 186.
65. "Slavery Justified," Appendix to *Sociology*, pp. 238–39.
66. *Ibid.*, p. 234. I have taken liberties here. Fitzhugh used these words to describe the English Puritans. I think them apt, from his point of view, right here.
67. Allen Tate, "Remarks on the Southern Religion," in Twelve Southerners, *I'll Take My Stand* (Harper Torchbook ed.; New York, 1962), p. 168.
68. *Sociology*, p. 206.

69. *Ibid.*, p. 109.
70. *Ibid.*, pp. 113–14.
71. *Ibid.*, p. 170.
72. "Southern Thought," *DBR*, XXIII (1857), 345.
73. *Cannibals*, p. 53; cf. *Sociology*, pp. 194–95.
74. *Cannibals*, p. 53.
75. *Ibid.*, p. 53.
76. *Ibid.*, pp. 107–8.
77. *Ibid.*, pp. 130–31.
78. *Sociology*, p. 198.
79. *Cannibals*, p. 131.
80. *Ibid.*, p. 132.

Chapter 4. The Defense of Slavery

1. Quoted in Jenkins, *Pro-Slavery Thought*, p. 210.
2. *Sociology*, p. 105.
3. Cf. J. Carlyle Sitterson, *Sugar Country: The Sugar Cane Industry in the South, 1753–1950* (Lexington, Ky., 1953), p. 96.
4. *Cannibals*, pp. 204–5.
5. *Ibid.*, p. 36.
6. *Sociology*, pp. 194–95.
7. *Ibid.*, pp. 205–6; cf. "Southern Thought Again," *DBR*, XXIII (1857), 449–62.
8. George Santayana, *The Life of Reason, or The Phases of Human Progress* (5 vols.; Collier paperback ed.; New York, n.d.), II, 32, 34–35.
9. *Ibid.*, II, 35.
10. Stampp, *Peculiar Institution*, pp. 162–63.
11. Santayana, *Life of Reason*, II, 38.
12. J. G. deRoulhac Hamilton, ed., *The Papers of Thomas Ruffin* (4 vols.; Raleigh, N.C., 1918–1920), IV, 255–57.
13. Prado, *Colonial Background*, p. 409.
14. Cf. C. Vann Woodward, "George Fitzhugh, *Sui Generis*," Introduction to Fitzhugh, *Cannibals*, pp. x–xi.
15. *Sociology*, p. 15.
16. *Ibid.*, p. 87.
17. *Ibid.*, p. 136.
18. *Ibid.*, p. 137.
19. *Ibid.*, p. 138.
20. *Ibid.*, p. 139.
21. "Southern Thought," *DBR*, XXIII (1857), 337–49, esp. p. 341. This article and others like it should be understood as representing Fitzhugh's immediate rather than his long-range view.
22. *Sociology*, pp. 190–93.
23. "Slavery Justified," Appendix to *Sociology*, p. 239.
24. *Cannibals*, p. 30.
25. "Public Lands of Rome and America," *DBR*, XXIV (1858), 428.
26. *Cannibals*, p. 245.
27. *Ibid.*, p. 246.

28. *Sociology*, pp. 17–18.
29. *Ibid.*, p. 31.
30. *Ibid.*, p. 202.
31. *Cannibals*, p. 58.
32. *Ibid.*, p. 248. Southern white labor in the late antebellum period did suffer from a lack of economic freedom. See Richard B. Morris, "The Measure of Bondage in the Slave States," *Mississippi Valley Historical Review*, LXI (September 1954), 219–40.
33. *Cannibals*, p. 202.
34. *Ibid.*, p. 243–44.
35. Hammond, *Pro-Slavery Argument*, p. 111.
36. Simms, *Pro-Slavery Argument*, p. 261, n.
37. *Sociology*, p. 170.
38. *Ibid.*, p. 179.
39. *Ibid.*, p. 180.
40. *Ibid.*, p. 178.
41. *Ibid.*, p. 185.
42. *Cannibals*, p. 133.
43. Fitzhugh certainly would have agreed with Henry Hughes, another theorist who took high ground on the social question: "Progress must be humane. . . . Evil ought not to be done, that good may come. There ought to be no tears. No blood: if betterment without blood, is possible. Progress loves peace; olive is its laurel. The spirit of progress is the spirit of love." *Treatise*, p. 73.
44. "Love of Danger and War," *DBR*, XXVIII (1860), 294–305.
45. Harper and other Southern theorists had long expressed great fear of the moral isolation of the South. See, e.g., *Pro-Slavery Argument*, p. 2.
46. "The Conservative Principle: Or, Social Evils and Their Remedies," *DBR*, XXIII (1857), 449–62.
47. *Cannibals*, p. 232.
48. "Southern Thought," *DBR*, XXIII (1857), 346.
49. From a letter to Horace Greeley, July 20, 1856, printed in *Cannibals*, p. 108.
50. *Cannibals*, p. 260.
51. "The Love Song of J. Alfred Prufrock," *Collected Poems of T. S. Eliot* (New York, 1936).
52. *Sociology*, p. 35.
53. *Ibid.*, p. 45.
54. *Ibid.*, pp. 47–48.
55. "Southern Thought Again," *DBR*, XXIII (1857) 450.
56. "Southern Thought," *DBR*, XXIII (1857), 346.
57. *Cannibals*, p. 11.
58. *Ibid.*, p. 238.
59. Quoted in Jenkins, *Pro-Slavery Thought*, p. 300.
60. *Sociology*, p. 48.
61. *Ibid.*, p. 68.
62. *Ibid.*, p. 65.
63. *Ibid.*, p. 66.
64. *Ibid.*, pp. 69–70.
65. *Ibid.*, p. 72.
66. *Cannibals*, p. 245.
67. *Ibid.*, p. 247.

68. "The Conservative Principle; Or, Social Evils and Their Remedies," *DBR*, XXIII (1857), 449–62.

69. *Cannibals*, p. 6.

70. Barrington Moore, Jr., *Social Origins of Dictatorship and Democracy* (Boston, 1966), pp. 140–41. Moore also notes greater Southern dependence on cotton exports to England rather than on those to the North.

71. Clement Eaton has argued that the hiring system was a step toward freedom, but Robert Starobin demonstrates that on the contrary it contributed to the stability of the system. See Eaton, "Slave Hiring in the Upper South: A Step Toward Freedom," *Mississippi Valley Historical Review*, XLVI (1960), 663–78; and Starobin, "Industrial Slavery in the Old South," unpublished dissertation, University of California, Berkeley, 1968.

72. Cf. Moore's chapter on Japan in *Social Origins* and the literature cited therein. I have relied most heavily on the work of T. C. Smith, Johannes Hirschmeier, and Robert Lockwood.

73. A. J. P. Taylor, *The Course of German History* (New York, 1962), p. 41. For a sketch of the economic shift, see J. H. Clapham, *Economic Development of France and Germany* (Cambridge, 1966), Ch. 2.

74. Max Weber, "Capitalism and Rural Society in Germany," in *From Max Weber: Essays in Sociology*, ed. and trans. H. H. Gerth and C. Wright Mills (New York, 1946), pp. 363–85, quote from p. 367; see also his appraisal, "National Character and the Junkers," pp. 386–95 of the same volume.

75. See esp. Hans Rosenberg, *Bureaucracy, Aristocracy, and Autocracy: The Prussian Experience, 1660–1815* (Boston, 1966).

76. Wish, *George Fitzhugh*, p. viii.

77. *Ibid.*, pp. 192–93.

78. Hughes, *Treatise*, pp. 187–98.

79. A good study of the radical, or left-wing, tendency within fascism has yet to be written. When it is written and when we can assess properly the ideology and social basis of the political tendencies associated with Röhm, the Strassers, D'Annunzio, Spirito, *et al.*, we should be able to make a better estimate of the content of such American movements as Populism and Share-the-Wealth, not to mention certain recent "revolutionary" movements.

Chapter 5. Last Thoughts

1. Stanley M. Elkins, "Class and Race: A Comment," *Agricultural History*, XLI (October 1967), 370.

2. Allen Guttmann, *The Conservative Tradition in America* (New York, 1967), p. 11.

3. *Ibid.*, pp. 154–55.

4. Russell Kirk, *The Conservative Mind: From Burke to Santayana* (Rev. ed.; Chicago, 1953), p. 15.

INDEX